UNIVERSITY LIBRARY
UW-STEVENS POINT

The establishment of the Japanese constitutional system

The Nissan Institute/Routledge Japanese Studies Series

Editorial Board:

J.A.A. Stockwin, Nissan Professor of Modern Japanese Studies, University of Oxford and Director, Nissan Institute of Japanese Studies
Teigo Yoshida, formerly Professor of the University of Tokyo, and now Professor, The University of the Sacred Heart, Tokyo
Frank Langdon, Professor, Institute of International Relations, University of British Columbia, Canada
Alan Rix, Professor of Japanese, University of Queensland and former President of the Japanese Studies Association of Australia
Junji Banno, Professor, Institute of Social Science, University of Tokyo

The establishment of the Japanese constitutional system

Junji Banno

translated by J.A.A. Stockwin

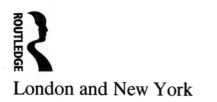

London and New York

First published 1992
by Routledge
11 New Fetter Lane, London EC4P 4EE

Simultaneously published in the USA and Canada
by Routledge
a division of Routledge, Chapman and Hall, Inc.
29 West 35th Street, New York, NY 10001

© 1971 Junji Banno

Translated from the original Japanese edition
Meiji kenpō taisei no kakuritsu
published 1971 by University of Tokyo Press, Tokyo, Japan
Translated by J.A.A. Stockwin

Typeset in Scantext Times by Leaper & Gard Limited, Bristol

Printed and bound in Great Britain by
Biddles Ltd, Guildford and King's Lynn

All rights reserved. No part of this book may be reprinted or
reproduced or utilized in any form or by any electronic,
mechanical or other means, now known or hereafter invented,
including photocopying and recording, or in any information
storage or retrieval system, without permission in writing from
the publishers.

British Library Cataloguing in Publication Data
Banno, Junji, *1937–*
     The establishment of the Japanese constitutional system.
     I. Title   II. [Meiji kenpō taisei no kakuritsu].
     English
     345.2022

     ISBN 0–415–00497–7

*Library of Congress Cataloging in Publication Data
has been applied for*

JQ
1624
.B3813
1992

Contents

Tables

General editor's preface

With growing speed, as we move into the 1990s, Japan in her many aspects is becoming a subject of interest and concern. The successes of the Japanese economy and the resourcefulness of her people have long been appreciated abroad. What is new is an awareness of her increasing impact on the outside world. This tends to produce painful adjustment and uncomfortable reactions. It also often leads to stereotypes based on outdated or ill-informed ideas.

The Nissan Institute/Routledge Japanese Studies Series seeks to foster an informed and balanced – but not uncritical – understanding of Japan. One aim of the series is to show the depth and variety of Japanese institutions, practices and ideas. Another is, by using comparison, to see what lessons, positive and negative, can be drawn for other countries. There are many aspects of Japan which are little known outside that country but which deserve to be better understood.

One of these aspects is the fine corpus of writing in Japanese by Japanese historians about the history of Japan. Most of this remains untranslated into English. This translation is an attempt to introduce to an English-speaking readership one of the acknowledged classics of modern Japanese political history by a leading historian of modern Japan. It is full of intellectual excitement.

J.A.A. Stockwin

Translator's introduction

Japan has developed from the backward and isolated group of islands that it was in the middle of the nineteenth century into a nation that today surprises the world with its modernity and economic power. The path taken has been uneven and at times tragic, but the decisions made have been pursued with extraordinary determination and resourcefulness. More than a century separates us from the key revolutionary year of 1868, in which the shogunate was overthrown and the imperial regime of Meiji established, and we may well marvel at the extent to which social and political developments covering centuries elsewhere was crammed into relatively short periods of time in Japan. Nowhere is this more true than of the reign of the Emperor Meiji, who ascended the throne in 1868 and died in 1912. Of the many experiments undertaken during his reign, one of the most interesting and important was the establishment of constitutional government with the promulgation of the Imperial (Meiji) Constitution in 1889. From our contemporary perspective, Japan may be regarded as having a depth of experience in constitutional government matching that of all but a few nations in the world today. Constitutional government, however, is not the same as democratic government. The policies of Japan's leaders in the 1890s were substantially driven by feelings of national insecurity, the need for nation-building, and nationalist ambition. This was a perspective from which 'democracy' lacked basic legitimacy. Leaders in some contemporary 'developing' countries share similar attitudes.

Professor Banno's book deals with the establishment of constitutional government in Japan during the turbulent decade of the 1890s. Essentially it is about how political experience was accumulated, by Government leaders, party politicians and their respective clientèles, in the formative decade of the Meiji Constitution. He tells an intensely 'political' story, full of power struggle and the clash of interests. It is also a story of the politics of compromise, pragmatism and fine calculation, in which political actors confronted by superior force rarely maintain rigid positions for ideological reasons, but rather trim their sails to the wind of reality, preferring even limited access to political power over principled confrontation. Nevertheless most participants play the political game with great intensity.

The book also details the tenacity of purpose possessed by a government determined to press ahead with an ambitious programme of military and industrial development. Government, in the early 1890s, was made up of members of the *hanbatsu,* or leaders from the small number of old feudal domains which had engineered the Meiji Restoration. The parties were mostly 'popular' parties, without access to power and locked in confrontation with the *hanbatsu* Government. Rather unexpectedly, the 'popular' parties discovered in the Constitution the means wherewith to challenge the 'transcendental' supremacy proclaimed by the more forthright elements within the *hanbatsu,* and whereas they could not securely win power themselves, they were well able to force the Government to a stalemate. Nevertheless, the *hanbatsu* learned how to use the weaknesses of the parties – and particularly their pragmatism (or, if one prefers, venality) – in order ultimately to spike their guns. The Constitution permitted the parties to hamper the Government in its task of governing but did not (at least in the 1890s) allow the popular parties to govern effectively in their stead, as was graphically shown by the brief experience of party rule in 1898. Whereas in some countries, no doubt, such a stalemate would have resulted in constitutional breakdown, in Japan it was resolved by compromise, in which the real prizes went to the more determined, stronger and less biddable elements, the *hanbatsu.* Two decades were to elapse after 1898 before the popular parties were to have another chance to take power. Even then they were ultimately unsuccessful, and only after Japan's defeat in 1945, followed by American occupation, did the parties obtain a secure place in government.

The main political issue which runs like a twisted skein through the politics of the 1890s was the land tax, and Professor Banno guides us through its infinite complexities with great skill. Most ironically from the perspective of the late twentieth century, it is the *hanbatsu* Government, authoritarian and politically conservative, which was determined to expand the budget and raise the necessary taxes for such expansion. The popular parties, by contrast, seen as a radical oppositional force, wished to cut expenditure and thus reduce taxation, or at least prevent it from rising. At least that was the situation in the first half of the 1890s. By the end of the decade the *hanbatsu* had hardly budged from its position, but the parties had found their principles seriously eroded. The logic of development, and the appeal of nationalism, together with objective changes in the economic situation of their clientèles, weakened their original determination to keep government expenditure within bounds. The political result was that power remained for the medium term in the hands of a narrow but highly motivated oligarchy. In the much longer term, indeed, it may well have inhibited the acceptance of the principle that freely elected parties should not only control government but also readily replace each other in government. It is not entirely concidental, perhaps, that a single party should now have controlled government continuously for over thirty years, even though Japan since 1947 has enjoyed a thoroughly democratic constitution. The history of relations between the contemporary Liberal Democratic Party and the opposition parties bears a curious resemblance in some respects to the history of relations between the *hanbatsu* and the popular parties during the 1890s. The rationale for government by bureaucrats, expressed so eloquently in Part I, Chapter 1 and Part II, Chapter 6 by Tsuzuki Keiroku, also finds echoes in Japanese politics today.

This book was originally published in Japanese in 1971. It was immediately recognized among modern Japanese historians as a pioneering work of acute and original analysis. Based almost entirely on contemporary documents, diaries and the letters which – in an age before the telephone – politicians in Japan, as elsewhere, wrote so voluminously to each other, it is also imbued with a remarkable subtlety of analysis about human motivation. Whereas much previous historical writing had tended to portray the relationship between the *hanbatsu* and the popular parties from a notably ideological standpoint, the Banno approach is based essentially on the understanding that politicians generally act to maximize political advantage within the constraints and opportunities provided by an existing political order. The precise nature of political institutions and how they worked in practice is crucial in his eyes. One important discovery revealed in this book is that although the Meiji Constitution provided in article 71 that if a government's budget were rejected by the House of Representatives it could carry on with the budget of the previous year, this was of little use to governments in times of rapidly rising government expenditure, such as was occasioned by the Sino-Japanese War of the mid-1890s. In a curious historiographic co-incidence, the same discovery was made slightly earlier and quite independently by an American historian, Dr George Akita of the University of Hawaii, in his *Foundations of Constitutional Government in Modern Japan.* Only following publication of their respective books did they meet and realize how similar on this issue their line of enquiry had been. Banno in his book, however, takes the argument one stage further by asking why, given this unexpected bonus vouch-safed to the popular parties by a Constitution which in other ways was designed to keep them in their place, did they nevertheless fail ultimately to press home their advantage.

This translation has been a long time in the making. It was begun in Canberra in the 1970s when Professor Banno was a Visiting Research Fellow at the Australian National University where I was then teaching. It was continued in Tokyo and in Oxford, where it was put into nearly final form during Professor Banno's Visiting Fellowship at the Nissan Institute of Japanese Studies in 1986–7. (Unforeseen circumstances then conspired to delay completion for a further period.) At all stages Professor Banno has been meticulous in checking my translation for accuracy and helping with such perplexing matters as the readings of personal names. We have had more sessions together on this translation than either of us cares to remember. Nevertheless, responsibility for any errors or infelicities that may remain rests entirely with the translator.

A few points need to be made about the translation.

No attempt has been made to render the Japanese written language of the 1890s into anything other than contemporary English. It should be remembered, however, that it was as different from contemporary Japanese as the English of Shakespeare (or even earlier writers) was from the English of today. A certain sense of historical distance, experienced by a Japanese reader of the Japanese text, is inevitably lost in translation.

The original book was written for a Japanese readership expected to be knowledgeable in some detail about the modern political history of Japan. A translation into English cannot make such an assumption about its readers, and indeed it is the intention of both author and translator that it should be read, not just by specialists on Japan, but by those interested in history – especially political history – as a common experience of mankind. Therefore, a number of appendices have been added to give basic information, about sessions of the Imperial Diet, prime ministers and their cabinets, election results in the House of Representatives, political divisions in the House of Peers and personalities encountered in the book.

Names of parties and other organizations have generally been left in their Japanese form, with translations, where appropriate, at first use. An attempt to use English translations of party names would have been likely to create more confusion that enlightenment. Important slogans, such as 'Enrich the Nation and Strengthen the Armed Forces' (meaning policies of financial expansion) and 'Lighten the People's Burdens' (meaning policies of financial retrenchment and cutting taxation), have sometimes been translated in full, but sometimes abbreviated to 'expansionist policies' or 'retrenchment policies', or terms similar to these, for the sake of readability. The term 'faction' needs a little explanation. In the 1890s the difference between 'faction' and 'party' was less clear cut than it is today, so that groups sometimes referred to as parties may elsewhere be called factions. Moreover, what is on occasion regarded as a 'movement' (for instance, the *Minken*, or Popular Rights, movement), may in other passages be designated a 'faction'.

Japanese names have been left in their original order, with the surname first: thus Itō Hirobumi, not Hirobumi Itō (except where Japanese authors of works in English are cited in footnotes). A macron over a vowel (e.g. ō) means that the vowel is approximately doubled in length when pronounced; many words are confused in meaning unless this convention is maintained. ('Tokyo', however has been left without macrons, except where it occurs in Japanese-language citations in footnotes.) All Japanese-language publications cited are published in Tokyo, unless otherwise stated. The original footnotes have been substantially abbreviated, and in a few cases eliminated altogether. Where this is the case, the original footnote numbering is preserved in brackets alongside the new numbering. Square brackets enclose explanatory notes by the translator. Where there are italicized passages within quotations from original sources, this indicates emphasis added by Professor Banno. Discrepancies in the given names of some individuals reflect the fact that given names were sometimes changed in mid-career, often to reflect rising status. Some writers also used pen-names.

Finally, we should like to thank our wives for their patience and support and to welcome the friendship that has grown between our families.

J.A.A. Stockwin

Introduction: Issues and methods

Consistently from the time of the Meiji restoration of 1868, Japanese governments led by the *hanbatsu*[1] pursued policies of economic and military expansion embodied in the famous slogan 'Enrich the nation and strengthen the armed forces.' These policies were made possible by virtue of the complete exclusion from the decision-making apparatus of those who bore the principal burden of financing the policies – namely the landlords and the farmers. Such a situation, however, could scarcely survive intact once the Imperial Constitution had been promulgated in 1889 and the Diet [parliament] had begun sitting in 1890. Through the medium of the 'popular' parties [parties other than those sponsored by the government], the landlords and farmers acquired, during the first session of the Diet, a firm base from which to force changes in the politics of 'enriching the nation and strengthening the armed forces', which had cost them so much sacrifice.

How then do we explain that these expansionist policies of the Meiji State continued to be pursued with ever-increasing vigour, and were hardly affected at all by the establishment of a parliament? The principal aim of this book is to find an answer to this question.

The Diet under the Imperial Constitution was not the purely formal and powerless body that some have suggested. It had the power to attack, within certain limits, the Government's policies of industrial and military expansion. Occasionally, the Government would attempt gross interference with elections, and yet the popular parties were always able between them to retain a majority in the House of Representatives. Why then did the popular parties, despite the clear powers granted them by the Constitution, and in spite of being able to keep a permanent majority in the Lower House, so conspicuously fail to achieve their most fundamental demands: retrenchment of government administration and lightening the burdens of taxation?

In this book the question will be approached principally from three angles, [those of the Constitution, political conflict and shifting policy positions].

The first will be an analysis of the actual functions of the constitutional system. Undoubtedly a new situation emerged with the Constitution and the Diet, which did impose certain restrictions on the realization of the Government's expansionist policies. Why therefore could the Government overcome such restrictions? Indeed, the situation clearly provided an opportunity for the former *Minken* [popular rights] movement to strike a blow against the policies of 'enriching the nation and strengthening the armed forces'. So why did its successors, the popular parties, fail to take sufficient advantage of such an opportunity? The answer does not lie in textual exegesis of the Constitution, but rather in analysis of its actual functions at the level of day-to-day politics. This aspect of the problem will be developed at length throughout the book, but here we shall outline the argument briefly.

The Government, anticipating that its policies of expansion could be frustrated by the Diet's use of its powers of budgetary deliberation, had written into the Constitution clauses designed specifically to prevent this, namely articles 67 and 71. Article 67 provided that the Diet could not, 'on the basis of constitutional sovereignty', reduce 'fixed expenditures' without the agreement of the Government, and this prevented the Diet from amending policies of heavy military expenditure. Article 71, giving Government the power to carry on with the budget of the previous year if the new budget were rejected by the Diet, was designed to provide all-round protection to the policies of industrial and military expansion. It would appear from this that the Constitution robbed the Diet of any chance it otherwise might have had to modify such policies. In practice, however, if the Diet were able to confine the Government's expansionist policies to the realm of 'fixed' expenditure, it would assuredly deal a serious blow to those policies. Expansionist policies could not, after all, be conducted simply by keeping the *status quo*. Even if the Diet could *not* act so long as it was within the ambit of articles 67 and 71, if it *could* still exercise an absolute veto on further increases in military expenditure and on expansion in the scope of the budget, then the policies of 'enriching the nation and strengthening the armed forces' would suffer a serious setback.

The only article of the Constitution from which the Government could here draw solace was article 7, giving the Emperor power to dissolve the Diet. Indeed, the Government made full use of the article, dissolving the Diet five times in the ten years following its inauguration; but in each of the five dissolutions the *hanbatsu* failed to alter fundamentally the balance of power in the House of Representatives. Leaving aside clashes of interest among the popular parties, the dissolution power enshrined in article 7 gave those parties, taken as a whole, little to fear. From this it may seem easy to argue that even under the Imperial Constitution the House of Representatives had every chance of modifying the policies of industrial and military expansion. That the popular parties failed so to do cannot be attributed entirely to the Constitution.

It would, however, be unfair to the popular parties to regard this question wholly from the standpoint of their right to debate the budget. As we shall show later, the popular parties demanded two things: retrenchment of administrative expenditure and reduction of the burdens of taxation. The first of these involved the power to debate the budget, while the second raised the question of the legislative power. Thus even though they might strike a blow against industrial and military expansion by using their power to debate the budget, unless they could succeed in cutting taxation as well (specifically, in reducing the land tax), this was but a hollow victory.

Now the Constitution provided an almost perfect defence against tax reduction, in the form of the House of Peers. It is true that from a literal reading of the Constitution it seemed that the Diet's legislative power (which included its power to debate proposed taxation) was quite untrammelled by comparison with its limited power to debate the budget. Although, formally speaking, it was restricted by the Emperor's power of giving sanction to laws (article 6), there was no instance during the period covered by this book of a bill which had passed both Houses being obstructed by article 6. It was, however, in the passage of legislation through both Houses that the problem lay. However many times the House of Representatives might pass a bill to reduce the land tax, once it was rejected by the House of Peers, there was no chance whatsoever of the land tax being reduced. The House of Peers consisted of hereditary members from the Royal Family, (princes and marquises), co-opted Members, (counts, viscounts and barons), Imperial nominees from the bureaucracy and representatives of the highest taxpayers. The Imperial Constitution, by automatically preventing reductions in taxation, indirectly helped to protect policies of 'enriching the nation and strengthening the armed forces', since if it was always going to be impossible to cut taxation, then the popular parties and their supporters were likely to find their will to oppose such policies diminishing.

In fact, however, total responsibility should not be placed on the Imperial Constitution over this issue. Although, as we have shown, the expansionist policies of the *hanbatsu* Government were rendered inoperable by a mere continuation of the *status quo*, the Government was not even able to maintain the *status quo* by raising further taxes. So when the issue of increasing taxation was put forward, the power of the House of Representatives under the Imperial Constitution rapidly increased. Articles 37, 62 and 63 of the Constitution made imperative the agreement of the House of Representatives for new and increased taxation. In fact the House had a veto power over all increases in taxation. For this reason it was clearly possible under the Constitution, by rejecting all increases in taxation, effectively to reduce the tax burden in proportion to the reduced value of the currency caused by rising prices. Legally, of course, it was possible for the Government as a last resort to increase taxes through the emergency ordinance power of the Emperor contained in article 8 of the Constitution. Article 8 also, however, stipulated that an emergency ordinance needed to be ratified by the Diet at its next session, and if it failed to receive ratification it would immediately lapse. Thus there were practically no prospects of increasing taxation by means of article 8. We may conclude, therefore, that scarcely any responsibility for the repeated taxation increases which occurred from the Sino-Japanese War onwards should be laid at the door of the Imperial Constitution.

The task of reinterpreting the process of conflict and compromise between the oligarchs and the parties over the policies of 'enriching the nation and strengthening the armed forces' during the ten years between the inauguration of the Diet and the founding of the *Rikken Seiyūkai* party will be the primary aim of this book, and will be attempted through analyses, such as that just presented, of the effective powers of the Meiji Constitution.

A second aim of the book will be to reinterpret the process of conflict and compromise over power between the oligarchs and the parties, centring on their policy confrontation over 'enriching the nation and strengthening the armed forces', and over reducing tax burdens. Once the Meiji Constitution had given the House of Representatives a certain degree of power to reject expansionist policies, the oligarchs could not in any case operate their basic policies without paying a price. They were forced gradually to abandon their monopoly of power in order to weaken the opposition of the parties and obtain their support. This was the reason why they needed gradually to revise their policy of 'transcendental' [i.e. non-party] cabinets, which had been the expression of their resolve to go on defending their power monopoly ever since the inauguration of the Diet. While attempting to place all kinds of obstacles in the way of the progress of the parties, they nevertheless toned down their 'transcendentalism'. These obstacles, however, for long afterwards remained a characteristic of constitutional government in Japan.

Thus the second object of this book is to explain the interrelationships between, on the one hand, 'enriching the nation and strengthening the armed forces' versus 'reducing the tax burdens of the people' and, on the other, transcendental Cabinets versus party Cabinets – the two great issues which had divided the oligarchs and the parties from each other ever since the first Diet session – and in this way to show what constitutional government was like in Japan in its formative period.

Thirdly, we shall investigate the changes that took place in the conflicts over expansionist policies, including changes in the sorts of demand emanating from the grass-roots support of the popular parties, and in the conditions of the grass-roots supporters themselves. As we have already suggested, if the main aim of criticism by the popular parties of expansionist policies was tax reduction, and specifically reductions in the land tax, then it is reasonable to suppose that changes in the levels of the tax burden falling upon the landlords and peasants would be reflected in shifts in the attitudes of the parties. The criticisms put forward by the parties, which based their support on the demand for a reduction in the land tax, as desired by those upon whom its burden directly fell, could be expected to weaken if the following developments occurred: a reduction in the real burden of the land tax caused by inflation of rice prices; a lifting of the burden which expansionist policies placed upon the landlords, because of increasing taxation of the masses – especially by indirect consumer taxes, and principally by the tax on *sake*; and, finally, a certain shifting of the base of support because of the political stirring of the commercial and industrial classes. In particular, with the establishment of parasitic landlordism and increasing taxation of the masses, a division emerged between those who bore the direct burden of taxation [landlords] and those who were direct victims of expansionist policies [the rest of the population paying indirect taxes], and this meant a big transformation in the popular parties. This is why I devoted considerable attention to analysing the political process involved in the issue of reducing the land tax [before the Sino-Japanese War] and the problem of increasing it [afterwards]. It is also with this in view that emphasis has been laid on the financial policies of the *hanbatsu* governments and the party government [of 1898].

A word needs to be said about the period which this book covers and the way it has been divided up. It embraces the ten-year period from the inauguration of the Diet in 1890 to the founding of the *Rikken Seiyūkai* party in 1900. The final year was chosen because the two major points of confrontation between the oligarchs and the parties had been resolved by 1900 with the passing of the Land Tax Increase bill in 1898 and the founding of the *Rikken Seiyūkai* in 1900 itself. The book separates the ten years into two periods, with the Sino-Japanese War (1894–5) as the boundary between them. The war marks a crucial turning point in the three problems mentioned above – the powers of the Meiji Constitution, the oligarchs' monopoly of power and the change in the support base of the popular parties. It goes without saying that a most crucial factor in the background of these changes was the rapid progress of policies of 'enriching the nation and strengthening the armed forces' after the Sino-Japanese War.

Part I

The political situation before the Sino-Japanese War

1 Some problems of transcendentalism

The fundamental attitude towards the Diet and the parties expressed by the Meiji Government at the time of the inauguration of the Imperial Diet [1890] was termed 'transcendentalism'. The word 'transcendentalism' was born out of a speech made to a gathering of prefectural governors on the day following the proclamation of the Imperial Constitution by the Prime Minister of the day, Kuroda Kiyotaka, in which he declared: 'The Government must always steadfastly transcend and stand apart from the political parties, and thus follow the path of righteousness.'[1] The word thus originated unaccompanied by any definition. As an official of the Ministry of Home Affairs pointed out in 1892: 'Already two years have passed under the Constitution, and in this time each Government has declared that it is observing what it calls "transcendentalism", but nobody has ever explained what doctrine it is that the word refers to. This is because the meaning of the word is extremely vague, and the same word "transcendentalism" can describe two doctrines having mutually quite opposite meanings.'[2] It was indeed, as he perceived, a multi-faceted term.

The Cabinet of Kuroda, who was the first to make a speech about 'transcendentalism', was complex in nature. The Foreign Minister in this Cabinet which had proclaimed that it must 'stand apart from the political parties' was Ōkuma Shigenobu, who in effect was president of the *Kaishintō* [party]. The *Kaishintō*, with the entry of Ōkuma into the Cabinet, aimed to 'make a start at realizing progressivism [*kaishinshugi*] from within the Government, and in the future gradually to remould the Diet on the English model'.[3] Moreover Inoue Kaoru, the Minister for Agricultural and Commercial Affairs, had planned ever since retiring from public office following the failure of his attempt to revise the treaties, [the 'unequal' treaties imposed on Japan by the Powers in the 1850s and 1860s] to organize a political party based on Europeanization and the politics of autonomy.[4] Tani Tateki writes as follows in his diary concerning the relation between the presence of Ōkuma and Inoue in the Kuroda Cabinet and the 'transcendentalism' speech:

> The notion of standing apart from the political parties ... should last for a time. But it is crystal clear that eventually it will change. Indeed, there are even signs of it already. Even if Ōkuma and Inoue are not formally enrolled as party members of the *Kaishintō* and *Jichitō* respectively, the fact that they protect their own positions by secretly giving assistance to their parties outside the Government, means that while Ōkuma, Inoue and others claim to stand apart from the parties, in fact nobody can doubt that Ōkuma belongs to the *Kaishintō* and Inoue to the *Jichitō*.[5]

Subsequently, about a month after the 'transcendentalism' speech, the leading advocate of the *Daidō Danketsu* [Grand Coalition], Gotō Shojirō, entered the Kuroda Cabinet as Minister of Communications. Although he came in for criticism from various quarters, Gotō himself said of his entry into the Cabinet:

> The best way to remove personal considerations and create a Cabinet properly founded in constitutional politics, is first, as a temporary measure, to build a coalition Cabinet which would sweep away old customs and old ways, introducing new laws and new procedures in their stead.[6]

Gotō also intended, as a first step towards the creation of a party Cabinet, to act as the advocate of the *Daidō Danketsu* faction within the Cabinet once he was a Cabinet member. Moreover, about the same time as Gotō entered the Cabinet, even Tani Tateki, a central figure in the opposition *Kokken* [Nationalist] faction, was approached through the Grand Chamberlain, Tokudaiji Sanenori, the Vice-Minister of the Imperial Household Agency, Yoshii Tomozane; and the Privy Councillor Motoda Eifu, with a view to persuading him to return to the Government as a Privy Councillor.[7] Although Tani's reaction was to maintain that 'in my opinion the Government wants me to join in the knowledge that in present circumstances I cannot support it', he nevertheless judged that 'it would be a quite a different question if the Privy Council were to accept my humble regrets ... and if my entry into the Cabinet were to be given honourable consideration',[8] Tani had a definite desire to join the Cabinet.

Tani's entry into the Cabinet did not materialize, but the Kuroda Cabinet, including as it did leaders of the *Kaishintō*, *Jichitō* and

Daidō Danketsu, was closer to a Cabinet of national unity than to a transcendental Cabinet, and more like a Cabinet that included the political parties than one that 'stood apart' from them. The composition of the Diet, which was to be inaugurated in 1890, was as yet unknown, and at the time when the Meiji Constitution was proclaimed there were various possibilities still open, as well as a variety of responses which might come from within the ranks of the oligarchs. It was not entirely out of the question that if the most important leaders of the *Kaishintō*, the *Jichitō* and the *Daidō Danketsu* could be included in the Cabinet, then friction between the Government and the Diet might be avoided. In fact, however, as the time for the inauguration of the Diet approached, the oligarchs became increasingly isolated. The inclusion in the cabinet of Ōkuma, of the *Kaishintō* (early 1888); of Inoue, who was planning the organization of the *Jichitō* (July 1888); and Gotō, who was actively promoting the *Daidō Danketsu* movement (March 1889), indicated a response to the activities of the former *Minken* faction, which was making rapid efforts to regroup anticipating the Diet inauguration and the general election. If it was impossible to suppress this regrouping even by bringing Ōkuma, Inoue and Gotō into the Cabinet, then the only course left open was to form a Cabinet which to outward appearances at least 'stood apart from the parties'. Whether the 'transcendentalism' speech meant that a tranquil Diet should be created by expanding the parties supporting the Government, or whether it meant that without bothering about party support, the Government should simply rely on the administrative bureaucracy and directly confront the legislature, was essentially a matter of demarcation. The speech itself appeared to come down clearly on the latter position, but the composition of the Cabinet which was responsible for the speech showed that the oligarchs were not completely ruling the former course out of account. As will be shown below, if one takes into account the political situation at the end of 1888 and the beginning of 1889, when the *genrō* [elder statesman] Inoue Kaoru had not entirely given up the idea of organizing a party similar to the *Kaishintō*, and Tani Tateki of the *Kokken* faction was placing high expectations on the *Daidō Danketsu* movement, this can be well enough understood. Thus on the one hand there was a type of criticism which interpreted the 'transcendentalism' speech in terms of a Cabinet of national unity; an example of this kind of criticism is that of Inoue Kaoru given in a letter to Itō Hirobumi of 2 September 1887. 'If politics is conducted by combining the main policies of each party, then it is likely to be a politics of many different colours, with centralization of power achieved in the morning, and regulations dispersing power to the provinces appearing in the evening, while budget expenditure would be similarly unco-ordinated.' On the other hand the speech was also interpreted as a defence of the executive against the legislature, as evidenced in the statement that 'there is no chance of controlling the Cabinet through the politics of the Diet'.[9] Since it became clear that the supremacy of the former *Minken* faction in the Diet was difficult to undo, the latter meaning of 'transcendentalism' became the accepted usage.

In what follows we shall first investigate the plan for oganiz- ing a party to be called the *Jichitō* ['independence party'], put forward by Inoue Kaoru, who was one of the Chōshū *genrō* along with Itō Hirobumi and Yamagata Aritomo. This may help us understand the variety of reactions within the *hanbatsu* Government around the time when the Meiji Constitution was promulgated, as well as their limits. After that, for comparison, we shall examine the more or less simultaneous reaction by the group centred on Tani Tateki, who was in some ways more conservative than the Sat-Chō clique and in some ways more progressive, had no connections whatever with the *Minken* movement, and was in a broad sense a member of the *hanbatsu* Government.

Finally, by comparison with these two groups, and as an example of bureaucratic transcendentalism after the opening of the Diet, we shall look at the transcendental argument of Tsuzuki Keiroku. Our aim is to show the contrast between the variety of responses by the *hanbatsu* before the inauguration of the Diet, and their unity of purpose afterwards, but we shall also attempt to explore why the clash that developed between the oligarchs and the parties from the outset of the Diet made for a sudden change of direction by one wing of the oligarchs.

INOUE KAORU AND THE PLAN TO FORM THE *JICHITŌ*

Inoue Kaoru, who resigned as Foreign Minister in September 1887, taking responsibility for the failure of the treaty revision negotiations, wrote the following letter of resignation to the Prime Minister, Itō Hirobumi:

> For the past few days I have been considering the future, and I have come to the conclusion that the present Cabinet too is

tending to become isolated, with the number of its attackers increasing as before. Occupying a position of weakness, it continually changes tack, but finds its room for manoeuvre more and more restricted. It therefore adopts an increasingly intransigent posture, whether it is attempting to deal with a situation by the use of the police, or is directing its attention towards the provinces. By leaving the Cabinet I shall become a private citizen, but I shall tour the provinces countering the Cabinet's attackers, and having conferred with the Cabinet Ministers I shall make speeches to the people in which I shall arouse them from their misconceptions and point out the errors commited by the newspapers. In this way I believe I shall be able to exercise a beneficial influence by circumspectly enlightening people about certain aspects of the course being pursued by the Government.[10]

He was saying, in other words, that in order to deal with the attacks on [incomplete] treaty revision being made by the *Kokken* and former *Minken* movements, the Cabinet had been relying on such tactics as the use of police power and issuing instructions to local officials, thus succeeding in isolating itself more and more. He himself would have to make speech tours of the provinces. In the same letter he also wrote as follows:

According to recent reports from the various regions, it is said that there is a tendency to circulate petitions and to stir up the people in the provinces, while Itagaki is even said to be embarking upon a plan to overthrow the Cabinet, and recently *Gotō* has been publishing speeches in the newspapers and elsewhere. Surely various measures ought to be taken. In particular it is most necessary to stop listening to all this and to establish administrative order. Consideration should also, in my opinion, be given to the problems of expanding our insignificant shell hole.[11]

Thus he thought that a resurgence of the former *Minken* movement was inevitable given the failure of the treaty revision negotiations, and in order to cope with it the Government needed to broaden its base of support. As a means of expanding 'our insignificant shell hole', Inoue thought first of all of having Okuma of the *Kaishintō* as his successor,[12] and secondly of making speeches in the provinces. It was clear to Inoue that the former *Minken* movement, which had re-emerged as a result of the campaign against his treaty revision policies, had been preparing for the inauguration of the Diet in 1890, and that as 1890 approached the movement would become increasingly active. At the close of 1888, Inoue wrote to Itō in the following terms:

> By next summer the temperature of politics can be expected to have risen to fever level, and the Government will be placed in the unfortunate position of having to choose between sitting back and doing nothing or of using force. The responsibility of both of us in acting as the vanguard of civilization, lies in the fact that the result of introducing civilization may well be to lead the nation into weakness and disorder. Thus looking to posterity, and taking our stand on morality and responsibility, we must not submit to this ultimate shame which looms ahead of us. *Today we must not allow the Constitution and the other laws which you have drafted to come into operation automatically without having the enterprise to develop active policies about them.* We must be clear-headed and not give way to anxiety, nor must we spend our days in inactivity. I intend independently to exert myself for this cause.[13]

Here may be seen very clearly the anxieties of the Chōshū *genrō* Inoue Kaoru just before the inauguration of the Meiji Diet. Neither the independence of the House of Representatives, as desired by the former *Minken* movement, nor the naked use of power in order to prevent the same thing, squared with the constitutional image painted by Inoue. He did not think, like Itō, that the situation could be dealt with simply by drafting a constitution and some laws. He well realized that in the field of practical politics, ultimately governed by power relationships, there was a limit to how far the Constitution and the law, however strictly administered, could control any situation. How then did Inoue intend to deal with this state of affairs? The answer lay in his plan to organize a party to be called the *Jichitō*.

The plan to organize such a party was first conceived about the time of Inoue's letter written in September 1887, and it reached its final form about the time of his letter of December 1888. In other words, it began at the time when the three-item petition movement came into prominence [The three items called for were: (1) equal treaties; (2) freedom of speech and other freedoms; (3) tax reduction], underwent temporary suppression because of the Security Regulations, and when the *Daidō Danketsu* movement, lead by Gotō Shōjirō, succeeded in regrouping the former *Minken* faction, Inoue's new party had practically reached the point where it was organized in opposition to that movement. To anticipate our conclusion: on the one hand, Inoue's plan for organizing a party called the *Jichitō* was to prove quite inadequate and totally incapable of grappling with the great wave of regrouping by the *Minken* faction, which increased in intensity as the Diet inauguration and the first general election approached. On the other hand, the movement to organize this party, planned principally by Inoue Kaoru between the latter half of 1887 and the beginning of 1889, is crucial to an understanding of the attitudes towards the setting up of constitutional government taken by the Kaimei [Enlightenment] faction within the *hanbatsu* Government.

The speech tours of the provinces, referred to in Inoue's letter of September 1887, were rather belatedly carried out between April and June 1888. Furusawa Shigeru, who accompanied him on these speech tours, reported on them in the following terms to Mutsu Munemitsu, who was at that time in the United States as minister plenipotentiary:

> Count Inoue, as you are aware, is spending his leisure time going out among the people, and is enthusiastically engaging in this task. In April he travelled to Nagoya, and thereafter visited Gifu, Kyōto, Osaka and Hyōgo. He has been meeting the important people in each place, and has been laying the foundations of *Jichitō* philosophy. He returned to Tokyo in the middle of June. (I accompanied him from start to finish.)[14]

In May of the same year Mutsu Munemitsu, shortly before taking up his new appointment in America, had written to Inoue in the following terms:

> While I was in Ōsaka I had general conversations and found that the people there of higher than middle rank were united in a tacit wish to support you. If you are now prepared to go to Ōsaka will you please co-operate with and assist wealthy merchants, lawyers and newspaper employees.[15]

As is clear from these quotations, Inoue, Mutsu, Furusawa and others were planning the organization of a political party by April 1888 at the latest, and the speech tours of Tōkai and Kinki by Inoue from April to June were part of this plan. In the background of these preliminary preparations was the fact that when Inoue entered the Kuroda Cabinet as Minister for Agriculture and Commerce, he insisted that it was 'necessary to unite property owners of the middle class and above, firmly maintain the principle of local autonomy, and form a conservative alliance',[16] thus officially advocating the formation of a Government party.

Miyake Setsurei called the plan to form the *Jichitō* 'no substitute for the hopes of Okuma',[17] but while the *Jichitō* was in competition with the *Kaishintō*, it also had co-operative relations with it. This is also clear from the letter written by Inoue to Itō at the time of the former's entry into the Cabinet:

> Even concerning the *Kaishintō*, which is currently the object of suspicion, I have told [Ōkuma] in Kuroda's presence that it should gradually merge with his party, it should eventually expand its base of support as a conservative party, and we should discuss whether to go so far as to make it into a government party.[18]

In another letter written to Itō the next day, Inoue wrote: 'I have been making the point very strongly Ōkuma that if the *Kaishintō* now sufficiently expands its base of support and if it is not to change its policies altogether, this may well sow the seeds of suspicion.[19]

As is obvious from these remarks, by the time he entered the Cabinet in July 1888, Inoue was, on the one hand, preparing the organization of the *Jichitō*, while, on the other, thinking how to turn the *Kaishintō* into a Government party. Among the conditions for bringing about an agreement between Kuroda and Ōkuma which Inoue Kaoru put forward on entering the Cabinet in July 1888 were the following:

> join together men of property from the middle class and above, promote a system of town and village autonomy, lay the foundations of independent autonomy, form a single conservative party at the centre, and eventually make it into a bulwark against political turbulence.[20]

This needs to be seen in the context outlined above. Indeed one of the things being considered for the future was the creation of a Government party through the amalgamation of the *Jichitō* and the *Kaishintō*. Borrowing the expression of Nomura Yasushi, while in the Kuroda Cabinet Inoue and Ōkuma were 'raising their banners and matching each other's superior strength'; the Inoue–Ōkuma relationship was that of the 'unity of extremes'.[21] Indeed the relationship brings to mind the circumstances surrounding the Atami Conference in January 1881, which may be called the first stage of the 1881 political crisis. At the outset of 1881, Itō, Inoue and Ōkuma were planning a double strategy of combating the burgeoning movement to establish a national Diet, and on the other hand combating the conservative faction among the oligarchs which stemmed mainly from the Satsuma group.[22] This plan finally resulted in the complete opposite of what was originally intended, since Itō and Inoue reacted against Ōkuma's argument that constitutional government should be quickly established. Nevertheless it is a fact that at least for a while at the beginning of 1881, this plan for a double strategy was being hatched by the *Kaimei* faction alliance within the oligarchy.[23] In the latter half of 1887, in order to counteract the emergence of the former *Minken* faction and the *Kokken* faction, Inoue sponsored Ōkuma, of the *Kaishintō*, as his successor; early in 1888 he set out to organize a political party himself, and then in July 1888, when he was at the stage of re-entering the Cabinet, he advocated a single large government party through the alliance of the *Jichitō* and the *Kaishintō*. This may be seen as a second attempt at the double strategy formulated by the *Kaimei* faction alliance within the oligarchy.

Such an attitude on the part of the *Jichitō* persisted for some time. Even in his letter of October 1888 (see page 16), Furusawa reported to Mutsu:

We consider that relations with the *Kaishintō* ... at the present time may be able to bring left and right together and promote the national interest. Count Ōkuma is also giving careful consideration to this. (But it seems that relations with the *Kaishintō* might be severed at any time.)[24]

Again, Mutsu advised Inoue, as late as May 1889: 'Until the *Jichitō* obtains a majority, there may well be serious conflict with the *Kaishintō*, and we are convinced that it is possible for you to have serious discussions with Count Ōkuma.'[25]

Exactly when the name *Jichitō* came first to be used, and whether it was a name applied by its own members or used by outsiders is by no means clear. In a letter to Mutsu from Aoki Shūzō dated 19 September 1888, there is the statement: 'We have recently become of the opinion that a single political party should be formed which should be called the *Jichitō*.'[26] However, in a letter sent by Inoue to Tsuzuki Keiroku at the beginning of January 1889, there is the following statement:

As you know from the newspapers, I have been meeting with the local aristocracy in each region, urging that local autonomy is the cornerstone of a nation, and persuading them that in the interests of peaceful progress, monarchical power should act in the Constitution as a strictly unsurmountable barrier to popular rights. *Public opinion has consequently identified me with the Jichitō, but as a result of being thus wrongly identified, I have suffered many extreme embarrassments even within Cabinet* [authors' italics].[27]

Again, in the previously cited letter of Mutsu to Inoue of May 1889, the *Jichitō* is clearly mentioned.[28] According to Aoki and Mutsu it was a name used by themselves, while Inoue claimed it was used [only] by others. At any rate, as is seen in Furusawa's letter to Mutsu of October 1888, which reads, 'We do not yet fly the flag officially, and before we do so we should use the name *Jichi Kenkyūkai*,'[29] although they did not officially use the name '*Jichitō*', they did use it internally, among themselves.

Nevertheless, in so far as it was a question of gathering supporters for the *hanbatsu* Government on the conditions which Inoue laid down for his entry into Cabinet – uniting property owners of the middle class and above in the spirit of local autonomy – this was not so very different from the expectations about putting into practice a system of local autonomy held by Yamagata Aritomo. Yamagata, too, thought that if the system of local autonomy which he had created were put into practice, 'the men who would occupy the position of Diet Members would be men of property, knowledge and influence', and that these men 'would naturally consider their welfare as one with that of the nation and would pay great attention to social order'. Once these upholders of local autonomy became 'members of the Imperial Diet after it is established', he thought it would be possible to defend the House of Representatives from the *Minken* movement.[30] As a matter of fact, among the public officials who participated in the *Jichitō* plan were the names of Aoki Shūzō, Nomura Yasushi and others who worked as members of the Local Autonomy System Compilation Committee under Yamagata. They emphasised that the *Jichitō* plan coincided to an extent with the aims of Yamagata, who was the promoter of a system of local autonomy.[31] Was it the case, then, that Inoue's *Jichitō* was intended to give a degree of party respectability to control by local influentials through Yamagata's local autonomy system? This was not necessarily so if we examine Inoue's advocacy of large-scale farmers.

From the time when he was Foreign Minister, Inoue spoke frequently on agricultural questions, advocating the unification of estates and concentration of arable land by landlords, and insisting on the adjustment of relations between landlords and tenants. In one of these speeches he said that the fact that 'the word "unification" (in other words the unification by rich farmers of the land of poor peasants) is thought of as if it constituted lèse majesté ... is unfitting in today's age of progress'.[32] 'For the sake of national progress, in some circumstances the suppression of the poor for the sake of the rich is inevitable in the order of nature and for the strengthening of the economy'.[33] Certainly Yamagata, too, hoped that the large landholders would be the upholders of the local autonomy system, and the *Daidō Danketsu* movement made local influentials the target of their organizing activities.[34] Nevertheless, to advocate openly, as Inoue did, the amalgamation of land by the big landlords, and openly to take the attitude that the ruining of poor peasants should be welcomed in the interests of economic development could hardly be expected to win over the villages. The demand for reduction of the land tax advocated by the former *Minken* faction was still understood as a slogan opposed to the ruin of peasants through heavy taxation, or the concentration of land in the hands of large landlords. As Tokutomi Sohō remarked, 'The *Jichitō* must be principally a party of farmers, but so far as Inoue is concerned, his interests must be seen as lying with commerce and industry.'[35] The organizers of the *Jichitō* were bureaucrats and entrepreneurs having close relations with Inoue Kaoru, and the target areas for party organization, apart from the home towns of those directly involved, were mainly city entrepreneurs, lawyers, newspaper correspondents and others. On this point there seems to have been a big difference between Yamagata and Inoue.

The civil servants connected with the *Jichitō* plan included, in the Foreign Ministry, Aoki Shūzō, Under-Secretary for Foreign Affairs; Mutsu Munemitsu, Minister in the United States; Saionji Kinmochi, Minister in Germany; in the Ministry of Agriculture and Commerce, Saitō Shūichirō, private secretary to the Minister; Furusawa Shigeru, secretary; also Nomura Yasushi, Transport Under-Secretary; Komatsubara Eitarō, private secretary to the Minister of the Interior; and others.[36] The businessmen involved included Shibusawa Eiichi, Masuda Takashi of Mitsui, Hara Rokurō of the Yokohama Specie Bank, and the leader of Kansai business world, Fujita Denzaburō.[37] Among the journalists were Seki Naohiko of the *Tōkyō Nichi Nichi Shinbun* and Arimatsu Hideyoshi of the *Jichi Shinshi.*[38] Areas where the *Jichitō* was able to penetrate to some extent were, according to Furusawa, 'Nagoya, Kyōto, Ōsaka, Wakayama and Chiba',[39] and to these may be added Yamaguchi, Shiga and Tokyo. As Mutsu said to Inoue:

In order to ensure that the *Jichitō* acts *en bloc* in the Diet, it would be better in present circumstances to pick localities rather than persons. For instance the Diet members from Yamaguchi Prefecture and Wakayama Prefecture are all for the *Jichitō*, and the Diet members of each prefecture should be organized as a group under your command.[40]

Wakayama and Yamaguchi prefectures were the home territory of Mutsu and Inoue respectively. In Ōsaka, Kyōto, Shiga, Nagoya and elsewhere, businessmen and the city middle class were the object of the party's organization drive, and Inoue's influence as Minister of Agriculture and Commerce was a considerable factor here. Mutsu submitted to Inoue on this point that 'the urgent task at the moment is to ensure that the prefectural governors and district heads in the areas under your influence – in other words the areas that must be brought over to the *Jichitō* – shall openly or secretly serve under your command, and thus, within legal limits shall exert themselves to further the election campaigns of the *Jichitō*.'[41] In order to show how Inoue's 'power' as Minister of Agriculture and Commerce came to be enhanced, one has only to look at the way in which the Governor of Shiga Prefecture, Nakai Hiroshi, promoted the *Ōsaka Dōyūkai*, the *Kyōto Kōminkai* and the *Ōmi Dōchikai*. According to a letter from Nakai to Inoue of the end of 1889, these activities were conducted along the following lines:

I wish you the best of health in this cold weather. I have come to present a request that the remaining money transferred to the prefectural governor, which I mentioned in confidence recently, should have its 50-year interest cancelled during the next month. As I reported, this year is already at an end, the time for next spring's elections is approaching, political parties will have to plan to exert all their efforts including paying sums of money, large and small, to attract businessmen from within the prefecture, and so expand their party strength. Happily in Kyōto and its hinterland, the *Ōsaka Dōyūkai*, the *Kyōto Kōminkai* and the *Ōmi Dōchikai*, formed by businessmen, have not yet affiliated with any political parties. Naturally, however, if we neglect them the situation for us may become quite irretrievable. Hitherto we have had enough money. *Even a small amount of gift money can make a certain difference to the direction in which a given party member goes, and we are putting some effort into this.* So far we have not had any money and we have not been able to help them. From the end of the year we have gradually tried to form an alliance of those groups on an unbiased, non-partisan, independent basis. For the future we deeply desire to work out a plan whereby distinguished people should be sent to the Diet. Without a certain amount of money this is impossible, but if evidence of this is revealed it may on the contrary create a hostile reaction, in which case the scheme would lose its effectiveness. Therefore our present duty is to keep the details strictly secret, and thus ensure future success. As I requested the other day, if the borrowers can pay the money back to the lender,* *would you please lend the money to the prefecture, keeping the transaction secret,* after listing and checking the amounts involved. We wish to *give some assistance, using this money, to newspapers, journals, clubs, etc.*[42]

It is not clear what exactly was meant by 'gift money' (*kanofukin*) referred to in the letter, but it was probably a kind of loan from the Ministry of Agriculture and Commerce for industrial projects in the prefecture. This money was used to assist the *Ōsaka Dōyūkai*, the *Kyōto Kōminkai* and the *Ōmi Dōchikai*. Since the *Ōsaka Dōyūkai* and the *Kyōto Kōminkai* were groups of businessmen connected with the *Jichitō*,[43] Nakai's activities may probably be seen as designed to promote the *Jichitō*.[44] Moreover, according to Nakai, the *Ōmi Dōchikai* of Shiga Prefecture was a political society comprising seven or eight hundred men of property and reputation.[45] If all this is so, then the remarks by Gotō Shōjirō of the *Daidō Danketsu* movement (a faction opposed to the *Jichitō*) about the previously mentioned speech tour which Inoue undertook between April and June 1888, through the Tōkai and Kinki regions, were perhaps not just a libel. Gotō wrote as follows:

Inoue from the time when he retired from the Cabinet promised not to enter the Ministry of Agriculture and Commerce, but has entrusted his pronouncements to speech tours, is linking up with his colleagues among the local rice merchants and is making a big profit by giving secret promises about reducing taxes. This is really to be deplored.[46]

As our researches have shown, the organizational target of the *Jichitō* was not so much the landlords and peasants, but, rather, the city merchants and industrialists; and thus the authority of Inoue as Minister of Agriculture and Commerce had plenty of scope. Turning to other regions, in Chiba Prefecture the Chiba *Chūseitō*, led by Ikeda Eiryō, Sakurai Shizuka, Narushima Giichirō and others, also had connections with the *Jichitō*.[47] The situation in Nagoya is not clear.

Nevertheless it is not known clearly how long the plan to form the *Jichitō* actually lasted. As mentioned above, in January 1889 Inoue himself had come to be annoyed with the fact that it was called

---

*[probably the Ministry of Agriculture and Commerce]

'*Jichitō*'. On the other hand, the detailed and concrete advice sent as late as May 1889 by Mutsu to Inoue has already been discussed. Also there is the fact that in the first general election for the House of Representatives in 1890, the newspapers in reporting the results listed M.P.s belonging to the *Jichitō*.[48] Perhaps what happened was that with the sudden emergence of opposition to Ōkuma's treaty revision negotiations from mid-July 1889, by the *Kokken* faction and the former *Minken* faction, the *Kaishintō* began to lose influence, and the *Jichitō* gradually withered without having taken the opportunity of holding an inauguration ceremony.

Thus, from about the spring of 1888 until mid-1889 there was this plan of Inoue, heading a group of Europeanizing bureaucrats and industrialists, to organize a *Jichitō*, which, it was hoped, would form a coalition with the *Kaishintō* to become the Diet majority. At the time that the Constitution was proclaimed, to be followed by the speech on transcendentalism, the political world was particularly volatile. The impasse in Ōkuma's treaty revision negotiations cost the *Kaishintō* the chance of becoming the majority party, and cost the *Jichitō* the reason for its existence.

TANI TATEKI AND THE JAPAN CLUB

As an attempt at party-political activity in this period of reorganization from a standpoint diametrically opposed to that of Inoue's *Jichitō*, we have the example of the Japan Club of Tani Tateki. At a time when Inoue's treaty revision negotiations were becoming a major political issue, they both used the issue as an opportunity for resigning – Inoue from the position of Foreign Minister, and Tani from the position of Minister of Agriculture and Commerce. Their reasons for resigning were completely the opposite, and the character of the political movements which they each developed after their resignations was utterly different, but at this point their respective activities bore a striking resemblance in that they were each thinking of organizing political parties. Neither of them found it possible to remain within the framework of 'transcendentalism'. Moreover while Inoue was contemplating the formation of a Diet-based party of government which would probably be linked with the *Kaishintō*, Tani was similarly placing considerable expectations upon the *Daidō Danketsu* movement. Differing from the transcendentalists of the early Diet period, they each directed their expectations to the aim of putting constitutionalism into practice.

Tani, who, as Minister of Agriculture and Commerce, toured the

Western European countries for more than a year from March 1886 to June 1887, wrote in his diary at the end of 1886 when he was in Germany:

> Radicalism in Japan at present must almost be considered as tantamount to national ruin. Every country is engaged in diligent preparations for war. But for Japan, which has yet to make any breakthrough in attaining Western rather than Eastern standards, even a naval loan of 1,700,000 [yen] would not provide enough for the building of one coastal port, the Army has less than 50,000 troops, and would be completely insufficient for one country's defence. If, however, one looks at what is actually happening, great public works are being carried out, whether it be urban reconstruction, the building of new Government offices, the improvement of drama, the remodelling of women's fashions, or diamonds, while everybody is working in peace and safety, and politics is being conducted in a selfish and self-indulgent fashion without regard for the people's welfare. This all results in a fearful diminution of the power of the Emperor, closes the mouths of the ordinary people and severely restricts their power, falsely clothes itself in the slogans of 'civilization and enlightenment' and is deceitful about treaty revision. When one considers that Western intellectuals have already set at naught the genuineness of their civilization, and for several years have retreated into fickleness and madness, one realizes that there is little prospect for a complete revision of the treaties.[49]

Thus Tani regarded as 'radicalism' the 'Westernization policies' adopted by Inoue as Foreign Minister with a view to bringing about treaty revision, and criticized them from the standpoint of 'military preparedness' and the 'people's welfare'. When he had an interview with Rudolf Stein [the German constitutional specialist] on 29 October 1886, he wrote the following in his diary: 'There is perhaps no nation with such heavy taxation as Japan. The burden of taxes which lies so heavy on the people is frittered away on the expenses of the various ministries. Is it possible to obtain happiness on the principle that the people are wicked and the officials are meritorious?'[50] In his diary entry for 10 November 1886, he agrees with the opinion of the German Minister of State for Agriculture that 'although Japan today is rapidly progressing, there is one point of historical experience which should be heeded. To rule by stealth, fear and force is not the road of truth, but leads rather to degeneration'. He replies that 'there is much to be learned from this, the way of progress being *to eliminate distinctions between high and low,* and to improve the position of the lower peasants.'[51]

It is clear from these points that what Tani acquired from his stay in Europe was the precise opposite of the conclusions arrived at by Inoue, which we have already discussed. An example of the difference is that whereas Inoue thought that 'progress' consisted in the amalgamation of poor peasants' holdings by the large landowners, Tani proposed 'to eliminate distinctions between high and low, and to improve the position of the lower peasants'.

On the other hand Tani was strongly advocating the expansion of military preparations. Should this not have been inseparable from higher taxation in Japan at that time? As we have seen, Tani concentrated his criticism on 'Europeanizing policies' which hastened the creation of the outward appearance of a modern State for the sake of revising the treaties. In other words, he was attacking excessive administrative outlays by the various ministries. When he met Stein in Austria, and heard his view that 'the size of Japanese administration is already larger than that of any European countries, and if her experience is similar, then if the common people become debilitated, the strength of the nation will be progressively destroyed',[52] Tani was much impressed, and became convinced that political expenditure should be retrenched by cutting back the administration. In other words what he was arguing for was a reduction in excessive administrative expenditure, with what was saved thereby being diverted to defence. He was not advocating a reduction in taxation itself. As Tani himself made clear several years later, the elements of his 'diligence and warlike spirit' policy were: 'a proposal to increase military preparedness, which was intended to stimulate a Government proposal'; 'an opinion – roughly the same as that of the popular parties – that the growth of the administrative organs had gone too far', and 'opposition to the senseless view of the popular parties that land tax should be reduced and the price of land controlled.[53] This 'diligence and warlike spirit' policy stood half-way between policies of industrial and military expansion on the one hand, and demands for reduced taxation, on the other. How it was used to cope with the inauguration of the Diet, and the kind of movement that was developed on the basis of it, will now be discussed.

Just like Inoue Kaoru, who was organizing a political party of Europeanizing bureaucrats and businessmen to counter the attacks of the *Kokken* faction, and who was considering the formation, together with the *Kaishintō,* of a Europeanizing faction which would have a majority, Tani Tateki too, whose 'diligence and warlike spirit' represented an onslaught upon policies of Europeanization, laid great store on the inauguration of the Diet. In January 1887, Tani wrote in a letter from Rome to Soga Sukenori:

> If we wish for real civilization, we must accept a true constitutionalism. Unless we bring about freedom of speech, freedom of publication and self-government, whatever is done will result in wasted effort and wasted expenditure. Even a person as stubborn as myself wishes only to change old thinking for new. Japan is the nation of His Majesty the Emperor, and a land of 37 million people. It is broad and large. It is dangerous to leave it in the hands of *petty* officials with meagre intellects. If one rejoices together with the people and grieves together with the people, the nation should be at peace. The petty officials think that if they dress their wives in Western clothes and make them sparkle with diamonds, foreigners will recognize this as civilization and culture and will respect them for it.[54]

Again, in a statement of opinion dated July 1887, he maintained that 'treaty revision is an aim steadfastly to be pursued, but now is not an appropriate time to accomplish it.... It should first become practicable to pursue this goal wholeheartedly in 1890, when the organization of the present Government has been changed, and after the new regime of constitutional justice has been established.[55]

Tani thought that constitutionalism 'respected conduct befitting superiors and inferiors, and [would probably] encourage the ordinary people to show reverence and respect in order that His Majesty the Emperor pursue the justice of the people individually, thus fostering the unity of high and low, as well as internal cohesion and external competition'.[56] In other words, rather than placing reliance on the 'meagre intellects of petty officials', the Constitution should guarantee unity of the whole nation through the co-operation of a single Emperor and the multitude of the people. For Tani, this was the means whereby pressure from the great powers of Europe and America could be overcome, and equal treaties could be concluded.

Nevertheless, support for a parliamentary system as a check to the despotism of government officials had been current ever since the criticism of 'official despotism' contained in the famous memorial on the establishment of a popularly chosen assembly in 1874, but since a cabinet system was introduced in 1885, critics of 'official despotism' were increasingly to be found even outside the *Minken* faction. An example can be found in the letter sent by the then Secretary of State for Foreign Affairs, Teraijma Munenori, to Itō Hirobumi in September 1887:

> In 1885 I put forward proposals for economizing, but nothing was done. In 1886 I wrote in plain language about national prosperity, and also made a great fuss about it, but the government took no notice.... As though I had written dead words on paper, however many proposals I made, no reply was ever vouchsafed me. *The fact that the government has nobody it can turn to to put its arguments, is a matter for genuine regret.* Even if a public enquiry is out of the question, it is desirable that *they should consult with people outside the Cabinet.* Even with the recent total breakdown of treaty revision it proved inconvenient [to consult]. Rather than making the national interest a matter of great secrecy, it should frequently be determined following the results of discussion. Other strategies result in a gulf developing between the bureaucracy and those out of power so that they enormously excite each other, compete in mutual tests of endurance and fall into a process which is self-defeating.[57]

Arrangements by the bureaucracy for the establishment of a cabinet system resulted in Terajima being excluded from the policy decision-making process, and he reacted against this by attacking 'bureaucratic despotism'. He even carried his criticism so far as to regret the 'gulf between the bureaucracy and those out of power' and to advocate politics based on public opinion. The same thing may be observed in the case of Nishimura Shigeki, adviser to the Emperor. Nishimura, who like Tani belonged to the camp of those who criticized Europeanization, reflected:

> The reform of December 1885 was the greatest reform since the Restoration. Throughout the nation people wiped their eyes and saw new politics; I myself place great store by the new politics. The new policies of the Itō Government, however, are an imitation of the legal system and customs and morals of Europe and America, and principally mean adopting the trappings of foreign culture. The bureaucrats who are emerging are mostly clever flatterers, while the straightforward and stout-hearted are always excluded.[58]

This shows clearly how far the establishment of a cabinet system in December 1885 and the subsequent reform of the bureaucracy outstripped the 'civilization and enlightenment' reforms of the early Meiji period. Thus a person like Nishimura could write in a statement of opinion at the time of the Ōkuma treaty revision issue: 'The

Imperial Diet will be inaugurated next year. Before the Diet begins, however, you gentlemen are making an effort to resolve major issues through cabinet decisions. I personally regret that you are making these preparations.[59] I hope that the opinion of the Imperial Diet will be asked, at least at the stage of ratification.'[60] There is a common thread running through Tani's repeated criticisms of the despotism of 'mere officials', and the views of Terajima and Nishimura. Even among the defectors from the bureaucracy one can detect a critical approach towards transcendentalism and a positive desire for the Diet to be opened.

As we have seen already, Tani Tateki, who reacted against the bureaucratic arrangements (his advocacy of administrative retrenchment was closely connected with this), accepted the argument that other expenditure should be retrenched to facilitate military spending, and held a view of Parliament based on 'one Emperor and the mass of the people', was making positive preparations for the opening of the Diet. At the time of the above-mentioned negotiations to install the privy councillors from 1888, Tani said:

'There are many reasons why I should decline the present offer, and when the political system changes next year a House of Peers will come into existence. What I should like above all is to become a member of the House of Peers and to perform the duties appropriate to that office. I have no desire to spend long relaxing in inactivity.'[61] Moreover, the fact that he declined the offer with the words: 'I respectfully beg you to release me before the national Diet is established',[62] shows that he was making some preparations for the opening of the Diet. So what kind of activities was Tani actually engaged in? It seems that he had the idea of running the out-of-power *Kokken* faction centred on the newspaper *Nippon*, co-operating with the *Daidō Danketsu* movement and expanding its influence. *Nippon* was started on 11 February 1889 at the same time that the Constitution was promulgated, as the organ of the *Kokken* faction. It gathered together a group of anti-Europeanizing intellectuals, headed by Tani Tateki, Asano Nagakoto and Miura Gorō, with Sugiura Jūgō, Fukutomi Takasue, Takahashi Kenzō, Kuga Minoru and others as leading participants.[63] At the same time it was a meeting point for regional organizations such as the Hiroshima *Kokken* faction led by Asano Nagakoto, Nomura Fumio and others (it later became the Hiroshima *Seiyūkai*),[64] also the *Shimeikai* of Kumamoto, through the good offices of Furushō Kamon and the *Kōyōkai* of Tosa, which was under the influence of Tani himself. Moreover, at the point when discontent had blown up within the *Daidō Danketsu* about the

entry of Gotō Shōjirō into the Cabinet, there was even a move to substitute Tani for Gotō as leader of the *Daidō* faction.[65] The fact that the
band of people running the *Nippon*, including Takahashi Kenzō,
Furushō Kamon, Kunitomo Shigeaki, Fukutomi Takasue, Sendō
Kiyoomi, Ono Michikazu, Kuga Minoru and others, gathered at Tani's
residence to protest against Gotō becoming a Cabinet minister,[66]
shows that this group was not only concerned with newspaper work,
but was also attempting political activities as one wing of the *Daidō
Danketsu*. After Gotō's withdrawal from the movement, Tani and his
friends, in alliance with Ōishi Masami, seem to have wanted to prevent
the infiltration of the former *Minken* faction into the *Daidō
Danketsu*,[67] and in May 1889 the *Kōyōkai* of Tosa, which was under
Tani's command, sent representatives to the *Daidō* Club[68] congress.[69]
From the time of the Tōhoku congress, the influence of the 'Nippon'
group on the *Daidō Danketsu* movement seems to have rapidly waned.
Tani's diary entry for 18 May 1889 reads:

> At five p.m. nine people came. Asano, Takahashi, Furushō, Sasa,
> Kunitomo, Fukutomi, Hirose, Shiba, Ono, etc. Made future
> arrangements. There still remains some hope of good changes for
> us at the next *Daidō* meeting due next February, our people must
> work hard to get political friends and take every opportunity to
> engage in united action. Definite arrangements to meet in Kyūshū
> in September and in October in Hiroshima under the *Seiyūkai* as
> host. Broke up after a little wine and food.[70]

The necessity of looking to the congress of the following February
was probably meant to indicate that the *Kokken* faction had been
expelled from the *Daidō Danketsu* movement, but it is worth noting
that at the stage reached in May 1889 the *Kokken* factions from
Kyūshū, Shikoku, Chūgoku and Tōhoku were coming together
around *Nippon* and Tani Tateki, and were planning to expand the
'party strength'.

Thus for Tani Tateki and others, who while keeping their connections close to the *Daidō Danketsu* movement were trying to consolidate the *Kokken* faction around *Nippon*, the increasing political
controversy surrounding Ōkuma's treaty revision negotiations from
July 1889 was an unexpected opportunity. On 7 July, the night before
Tani returned to his own town, Fukutomi Takasue, Takahashi Kenzō,
Sugiura Jūgō, Hirota Masao, Ono Michikazu, Kuga Minoru and
others gathered at Tani's residence and arranged to organize a
movement against the Ōkuma proposal.[71] Tani then returned to his
native Tosa and was away from Tokyo, while in the meantime Kuga

Minoru marshalled arguments in the editorials of *Nippon*, and Sasa
Tomofusa worked madly to rally the *Kokken* faction at the centre.[72]

Tani Tateki returned to Tokyo on 6th August; and amid an
upsurge of activity against the Ōkuma treaty in the form of a five-
group league comprising both *Minken* and *Kokken* factions,[73] he
took the initiative in forming the Japan Club, together with Asano
Nagakoto and Miura Gorō. For Tani this may have been in
anticipation of the expected formation of a political party. In his diary
entry for 22 August, he records: 'Within the limited objectives with
which the Club has been founded, *there is included a long-term
plan.*[76] Miura Gorō reflected:

> Tosa is under the thumb of Itagaki's Liberal party, and Tani's
> control there has withered; it is the same story in Higo. He wanted
> to enter into an alliance there with the *Kokken* party of Sasa
> Tomofusa, Furushō Kamon and others, and form a new single
> party, but Tōhoku is opposed to this. Abei Iwane, Shiba Shirō and
> others are disinclined, saying: 'there is insufficient prospect and
> therefore no need to form a party; an association designed to
> rescue the Tosa and Kumamoto people from their plight is
> completely unacceptable'. Tani is using the treaty revision question
> as a tool, but his real intention is to organize a single party,
> bringing together under one roof all those who say they are
> opposed to Treaty revision.[75]

Now if one considers these reflections of Miura alongside Tani's diary
entry for 22 August, the Japan Club may be seen as a compromise
between Tani and Sasa, who planned to form a political party, and
those who were opposed to the idea. The ending of Ōkuma's treaty
revision negotiations towards the end of October also brought to
naught the hopes which Tani had been pinning on the Japan Club.
Once the Diet was inaugurated, Tani, as leader of the House of Peers
Konwakai [Discussion Group] became a force within the House of
Peers critical of the *hanbatsu*-based Government.

As we have seen, therefore, at the stage just previous to the Diet
inauguration, rival Europeanizing and Japanizing groups were
formed among *hanbatsu* leaders, and each group planned to form
political parties. Both these groups, however, with the approach of
the first general elections in July 1890, gradually lost effectiveness in
the face of the vigorous electioneering of the old *Minken* movement,
and tendency of the various individual *Minken* factions to unite. By
the time the first Diet was assembled, they were unable to preserve
the image of independently formed intra-Diet bodies. Nevertheless,

these two streams by no means disappeared without trace during the first stage of the Diet. Speaking broadly, the *Jichitō* stream was inherited by Itō's bureaucrat followers, while the Japanizing faction stream was inherited by the *Sanyōkai* [Third Day Group] and *Konwakai* in the House of Peers, as well as by a section of journalists. When Itō on two occasions tried to form a political party, he was able to use Inoue's *Jichitō* as a model, and the *Sanyōkai* and *Konwakai* in the House of Peers, both led by Tani, putting forward their own form of constitutionalism and a hard-line foreign policy, developed criticisms of the *hanbatsu* Government from that Government's side. Both of them however, completely reversed their relationships with political parties. The Itō-line bureaucrats shifted from the *Kaishintō* [Progressive Party] to the *Jiyūtō* [Liberal party], while the Japanizers took their patronage from the Liberals to the Progressives. This was because on foreign policy – meaning principally the treaty revision question – the positions of the *Jiyūtō* and *Kaishintō* had been reversed. Co-operative relationships linking the Itō-line bureaucrats on the one hand with the Liberal party, and on the other the Tani groups in the House of Peers with the *Kaishintō* and *Shinpotō* (Reformist party) lasted as a stable fact of life from the twenties of Meiji (1887–96) to the early thirties (1897–1906). The Matsukata, Saigō, Kabayama, Takashima and other groups which are generally listed under the label of 'Satsuma faction' were also in existence, but if one excludes firm combinations based on place of origin, some of them took the same attitudes as Yamagata-line bureaucrats, while others allied themselves, like Tani and his friends, with the *Kaishintō* and *Shinpotō*, and like him advocated their own form of constitution-alism. Because of the existence of these streams within the *hanbatsu* Government, against a background of what seems at first sight a clear confrontation during the first stage of the Diet between the *hanbatsu* and the popular parties, there was a complex web of compromises constantly being devised. Thus with unexpected suddenness, given the extent of clashes between the two of them in the first and second Diet sessions, a movement towards realignment of the political world took place. We shall examine this tendency in detail in the next chapter, but before that, we shall discuss the third stream, that of the 'transcendentalism' of the Yamagata-line bureaucrats, taking as our central example the 'transcendental argument' of Tsuzuki Keiroku.

TSUZUKI KEIROKU AND BUREAUCRATIC TRANSCENDENTALISM

The situation described above underwent substantial change as a result of a political reshuffle which took place from the end of 1889 into 1890. This involved the retirement of Ōkuma as Foreign Minister, following the failure of treaty revision, and the relegation of the *Kaishintō* to opposition status, the failure of Inoue Kaoru's plan to create a *Jichitō*, the formation of the *Rikken Jiyūtō* and the resultant dissolution of the *Daidō Danketsu* movement and the decline of the *Kokken* faction. The mixing of Government and oppositions which accompanied this political reshuffle was once more sorted out at the stage when the inauguration of the Diet was anticipated; and when it became clear that the lines of conflict in the early Diet sessions were focused upon confrontation between the *hanbatsu* Government and the popular parties, the term 'transcendentalism' became established usage, meaning a fundamentally antagonistic posture on the part of the *hanbatsu* Government towards the Diet and the political parties. This was not 'transcendentalism' in the sense of the adjustment of forces within a cabinet of national unity, such as happened under the Kuroda Cabinet. 'Transcendentalism' was not merely a denial of party cabinets, but expanded its meaning to indicate the ignoring of the legislature by the executive. In practice it became daily clearer that the legislature could not be ignored, but this in itself seems to have resulted in the expansion of the meaning of the term. One example is an article entitled 'Transcendentalism', written by Tsuzuki Keiroku,[76] official of the Ministry of Home Affairs, in July 1892. Later Uzaki Rojō wrote of Tsuzuki:

> They say that you are the personification of the bureaucracy, and since you twist logic and make auspicious selections for the sake of bureaucratic politics, this reeks from head to toe of an executive eulogy. Bureaucratic politics, meaning that the Minister blindly affixes his seal and officials manage everything, is basically what you and others have been aiming at.[77]

As this suggests, Tsuzuki was representative of a certain type of bureaucrat of the twenties of Meiji [or 1890s].

His article 'Transcendentalism' which was written for the purpose of 'showing what kind of doctrine transcendentalism is, explaining where its rationale lies, and acting as a reference for those who in the future wish to govern the State according to its principles';[78] espoused thoroughgoing monarchicalism: 'People who are ministers of state have a duty only to assist the Monarch ... In no case ought they to assume a responsibility towards other bodies such as the Diet; still less can one see any reason why they should undertake any responsibility towards the people as a whole.'[79] So the duties of a Government official who shouldered responsibility towards the Sovereign, but none towards the Diet or the people, were to ensure the execution of national policy. As the article put it:

> A minister of state in a constitutional nation must always in domestic policy make national interest *the aim of his administration*, make his opinions known to the whole country, study the means of accomplishing *what he believes to be* the national interest, put into practice what he himself believes without modification, and however much it may offend the Diet or public opinion, he must unbendingly petition the Emperor for what he believes right, express his disagreement with the Diet, and ultimately if a situation should arise where because of disagreement an enterprise which he believes to be in the national interest were put in jeopardy, he must petition the Emperor for as many successive dissolutions of the Diet as necessary to bring it round to his way of thinking. He must neither follow the wishes of the political parties, nor follow the will of the Diet, nor indeed the opinion of the people; but rather it is up to him to formulate resolute proposals directed towards national goals, to issue orders to his officials, to make specialist investigation of the affairs of state, and thus realize the goals of the State.[80]

This means, in effect, the absolute superiority of 'national interest' over 'public opinion', and of the executive over the legislature. Immediately following the inauguration of the Diet it was probably impossible to find as clear a statement as this of the view that the Diet and public opinion should be ignored. Certainly since the Meiji Restoration the superiority of 'national interest' over 'public opinion' had been the consistently held position of the Meiji Government, but the Restoration leaders candidly admitted that this was an unavoidable 'anomaly' accompanying the modernization of an underdeveloped country.[81] At the time of the Restoration the 'principle of political concentration' went along with the 'principle of political expansion', and the latter meant the achievement of some citizens' rights.[82] Even compared with the leaders at the time when centralized government was first established, Tsuzuki's belief that public opinion should be ignored was exceptionally harsh. Such an extreme view probably arose from a sense of crisis among bureaucrats experiencing the unexpected strength of the political parties once the Diet had been inaugurated.

Transcendentalism in Tsuzuki's extreme sense of disregarding the Diet and public opinion was connected with his own special interpretation of the Constitution. This can be seen in the way he interpreted the power of budget deliberation. Tsuzuki explains as follows:

> The Imperial Constitution does not determine what burdens should fall on the people as a result of the budget, but always determines it as a result of the law, and until there is a change in the law relating to taxation, irrespective of the year's budget, irrespective of the year's receipts and expenditure, because the duty to levy taxation rests with the Government, *one cannot regard the budget as determining the burdens to be borne by the people.* Increases and decreases in the annual expenditures in the budget have hitherto not necessarily had a direct relationship to increases and decreases in the burdens falling upon the people. Consideration of taxation changes should take place when legislation concerning revenue is being put into effect, and does not refer to the determination of the budget. In other words, the Diet's most important duty in relation to the budget is a negative one, namely to check from the sidelines on any mistakes made by officials.[83]

What this meant was that since decisions about taxation were to be taken at the level of discussion about legislation, and not at the level of budget discussion, the right of the Diet to engage in budgetary deliberation was strictly limited. In other words, the Diet and the people had political rights only over the total amount of taxation to be levied; on the way tax revenue was to be spent they had at most the right of 'inspection'.

In order to give concrete backing to this interpretation, Tsuzuki, in an article written at about the same time as the 'transcendentalism' article, developed an interpretation of articles 64 and 67 of the Constitution. On the general definition of the power of budget deliberation contained in article 64, he latched onto the use of the word 'consent' (*kyōsan*) in the article, and wrote:

> Consent does not mean approbation (*shōdaku*), because the power of consent does not indicate the power of arbitrary decision.... The Diet possesses only the power to be consulted on questions relating to the budget, and completely lacks the power to determine the budget on its own account.[84]

In other words, he held that article 64 itself, which determined in a general way the Diet's power of deliberation on the budget, established limits to that power. If this is the case, then article 67, which was designed specifically in order to limit the Diet's deliberative powers relating to the budget, becomes a double limitation clause. Tsuzuki explains article 67 as establishing a partial power of implementing bills. As he put it:

> If the Government does not have the consent (agreement) of the Diet, it must have the item of expenditure defined as an item under article 67, and because items of expenditure under article 67, which concerns Government proposals, are settled by the will of the Government alone, *even when the budget itself fails to pass, items under article 67 must be regarded as being previously established by the Government's budget of that year.*[85]

Article 67 provided that 'those already fixed expenditures based by the Constitution upon the powers appertaining to the Emperor, and such expenditures as may have arisen by the effect of law, or that appertain to the legal obligations of the Government, shall be neither rejected nor reduced by the Imperial Diet, without the concurrence of the Government'. This was one of the important issues during the first Diet between the Government and the Diet. Since, however, the argument focused mainly upon the timing and method of expression of the 'concurrence' or 'non-concurrence' specified in the text of article 67, even today the interconnection between items of expenditure under article 67 and the power to carry out the budget of the preceding year contained in article 71, remains fairly unclear. Nevertheless, Watanabe Kunitake, Finance Minister in the second Itō Cabinet, insisted that the phrase in article 67, 'Those already fixed expenditures based by the Constitution upon the powers appertaining to the Emperor'[86] must be considered together with the power to carry out the budget of the preceding year, and arrived at a view which was diametrically opposed to that of Tsuzuki. In his words:

> If this article is simply provided in order to guarantee the total sum which is determined by laws, orders and contracts, and which, therefore, cannot be altered without changes of laws, orders and contracts, it was introduced for the purpose of making the total sum unalterable, and as a guarantee that every year along with the budget it is extremely difficult to effect alterations over and above the laws, orders and contracts. But in connection with the expenditure based upon powers appertaining to the Emperor, the word 'fixed' has been added, which restricts the constitutional

guarantee to the already determined budget and gives sufficient strength to the Diet's power of consent so far as new or increased expenditure is concerned. This seems to be the most proper interpretation.[87]

Watanabe proceeded to give a concrete example: 'Fixed expenditures based upon the powers appertaining to the Emperor' include (1) salaries of officials with the ranks of *chokunin, sōnin* and *hannin* [government officials of first, second and third rank] and (2) salaries, provisions, clothing and upkeep of horses within military and naval expenditure,[88] and these are clearly items 'determined [within the total sum of] the budget of the preceding year'.[89] It is [now extremely] difficult to be sure whether it was Tsuzuki's interpretation or that of Watanabe which was the prevailing one within the Government at that time, but clearly, compared with Watanabe, the Finance Ministry official, the interpretation of article 67 by Tsuzuki of the Ministry of Home Affairs was the more transcendental.

Tsuzuki's insistence on absolute executive superiority over the legislature, and on absolute superiority of the national interest over public opinion, was obviously connected with the view that officials were far superior beings to Diet members. His transcendentalist argument was supported by self-confidence and a sense of élite superiority in his position as a specialist official. Even in his previously cited article 'Transcendentalism' Tsuzuki advanced as a proof of the superiority of 'national policy' over 'public opinion', that 'national policy' is established as a result of 'Government officials', making 'specialist investigations'; but in an article written about the same time entitled 'On Civil Administration', he covers the same point in greater detail:

What the popular rights supporters argue is that people, as many as possible, should be consulted in the administration of political affairs. The thinking, however, which underlies this doctrine is the idea that irrespective of their wisdom or folly, irrespective of their poverty or wealth, irrespective of their education or the lack of it, men are creatures on an equal footing.... On the contrary, the majority in any country are always humdrum people, while men of wisdom are in a minority. The majority are poor, while the rich are always a minority. The majority are uneducated, whereas those who have received education are always a minority. Majority politics always means the repression of the minority of men of intelligence by the majority of ordinary people, and repression of the minority of rich people by the majority of poor. Therefore it is nothing strange that any country which is administrated by its majority will always fall under oppression.[90]

His general argument contrasting the ignorant, uneducated and poor majority with the knowledgeable, educated and well-off minority was developed into a contrast between Diet Members and journalists, on the one hand, and Government officials, on the other. Diet Members 'never approach a country's political problems by means of specialist study, but merely obey the dictates of public opinion',[91] while journalists 'in the bulk of cases have no other means of making a living while they are young, and try to make their reputation by having their names in the newspaper, and thus gaining influence in the world. The explanations are usually shallow and easy to understand, and it is extremely rare to see a deep and penetrating argument on the pages of a newspaper.'[92] The repeated use of phrases like 'specialist investigation', or 'a deep and penetrating argument' clearly provided the ground for believing in the superiority of Government officials over other forces.

We can see, therefore, that Tsuzuki's 'transcendentalist' argument presented in an extreme form the supremacy of 'national interest' over 'public opinion', of the executive over the legislature, and of the bureaucracy over Diet Members and newspapermen. In other words, a Government which dealt with national issues formulated on the basis of proposals emanating from the specialist research of the bureaucracy, without making any concession to the Diet or to public opinion, was a 'transcendentalist' government, and was Tsuzuki's ideal.

As we have already seen, transcendentalism in this sense attracted a considerable number of opponents within the *hanbatsu* Government and on its periphery. One of these was Tani Tateki, whom we have discussed in the preceding section. Tani put forward a strong counter-argument against Tsuzuki's 'fixed expenditure principle' in the following terms:

> Tsuzuki's argument is uncouth in the extreme. This kind of argument amounts to disloyal nonsense which puts the Constitution and the Imperial House in danger.[93]

Remembering that the character of Tsuzuki's transcendentalism, seen as bureaucratic absolutism, was typically revealed in his interpretation of article 67 as granting the power of executing bills, it can readily be understood that Tani Tateki, who opposed bureaucratic absolutism and therefore placed expectations on constitutional government, should have attacked Tsuzuki's interpretation of article 67. In other words, the debate about article 67 constituted a crucial point of dispute in the debate about transcendentalism. Tani in his article started from an 'Emperor and people' interpretation of constitutional politics, using the phrase 'Agreement between Emperor and people, absence of rancour between high and low',[94] and although he admitted that there was a contradiction in the Constitution between the definition of powers appertaining to the Emperor and the definition of the Diet's power of consent, he feared that if the Government were to operate using a literal interpretation of the powers appertaining to the Emperor, the Diet would engage in the same kind of behaviour and the result would be conflict between the Emperor on the one hand and the Diet and People on the other.

However much Tsuzuki may have repudiated the notion of restraint by the legislature over the executive, articles 38 and 64 of the Constitution gave legislative power and the power of budget deliberation to the Diet, and in any case the matter was not such as could be resolved by constitutional interpretation alone. The relationship between the executive and the legislature was no longer a question of 'law' but had become a question of 'politics'. This point was made by one of the Itō faction bureaucrats, Inoue Kowashi, who wrote:

> The kind of theory which holds that the Government should maintain strict neutrality, standing aloof from the political parties, can be applied legalistically (the notion that one can govern according to the same law whether in relation to political friends or political enemies), but it is fantastic nonsense to argue that it can be applied to the dictates of political strategy.'[95]

In the same statement of opinion, Inoue wrote: 'If the previous supporters of the Government are not strong enough to rely on, and if the popular parties make some concessions and are prepared to unite with the Government, the Government should not hesitate to enter into an alliance with the popular parties, and there is nothing that politicians should be unduly anxious about in pursuing such a policy.'[96] As this suggests, in the arena of practical politics, not only the formation of parties supporting the Government, but even coalition with the popular parties, had become a real issue. The tendency which Tsuzuki so strongly attacked, whereby 'in order to obtain a majority in the Diet they try to obtain an accord with [the parties], and in order to gain such an accord they themselves end up by constricting their own administrative powers',[97] was something which those actually holding political power were not able to avoid.

Just as Inoue thought Tsuzuki's transcendentalism was 'legalistic', and set up a 'political' interpretation in its stead, so Mutsu Munemitsu from an early stage criticized transcendentalism as 'academic', and counterposed a 'realistic' view. Mutsu summarized Kuroda's transcendentalism speech (see p. 8) in the following terms: 'The Cabinet assists and serves the Imperial House, and oversees the whole of the "State", but the political parties, which represent a part of that "State", cannot, whatever party it may be, enter into any relationship with the Cabinet.' He criticized this view in the following terms: 'Quite apart from the fact that this may be true as an academic opinion, in actual practice how is it possible to obtain a Diet majority in isolation from various parties?'[98]

Thus Tsuzuki's transcendentalist argument encountered criticism even from among officials such as Inoue Kowashi and Mutsu Munemitsu. When we have Mutsu saying that 'first of all politicians are practical not theoretical people',[99] we can clearly observe the fundamental difference between Tsuzuki and Mutsu.

During the later period of the first Matsukata Cabinet and into the second Itō Cabinet, within the arena of practical politics those in the *hanbatsu* Government who were advocating the formation of Government parties or wanted closer relations with the popular parties were gradually increasing in number. As Inoue wrote, 'The Government should not delude itself into thinking that it has political friends and that a political party Cabinet is still a distant prospect,'[100] in other words, although they were still repudiating the notion of a party Cabinet, it was clear for them that unless they allied themselves with the majority party in the Diet it would become harder and harder to govern. We should remember that Tsuzuki's extreme statement of bureaucratic absolutism was written as a reaction against concessions in the arena of practical politics made to the parties and the Diet. Even though it was an unrealistic attitude, it has a significance which cannot be ignored. Paradoxically, the more it became necessary to make concessions to the parties after the Sino-Japanese war, the more support for Tsuzuki's kind of transcendentalism emerged within the bureaucracy. The bureaucratic group known as the *Yamagata* faction will be discussed in Chapter 4, but the transcendentalism of Tsuzuki may be regarded as a precursor of it.

2 'Enrich the Nation and Strengthen the Armed Forces' and 'Lighten the People's Burdens' as issues in the early Diet sessions

From the time of the first Diet session the popular parties – principally the *Jiyūtō* and the *Kaishintō* – proclaimed as their fundamental policies retrenchment of expenditure and reduction of the people's burdens [of taxation], and they vigorously attacked the *hanbatsu* Government to this end. Between the first Matsukata Government, however, and the second Itō Government, relations between the *hanbatsu* and the popular parties entered a period of significant change, both in the nature of policy confrontations and in their attitudes towards 'transcendental' versus party cabinets. First of all the *Jiyūtō* began to acquiesce in the 'positive policies [translated hereafter as 'expansionist policies', or 'expansionism'] being propounded by the *hanbatsu* Government, of armaments expansion and development of industry. In contrast, the *Kokumin Kyōkai*, which had previously occupied a pro-Government position in support of the Government's policies of enriching the nation and strengthening the armed forces, swung round to a position of hostility to the Itō Cabinet by introducing the treaty revision problem as a new issue. A little after the *Jiyūtō* had moved to a pro-Government position, the *Kaishintō*, which now occupied the status of the only remaining popular party, shifted the focus of dispute at the inauguration of the fifth Diet from the budget to foreign policy, and, aligning itself with the pro-Government *Kokumin Kyōkai*, became a wing of the hard-line foreign policy faction.

This chapter will examine the relations of each party between the fourth and fifth Diet sessions, by looking at its basic policies. We shall see how the conflicts and contradictions between the Government policies and the policies of the popular parties developed, in order to illuminate the changes in relationship between the *hanbatsu* and the popular parties.

EXPANSIONIST POLICIES

As is well known, during the first Diet session the *Jiyūtō* and the *Kaishintō* strongly attacked the *hanbatsu* Government, advocating policies of retrenching expenditure and decreasing taxation. Opposing this, Prime Minister Yamagata attempted to reject their demands by stressing the nation's goal ever since the [Meiji] Restoration, of 'enriching the nation and strengthening the armed forces', as well as of industrialization. Yamagata, reacting against the action of the Diet in cutting the budget, spoke as follows:

> Since the opening of the country by Imperial command at the Meiji Restoration, the Government has concentrated on advancing the progress of civilization, has built up armaments and introduced education, broken down old prejudices and reformed hundreds of institutions, and in the whole of these twenty-four years there has not been a single day when these national goals have been altered. Following our national goals, we are seeking externally to expand our national power, while internally we are striving to follow the path of civilization. If we are steadily to realize these aspirations, we cannot accept this extreme reduction of expenditure, which has been essential for management hitherto. My colleagues and I deeply regret the obstacles to our national goals which have been placed against our policies. Reduction of expenditure contradicting our national goals will reduce the strength of our nation, lose us the respect of the Powers, and in the long term will constitute a grievous error. The Government can never agree to any such policy.[1]

This speech was made for the purpose of expressing disagreement with article 67 expenditure items in the revised budget proposal in the House of Representatives.[2] In other words, because it would have lacked persuasiveness merely to have expressed disagreement with article 67 of the Constitution, he spoke in terms of the post-Restoration 'national goals' of 'enriching the nation and strengthening the armed forces', as well as of an 'open country and progressive spirit', appealed to the need for armaments expansion and industrialization, and thus appealed to the Diet not to accede to any reduction of expenditure.

The revised budget draft, however, in the Budget Committee of the House of Representatives, sought essentially to make up the shortfall in land tax by reducing public service expenditures and salaries, and did not directly require a reduction in military expenditure and public works.³ Of course this revised budget, which attempted to reduce the numbers and salaries of public servants, could not be passed without the concurrence of the Government, because it fell under Constitution article 67, section 1: 'Those already fixed expenditures based by the Constitution upon the powers appertaining to the Emperor....'⁴ This, however, did not directly conflict with the 'national goals' proclaimed by Yamagata. When Inoue Kowashi, head of the Legislative Bureau, was shown the draft of the speech by Yamagata and asked his opinion of it, he made the following points and wrote these criticisms:

> For the Government to establish national goals and to say that reduction of expenditure is incompatible with the expansion of national power, is acceptable in relation to certain areas of expenditure (such as expenditure on the Army and Navy, and on education), but it should not apply to reductions in excess public service numbers and expenditure, in the cutting of luxuries and waste, and if it is mistakenly applied to these categories we may expect a strong reaction. The Diet has avoided making cuts in industrial and military expenditure, just as the Government had insisted in its speeches; in other words we have to say that it has been at pains to follow the common goals which the Government is putting forward, and it is limiting its budget cuts to the bureaucracy. Therefore if it wants to reject the budget resolution, the Government must base its position on the following three reasons: (1) that there is a tendency for Imperial rights to be violated; (2) that the smooth working of the bureaucracy is being hindered; (3) that even if the Government were prepared to accept this argument, a long period of investigation and preparation would be necessary. 'An open country and progressive spirit' is unrelated to this question.⁵

In Inoue's criticism of Prime Minister Yamagata's speech, the problems inherent in the call to reduce expenditure, (one of the popular parties' principal policies in the early Diet sessions), were clearly revealed. What this meant was a call, not for a general reduction in expenditure, but for cutting down 'political expenses', in other words too much administrative expenditure. Since the powers of the Diet in matters relating to article 67 of the Meiji Constitution, which refers to 'ordinary expenditures required by the organization of the different branches of the administration, and by that of the Army and Navy, the salaries of all civil and military officers and expenditures that may be required in consequence of treaties concluded with foreign countries',[6] were restricted, the Government had the constitutional powers to reject demands for reduction in expenditures in these areas. But on the other hand it was difficult to obtain the agreement of Diet Members and electors for administrative expenditures, by comparison with military and industrial expenditures. The image of lavish expenditure by officials, and of administrative waste, had permeated the popular consciousness ever since the *Minken* [popular rights] movement, and had been strengthened by the impression left from the *Rokumeikan*[7] period. Therefore, it was not particularly persuasive to reject the Diet's demands for budget cutbacks simply because of article 67 of the Constitution. This was why Yamagata was so passionate in his defence of 'national interest' when he demolished the Diet's proposals. As Inoue Kowashi said, however, the parties were not opposed to the 'national interest' as such. In fact, of course, since the call to reduce expenditure did imply the restructuring of the Army and Navy, and a reduction in salaries of their personnel, it did mean reducing military expenditure. Its aim, however, was not the reduction of military strength, but it was put forward as a way of tightening up on wasteful administrative procedures. For this reason it did not make sense for the *hanbatsu* Government to use 'national interest' as its reason for rejecting the popular parties' demands for cutting back the budget.

The expansionism of the first Matsukata Cabinet was specifically put forward in an attempt to overcome this weakness of the *hanbatsu* Government in its struggle with the budget reduction arguments of the popular parties, and this, as we have seen, was clear in the thinking of Inoue, who was a principal advocate of expansionism. In July 1891, Inoue Kowashi proposed to Itō Hirobumi (President of the Privy Council) and to Matsukata Masayoshi, (Prime Minister) policies for the second Diet session, and in these proposals an expansionist approach was clearly evident. In a letter sent to Itō on 5 July 1891, Inoue wrote: 'We must change the Government's defensive posture in the second Diet session, and must move over to the initiative. . . .'[8] Expansionist policies are more dangerous than passivity, and if we do not have the right person to lead us we shall be in trouble.'[9]

It is clear that he was criticizing the policies towards the Diet of the Yamagata Government as 'negative' and defensive', and was advocating instead the need for expansionist measures. These could be summarized as follows:

1 Since the Government agreed to the expenditure reduction

proposal of the first Diet session, and since on the revenue side the land tax reduction proposal was defeated in the House of Peers, the resultant excess revenue should be used for one of the following items in a supplementary budget:

(a) riparian works
(b) capital for the Agricultural and Industrial Bank
(c) buying up private railways
(d) development works in Hokkaidō.

2 If it is impossible to reduce the land tax, we must put forward reasons which are sufficiently comprehensible. If it is possible to agree to a reduction in the land tax, this should be only on condition that the bulk of the capital from the tax reduction be used for insurance and savings.

On the question of riparian works (1a), it was proposed to create a Central Riparian Council, consisting of five officials and seven leading party personalities, the party members to be given responsibility for the riparian problem, so as to make them more understanding of the Government's point of view. On (1b) – the Agricultural Bank – there was no explanation in the document, but an explanation was attached to the very similar statement of opinion given to the Prime Minister, Matsukata, on 18 July. According to this, the bank was to lend only to co-operative unions run by local authorities for the purpose of agricultural improvement and Government-run construction projects. It should be noted that the reason why industrial construction projects were excluded from the bank's lending activities was that the Diet's opposition was being taken into consideration.[11]

As has already been noted, the excess revenue of ¥6,500,000 with which Inoue was concerned had come about because of the failure of the first Diet to pass a bill for the reduction of the land tax. Thus it was clear that the popular parties were now using the excess revenue as an argument for their goal of reducing the land tax. Having more or less foreseen that this would occur, Inoue was now proposing to make use of the excess revenues for undertakings closely connected with local interests, such as the establishment of a bank directed towards riparian works as well as agricultural and construction projects. As was clear from Inoue's statement that 'when compared with reduction of political expenditures, the proposal to move the burden of expenditure on prisons from the prefectures to the central Government is not as attractive',[12] he thought that he could face the popular parties by using the excess revenue left over from the first

Diet session for policies more attractive then the tax reduction policies of the parties themselves. Rather than giving the people 'relief', he proposed, as it were, to give them stimulus for development.

The Yamagata Government, with the aid of Gotō Shōjirō and Mutsu Munemitsu, was successful in removing the first Diet session from the manipulations of the *Jiyūtō* Tosa faction, but this was only a temporary respite, and the confrontation between the *hanbatsu* Government and the popular parties did not abate. Rather the fact that ¥6,500,000 was cut from expenditure provided an impetus for the popular parties to demand a reduction of land tax. Immediately before the second Diet session, Itagaki of the *Jiyūtō* and Ōkuma of the *Kaishintō* entered once again into an alliance with each other, and as a result co-operation between the popular parties was strengthened. On the other hand, the *Taiseikai*, which during the first Diet session had wholeheartedly supported the *hanbatsu* Government, split into two factions before the second Diet session: a completely pro-Government party and a quasi-Government party. The latter, in November 1891, formed itself into the *Tomoe* Club and assumed an opposition party colouring.[13] Thus the *Taiseikai*, which had had seventy-nine Members in the first Diet,[14] was reduced to sixty seats at the start of the second Diet[15] and to fifty at its close.[16] Inoue Kowashi reported to Itō Hirobumi: 'There is a rumour that a meeting took place recently between Itagaki and Ōkuma; I checked with the Security Bureau [of the Home Ministry], who knew nothing of it, but it was also reported in yesterday's *Kokumin Shimbun*. Whether or not there was any meeting, the tendency to form an alliance is clear. Also the *Taiseikai* is not holding together.'[17] Itō Miyoji also wrote to Itō Hirobumi:

> 'Even if the *Taiseikai* is to exist as a small group, at present it has split asunder and nothing can be done about that. The activities of Ōhigashi Yoshitetsu and the rest of the Kyōto group have so much hurt the feelings of the rest of the *Taiseikai* members, that the members who wish to help the Government can do very little about it, and since Suematsu and others are not in a position to help the Government, if things continue as at present we shall not be able to find anyone to support us during this session.'[18]

In contrast to the fact that the popular parties, split in the first Diet, had reunited, the *Taiseikai* had split and its pro-Government faction was isolated. In this situation the Government had no prospect of devising a political strategem to extricate itself from its predicament.

It was for this reason that the 'expansionist' policies put forward by Inoue Kowashi were essential for the *hanbatsu* Government during the second Diet session.

The budget bill presented to the first Matsukata Cabinet was a way of combating the demands of the popular parties for a reduction in the land tax, by broadly accepting the proposals of Inoue Kowashi, and boldly asserting the necessity of military expansion and industrial development. Reflecting the fact that the first Yamagata Government had failed in its attempts to substitute its own preferred option of military and industrial development for the administrative retrenchment policies of the popular parties, the first Matsukata Government counterposed policies of military and industrial development against the tax reduction policies of the popular parties. Specifically, the Government planned to spend the surplus which the popular parties had hoped, in the first Diet, to obtain from reduction of administrative expenditure, in order to reduce the land tax, to expand the Army and Navy, to establish a steel works, for riparian works and for the development of Hokkaidō. In the Diet they presented a simple choice between military and industrial expenditure and tax reduction. Table 1 shows the continuing projects planned by the Matsukata Cabinet, to be financed from the total of ¥11,660,000, which was made up of ¥6,450,000 surplus revenue from administrative savings made during the first Diet session, and ¥5,210,000 surplus of 1890. About one third of this, or ¥3,150,000, was put into the budget of 1892.

Moreover, apart from these long-term proposals, the Government brought down a private railway purchase law and a railway public loan law, in order to expand public transport by railway nationalization. The Government also promised a credit union law and an agricultural society law, in order to improve the condition of

Table 2.1 The long-term expenditure proposals of the Matsukata Cabinet

Army expenditure	¥3,000,000
Expenditure on battleship construction	¥2,750,000
Expenditure on construction of steelworks	¥2,250,000
Riparian works	¥ 945,000
Hokkaidō land research expenditure	¥ 131,991
Total	¥9,076,991

Source: *Meiji zaisei shi*, vol. 3, p.569

agriculture, and proposed that the State should take over the cost of prisons, in order to lighten local taxation.[19]

It is clear therefore that the Matsukata Government in presenting its 1892 budget, countered the demand of the popular parties for a reduction in land tax by not only declaring the necessity of increasing military and naval expenditure, but also putting forward a fairly large-scale plan for industrial development. As Matsukata said in his keynote address to the second Diet session: 'Happily these last two or three years – and especially this year – we have achieved a surplus over our planned revenue by cutting expenditure, and we propose to use these surplus funds principally for the previously mentioned essential projects.'[20] So the special characteristic of the Matsukata Government's expansionism lay in the fact that it used all the surplus which had derived from compromise with the popular parties in the previous Diet, for the purposes of military and industrial development. The meaning of expansionist policies in order to counter the popular parties, was expressed succinctly by the pro-Government paper *Kokkai* at the time of the Diet dissolution:

> The Government has adopted a policy of positive progress.... Even if it adds to the burdens of the people, it will result in the promotion of all kinds of new undertakings so as to develop our nation. The popular parties have adopted a negative strategy of regress, desiring to cancel almost all the projects and so achieve tax reductions.... We believe that from now on both Government and Opposition parties should confront the electorate and seek its verdict.[21]

As is evident from the above, the bulk of the ideas contained in the 'post-war planning' which followed the Sino-Japanese War was contained in the budget which was presented to the second Diet session by the First Matsukata Cabinet. There was a decisive difference, however, between the expansionist policies of these two periods, in both the scope and the nature of the surplus. It is clear if we compare Tables 2 and 3 with Table 1 that the expansionist policies of the first Matsukata Cabinet were incomparably smaller in their scope than those which followed the Sino-Japanese War. This was particularly so in the case of industrial development.

Fukuzawa Yukichi [in 1891] judged that 'if we just look at the words, it would appear as though the Government is putting forward expansionist policies, but if we consult reality this is certainly not the case, since those which can be called new projects amount to no more than a single steelworks.'[22] That, however, the construction of the

Table 2.2 Purposes for which Chinese reparations were spent

War expenses	¥ 55,000,000
Army expansion	¥ 50,000,000
Naval expansion	¥130,000,000
Construction of steelworks	¥ 5,000,000
Contingency fund	¥ 50,000,000
Supplementary capital for Agricultural Bank	¥ 10,000,000
Total	¥300,000,000

Source: *Meiji zaisei shi*, vol. 1, p.21

Table 2.3 Projects for which public loans were earmarked (7-year plan from 1896)

Army and naval expansion	¥ 77,458,907
Construction of steelworks	¥ 3,516,031
Hokkaidō railway construction	¥ 1,178,330
Tobacco Control Bureau establishment and capital	¥ 12,123,550
Expansion of telephone exchanges	¥ 12,802,102
Repairs to the National railways	¥ 26,553,000
Other	¥ 1,278,080
Total	¥135,000,000

Source: *Meiji zaisei shi*, vol. 3, p.836

steelworks was regarded not so much as industrial development as military expenditure is shown graphically by the fact that the expenditure was included in the naval category and was under the jurisdiction of the Navy.[23] Indeed Kabayama, the Navy Minister, appealed to the Diet concerning the necessity of building the steelworks, and this is a clear indication of the same thing:

If a ship were to be damaged either by accident or in the course of naval action, it is hard to see how the repairs could be carried out. Despite the assiduous efforts of our officials, who have endeavoured to build a Navy worthy of the name of Navy, the lack of materials has practically brought these efforts to naught. Even though some say that it is sufficient to build up peacetime stockpiles, this is not enough to maintain Japan's independent military capacity, and if we cannot do this, we might as well fight the enemy with weapons which we borrow from him. Indeed, if our weapons are damaged we shall not be able to replace them.[24]

In other words the purpose of building a steelworks was to create self-sufficiency in arms production. Among the continuing projects, only riparian works and Hokkaidō development could really be called development expenditure, and these were less than 16 per cent of the total. Apart from these there was a plan for railway nationalization, but this was conditional on the private railways purchase bill and the railways public loan bill passing the Diet. In the proposal put forward by Inoue Kowashi which we cited above, he argued that the whole previous year's surplus of ¥6,500,000 should be put either into riparian works or into a development bank, in order to produce a programme which would compete effectively with the arguments and policies of land tax reduction. The Matsukata Cabinet, however, spent only ¥950,000 on riparian works. The 'expansionist' policies of the Matsukata Cabinet, which were aimed at combating the tax reduction policies of the popular parties, leaned heavily towards military expansion, and so the expectations which Inoue Kowashi had entertained were not realized. It had become futile to expect to overcome the land tax reduction arguments with 'expansionist' policies which had become virtually synonymous with military expansion.

Comparing the expansionism following the Sino-Japanese War with those of the first Matsukata Cabinet, we see that there was a difference in the nature of the finance involved. The former was at first financed from the Chinese indemnity and the public development loan, and it was possible to construct a plan whereby the indemnity was used for military expansion and the loan for industrial development. On the other hand, the latter needed to finance both military and industrial expenditures from the sources of finance expected by the popular parties to realize their demands for tax reduction.[25] The reason why the popular parties demanded large-scale reductions in expenditure during the first Diet session and clashed with the *hanbatsu* Government over this was that they wished to make reductions in the land tax by the use of such expenditure cuts. Thus whereas in the first Diet session the popular parties succeeded in reducing public service expenditure by ¥6,500,000, and therefore produced a revenue surplus of the same amount, it is quite clear that in the second Diet session they very much wanted to use these revenues for land tax reduction. Since the Government's expansionist policies and the tax reduction policies of the popular parties were competing for the same revenue, this made compromise between them extremely difficult. Moreover, as we have seen, the Matsukata Cabinet, against the advice of Inoue Kowashi, was using the bulk of the ¥6,500,000 not for industrial development but for military expansion. Even if the question had been framed along the lines favoured by Inoue Kowashi, namely *either* riparian works *or* land tax reduction, or *either* the establishment of an industrial bank *or* land tax reduction, in the second Diet session the Government would probably have lost. Moreover, if it had been a straight choice between military expansion and land tax reduction, there is no doubt that the popular parties would have rejected the former in order to realize the latter.

On the other hand, as we saw in Chapter 1, the expansionism of the Matsukata Cabinet was not sustained by article 67 of the Constitution. What was protected by the Constitution was only the fixed element in military and naval expenditure, whereas the construction of gun emplacements or of battleships, being 'new projects', went beyond the definition of 'fixed expenditures'. Obviously things like the construction of a steelworks or riparian works came outside the article 67 category. For this reason the House of Representatives, in its scrutiny of the budget, slashed most of the surplus expenditure, with the exception of part of the planned spending on gun emplacements.[26] Later the Diet rejected both the private railways purchase bill, which was part of the Government's expansionist policies, and the bill for State financing of prisons, which the Government had put forward as a tax reduction measure instead of reducing the land tax. Since these were legislative bills, the power of the House of Representatives was stronger than in the case of the budget. It is here that the contradictions between the expansionist policies of the Government and the dictates of the Imperial Constitution were revealed in their most concentrated form. As we have already seen, the Matsukata Cabinet's expansionism was not confined to those areas protected by the Constitution, and the Government was trying to progress beyond a mere defensive strategy in the face of the popular parties' attacks. When, however, the Government sought to progress along these lines, it found that the only guarantees given it by the Constitution were its powers of Diet dissolution and of carrying on with the budget of the previous year. Of course even the second Diet was not entirely without controversy on the article 67 question, but when we look at the explanations given by the Cabinet for dissolving the Diet, it seems that the principal reason lay in the

Diet's rejection of those aspects of expansionist policies lying outside the purview of article 67.[27] Indeed it seems highly likely that after the Diet had been dissolved the main reason why the Matsukata Cabinet attempted to reverse the power relationships within the Diet by its notorious interference with the elections was precisely this. When the Government wanted to build up the armed forces and to develop various projects, article 67 was of no avail, and it had to resort to Diet dissolution or carrying on with the previous year's budget. Moreover, as should be clear from our previous discussion, the option of carrying on with the budget of the previous year was for the Matsukata Cabinet a mere recipe for continuing spending at the lowest level, and this meant that any plans for expansionism could be consigned to oblivion. The financial condition which initially enabled the Cabinet to propose expansionist policies was that as a result of the concessions it had made to the Diet in the previous year in reducing expenditures, there was an unspent surplus. If then they had continued with the budget of the previous year, there would have been no possibility of carrying out expansionist policies simply from accumulated surplus revenue of approximately the same amount. If, as we have previously argued, the emphasis of the Cabinet's expansionism was on Army and Navy expansion, and particularly upon plans for battleship construction for the Navy, this could have been accomplished neither through article 67 nor through the previous year's budget provisions of article 71. If military and naval expansion were an absolute necessity for the *hanbatsu* Government, it had two choices: either it could seek to force a rectification of the Diet by interfering with elections, or it could attempt to arrange with the Diet some sort of compromise.[28] The famous 'indignation speech' of the Navy Minister, Kabayama [see pp. 47–8], was a revelation of the astonishment and indignation of Kabayama at the time that he discovered that expenditures for battleship and steelworks construction had been completely cut out by the Diet, and that no effective policy existed to deal with this.[29]

As we can see, therefore, the Government's policies of expansionism met a total rebuff during the second Diet. Moreover, even the notorious electoral interference, which was practised subsequently, failed in its aim of effecting a fundamental change in the balance of power in the House of Representatives. The Government's attempts to pull out from the *status quo* received almost no help from the Imperial Constitution, which had been so carefully prepared.

Nevertheless, the expansionist policies of the Matsukata Cabinet were not entirely without significance for the *hanbatsu* Government as a whole. As Itō Miyoji wrote in reporting the internal situation of the *Jiyūtō* to Itō Hirobumi, 'Even though the party is totally opposed to the new projects for 1892, public opinion is tending towards the Government position on the question of railways, and the Party is reluctant to make enemies of influential businessmen. The Party, therefore, is most hesitant, in this respect.'[30]

Thus expansionist policies in the same sense of opposition to the retrenchment and tax cutting views of the popular parties should not be ignored. The real nature of the first Matsukata Cabinet can be demonstrated by a later party report of the *Kaishintō*:

> When the Matsukata Cabinet was formerly in office, it proposed to the Diet a radical programme of legislation, including a steelworks bill, railway bills, a bill for transferring to the State the burden of prison administration, and a battleship construction bill, and it has subsequently continued its efforts to have the legislation passed by such means as dissolving the Diet and interfering with elections. The general tendency, however, is running contrary to that of the Matsukata Cabinet, and over half the bills have been consigned to the rubbish heap. Nevertheless, the Cabinet certainly has the nature and policies of a Cabinet secure in its opinions and determined to carry them out.[31]

THE TAX REDUCTION ARGUMENT AND ITS CONTRADICTIONS

Just at the time when the expansionist policies of the first Matsukata Cabinet had been defeated as a result of the vigorous opposition of the popular parties in the second and third Diet sessions, retrenchment and tax reduction also – considered to be a 'life and death matter'[32] for the popular parties – were entering into a difficult period. The policies championed ever since the first Diet session by the popular parties could be summed up as a reduction in both the numbers and salaries of officials, whereby land tax could be cut and land assessment could be revised.[33] If we broadly divide budget expenditures into those relating to administration, government projects and the armed forces, the parties did not wish to reduce either government projects (rivers, riparian works, roads, shipping, harbours, railways, etc.) or military spending, but they wanted to achieve tax reduction principally by means of cutting the numbers and salaries of officials.[34] In the words of Ozaki Yukio: 'In order to achieve reductions in expenditure it is necessary to bring about administrative retrenchment, whereas to cut back on project expenditure is always harmful and without benefit.'[35] As we have seen, the budget investigation conducted by the popular parties in the first Diet was based on this very principle. Since according to article 67, paragraph 1, of the Constitution it was not possible to cut administrative expenditure without the concurrence of the Government, from a constitutional point of view administrative retrenchment was problematical. As was admitted, though, by Inoue Kowashi, a member of the *hanbatsu* Government, it was politically impossible for the Government to ignore the insistence of the popular parties that superfluous officials should be dismissed. When, however, the popular parties came to confront the expansionism of the Matsukata Cabinet in the second and third Diet sessions, their retrenchment and tax cutting arguments became unable to bear the weight of such a principle, because since the Matsukata Cabinet was redirecting the surplus acquired as a result of administrative retrenchment towards military and industrial development, a reduction in the land tax could be achieved only by cutting these administrative expenditures. At a time, however, when the unequal treaties were still in existence and Japan was still working towards the status of an independent state with respect to the outside world, it was extremely difficult to oppose directly any expansion in military spending. Moreover, to reduce project spending connected with local interests, such as the completion of riparian works and development of the railway network, was coming to be regarded with caution from within the popular parties themselves. The fact that it became impossible to restrict budget cuts to the sphere of administrative retrenchment was one of the reasons why the tax cutting proposals of the popular parties became problematical.

Before we go into this argument, however, we must first explore another contradiction of the retrenchment and tax cutting argument. As we noted when we were discussing the transcendentalist argument of Tsuzuki Keiroku in Chapter 1, the Imperial Constitution, 'in providing for taxation, does not do so through the budget, but by individual pieces of legislation'.[36] This meant that the two policies of administrative retrenchment and cutting taxation, though they were both part of the same thing so far as the popular parties were concerned, nevertheless differed from each other in the procedures required for their attainment. The former required the use of the budget investigation power, whereas the latter required the use of the legislative power. As we have already pointed out, despite the limits imposed by articles 67 and 71 of the Constitution, the power of the

Diet in budget investigation was really quite strong. The government did not have the power of executing bills, but since the administration of the previous year's budget represented in practice a reduction in the finance available, a supplementary budget had to be presented, and even that could be cut back by the Diet. For this reason the administrative retrenchment demanded by the popular parties was something which the Government had to acknowledge and with which it needed to compromise. The problem was that the saving on administration thus effected was not linked with tax reductions. Reduction in the land tax and reform of land assessment – the form of tax cutting which the popular parties were insisting on – could not be brought about without the presentation of a bill, which had to pass both the House of Peers and the House of Representatives. Therefore, although the Government could be made to accept administrative retrenchment up to the point where land tax reduction and land assessment reform were budgetarily possible, once the two crucial bills had been defeated in the House of Peers, that was as far as it could go. Only the surplus revenue produced by administrative cutbacks could be carried over to the following year. The Land Tax Regulations Amendment Bill passed the House of Representatives in the first, third and fourth Diet sessions, but in each case was either talked out or defeated in the House of Peers and therefore did not become law.[37] We have already seen how the administrative cutbacks brought about in the first Diet session provided finance for the expansionist policies of the Matsukata Cabinet in the second. Diet members from the popular parties must have been incensed to read in the newspapers representing the *Taiseikai*, 'Although the first Diet pruned administrative spending by ¥6,500,000, *because the money saved was not added to revenue, it in no way served to benefit the people* during this year: in other words the hopes of those who were expecting tax reductions over a number of years were completely dashed.'[38] In fact not only were the monies saved not added to revenue, but this happened because the House of Peers prevented it. This was not just a question of the land tax, but was connected with the nature of the whole legislative power under the Imperial Constitution. The treatment received at the hands of the House of Peers by bills presented by members of the House of Representatives, which were passed by that House between the first and the fourteenth Diet sessions, is set out in Table 4. Before the Sino-Japanese War (that is, up to the sixth Diet session), of 53 bills which passed the House of Representatives a mere 13 were passed outright or with amendments by the House of Peers. The remainder were either rejected or talked

Table 2.4   A history of bills presented by Members of the House of Representatives to the House of Peers

Diet no.	Passed	Amended	Rejected	Talked out	Total
1	2	–	–	5	7
2	–	–	–	6	6
3	2	–	2	8	12
4	2	5	8	1	16
5	1	–	–	6	7
6	–	1	1	3	5
7	–	–	–	–	–
8	15	3	16	9	43
9	2	1	9	5	17
10	4	1	6	6	17
11	–	–	–	–	–
12	3	2	–	2	7
13	8	4	7	11	30
14	24	2	8	5	39

Source: Calculated from *Gikai seido nanajū nenshi, teikoku gikai anken meiroku*

out. In contrast there was a considerable increase after the the Sino-Japanese War in the number of bills from the Representatives which the House of Peers let through. This may have been connected with the parties' own change of direction. During the early Diet sessions the House of Peers faithfully played the role of 'bulwark' for the *hanbatsu* Government, which meant that for the time being article 38 of the Constitution, providing the House of Representatives with the power of initiating legislation, was practically a dead letter. Because of the existence of the House of Peers it was extremely difficult for the political parties to bring their politics to fruition through use of the legislative power, and this was the primary reason why the popular parties were frustrated in their attempts to cut back taxation.[39]

We shall now discuss more specifically how the strategy of administrative retrenchment and tax reduction broke down under the onslaught of expansionist policies. These policies, as advocated by the popular parties, were inescapably contradictory by virtue of the fact that during the second and third Diet sessions military and industrial spending had to be reduced. Although the popular parties from the second Diet session onwards were insisting on tax cuts without reducing military and industrial expenditure, by utilizing the surplus, in actual practice wide-ranging reductions had to be made in military and industrial spending. The reason for this was that since the confrontation that took place during the second Diet session was a dispute about whether to use the administrative retrenchment surplus for military and industrial expansion *or* for reducing taxation, there would be no money available for tax cuts unless military and industrial spending were cut back. The logic of the popular parties in their attempts to rationalize this contradiction can be seen from the following quotations:

> Whether a given project is effective or ineffective depends upon the skill or incompetence of those in charge of operations, and in order to judge the worth or otherwise of the present Government's projects, rather than concentrating on the nature of the projects themselves, we should examine the good and bad points of those in charge.[40]

> In examining project expenditure we need to distinguish between what is fundamental and peripheral, thrifty and extravagant.[41]

Originally when the popular parties so vigorously attacked the *han-batsu* Government, calling for administrative retrenchment and tax reductions, they avoided direct confrontation with the Government when the latter appealed to 'national interest' under such slogans as 'enriching the nation and strengthening the armed forces' or 'promotion of industry.' According to Inukai Tsuyoshi, 'The projects which our Government has hithero sought to carry out, such as promotion of industries, the expansion of railways, the building of ships, the construction of gun emplacements and the expansion of the armed forces, are all useful projects for which the Government needs to take responsibility, and it is nonsense to call any of them superfluous.'[42] For this reason criticism of expansionist policies which were justified in terms of military and industrial developments had to resort to probing of Government untrustworthiness and alleged mishandling of planned projects, and such criticism lacked persuasive power. At the time when spending on battleships and steelworks was being cut back during the second Diet, Sugita Teiichi of the *Jiyūtō* spoke as follows:

> Generally speaking we, as Japanese people, are supporters of the expansion of the Navy. Considering, however, the chaos in the Naval Ministry, and the inability of the Navy to assuage anxieties, we cannot sanction enormous appropriations.[43]

The problem for the popular parties was that they were supporters of naval expansion, but they found they had to argue for retrenchments on the grounds of chaos in the Naval Ministry.

The adverse influence of the Government's policies of expansion upon tax reduction was not confined to the level of logic. Among the industrial promotion policies of the Matsukata Cabinet during the second Diet session were included a private railway purchase bill and a railway public loan bill, but both of them were either talked out or rejected by the second Diet, and at the same time these two bills provoked internal dissent within the popular parties. The *Jiyūtō* held a general meeting of its Diet Members on 16 December 1891 in the very middle of the second Diet session, and they resolved to oppose both bills on account of their policy of opposition to new works. Hoshi Tōru, however, representing the views of businessmen who were demanding that railways be bought up by the Government as a rescue operation at a time of economic recession, vigorously asserted the need to purchase private railways.[44]

At the same time there were quite a few Members who, even if they were not interested in rescuing the railway capitalists, were nevertheless strongly in favour of the railway public loan bill as a means of railway expansion in order to develop local industry.[45] Moreover, outside the parties there was a petition movement by local chambers of commerce in various regions[46] demanding the purchase of private railways, and a movement by the Railways Construction League centred on local notabilities,[47] both of which constituted a source of pressure on the popular parties. Quite apart from the railway capitalists, a petition movement for the abolition of cotton import duties and silk export tax was centred upon the cotton spinning industry, and was active in relation to the Government and the Diet.[48] Since the expansionism of the Matsukata Cabinet created certain expectations among the supporters of the popular parties, it gradually became difficult for those parties to restrict their policies to administrative retrenchment and tax reductions.

The fact that a split developed over the tax reduction proposals themselves was one cause of the weakening of the popular parties' position. In fact within those parties there were individuals who regarded policies of administrative retrenchment and tax reduction as a means of embarrassing the *hanbatsu* Government and paving the way for party cabinets. An example of this was the insistence of Minoura Katsundo of the *Kaishintō* that 'our aim ultimately is not revision of land assessment or reduction of land tax'.[49] In this case it was not tax reduction but administrative retrenchment that became of prime importance. This can be seen in the statement that 'Those who, in pursuit of economic retrenchment, seek to reform land assessment and reduce the land tax, and in order to make up the revenue forgone need to increase other tax rates or impose completely new taxes, are mistaken in their aim'.[50] We have already seen, however, how embarrassing it could be to the *hanbatsu* Government if the parties were to adopt such a position of principle. If, nevertheless, the Government were to place emphasis on tax reduction, treat administrative retrenchment as a means to it and bring about some lightening of the burdens borne by landlords and peasants, then some progress would be made in the direction of reducing taxes within limits that the Government could agree to.[51] On the other hand, the amount of the reductions was bound to be very small, and this led to internal conflict among the proponents of tax reduction. Moreover, not only land tax reduction and land assessment revision, but also the bill for State financing of prefectural gaols advocated by the *Taiseikai* and the *Kokumin Kyōkai* were presented as a means to some tax reduction. For instance: 'If surplus revenues which are available can be used for the State to take over the running of prisons, it should be possible to reduce local taxation a little, whether it be the local land tax, or local business tax, or miscellaneous local taxes, and so reduce the burdens which the people are carrying.'[52] If prefectural expenditure on prisons were to be taken over by the central Government, this would improve local finances and lighten the local tax burden. Since taxation at the national level would remain as it was previously, a reduction in taxation as a whole would have been achieved. One reason why the *Taiseikai* and the *Kokumin Kyōkai* pushed for the State to take over the financing of prisons, and why the first Matsukata Government, presented a Government-sponsored bill to that effect to the second Diet session, was that this bill contained a crucial ideological point. If the land tax were reduced and land assessment revised, as the popular parties were advocating, the share of the land tax in local taxation would automatically be reduced, and 'the landlords would find their burdens doubly reduced'; the shortfall would have to be made up by supplementing household tax, business tax and miscellaneous taxes, so that 'the small man would groan under ever heavier taxation burdens.'[53] How far the *Taiseikai* and the *Kokumin Kyōkai*, as Government parties, were really thinking of the interests of 'the small man' is open to question,[54] but an attack of this kind upon the popular parties was probably quite effective at a time when memories of the *Minken* [popular rights] movement still remained. Ueki Emori, who had been a theorist for the *Jiyūtō* ever since the time of the *Minken* movement, admitted that the attack on the popular parties had reached its target, and he called upon the landlords who were also Diet members to 'pledge that if the land tax were ever reduced, tenants should also be granted relief.' From this he continued:

> Gentlemen, you have rightly been clamouring for a lightening of the people's tax burdens. You must clamour for relief of poverty among the peasantry. But now that you have become members of the Imperial Diet, you want to argue about reduction of the land tax in the Diet. Even if you accomplish a reduction in the land tax in this way, if the small farmer should fail to obtain the benefit of it, your use of the argument in favour of reduction of the land tax that the tax impoverishes the small farmer will be seen to have been an excuse for you yourselves to grow fat, and you will have no answer to make to such an accusation.[55]

Even though this attack on the tax reduction arguments of the popular parties for allegedly ignoring the interests of the small farmers came from the spokesman of the Government parties, they did have a certain degree of effectiveness. Moreover since both the tax reduction faction and the faction which wanted the Government to take over the finances of the prisons relied upon limited surplus revenue to be derived from administrative retrenchment, they were not in a position to unify their forces.

Between proponents of the land tax reduction and proponents of the land assessment revision there existed a relationship similar to that between those who wanted to reduce the land tax and those who wanted the State to take over the running of the gaols. The popular parties advocated officially both land tax reduction and land assessment revision, but the Government was unlikely to concur with such a double reduction, and therefore it was unlikely to pass the House of Peers. If, however, it were merely a question of land assessment revision on its own, then the Government, ever since the first Matsukata Cabinet, had been considering some sort of concession on this front. Many Diet members from the local regions stood to gain an actual reduction in tax from a revision of land assessment, even though there was no reduction in the rate of taxation, and they came into intense conflict within the popular parties with members who, without reduction in rate of tax, would enjoy no reduction in taxation whatsoever.[57] The land assessment reduction faction, because its demands were more practical, was more prepared to compromise than the land tax reduction faction, and was in a mutually hostile relationship with the faction that wanted the State to assume the prison finances, since that demand, too, was equally well realizable.

The two sides, therefore, were 'completely unable to unite.'[58] Both of them would co-operate with the Government and could satisfy their demands within the bounds permitted by the Government, and since there was a limit to the degree of compromise which could be allowed by a Government which pursued policies of industrial and military expansion, the two of them found themselves in a mutually exclusive relationship with each other.

Thus during the second and third Diet sessions a number of contradictions emerged in the basic policies being pursued by the popular parties, namely administrative retrenchment and tax reduction. When the expansionism of the first Matsukata Cabinet ended in complete failure because of the opposition of the popular parties, it gradually became difficult for those parties themselves to continue to maintain their old policies. The kind of stalemate that developed during the second and third Diet sessions between the Government and the popular parties came to necessitate fundamental political restructuring in the fourth and fifth sessions of the Diet.

FROM TAX REDUCTION TO EXPANSIONIST POLICIES: THE *JIYŪTŌ*

It was the *Jiyūtō* which decided to break the tax reduction stalemate by a concerted move towards the expansionist policies advocated by the Government. The 'Policy of the Policy Affairs Committee of the *Jiyūtō*', published when the first Matsukata Cabinet resigned, included the following statement:

> 'We must not be a party self-satisfied with negative measures of reform. We must take on ourselves the task of directing positive expansionist projects. We must aim to reform and develop Japan's agriculture, industry and commerce, and thus cultivate the people's strength and create a wealthy nation.'[59]

This was a clear sign of a change from negative [retrenchment and tax cutting] to positive [expansionist] policies, from 'conserving the people's strength' [tax reduction] to 'cultivating the people's strength' [public works]. Subsequently towards the end of the year, at the Party Congress, which was held before the opening of the fourth session of the Diet, the following policy was resolved:

> 'Although hitherto our policies have been based on administrative retrenchment and tax reduction, we must now, despite our mistrust of the Government, take positive measures concerning problems

of national interest, in particular those relating to the standard of living, education, foreign policy and defence.'[60]

According to a report which the Government received from Takeuchi Tsuna of the *Jiyūtō*, a meeting of party executives took place at Itagaki's house on 9 November 1892, including Hoshi Tōru, Kōno Hironaka, Matsuda Masahisa and Takeuchi Tsuna. The meeting resolved that:

> The *Jiyūtō* must adopt Positive Constructive [in English in the original] policies without reference to the whims of popular prejudice, and all our policies must be chosen to fit this outlook. Whether we shall be called a government party or a popular party is of no consequence.[61]

What was meant by 'positive policies' or 'positive projects' was, according to Itagaki, 'expansion of railways, development of industry, reform of agriculture, and encouragement of silkworm cultivation',[62] and according to Hoshi Tōru, also included 'the expansion of shipping lines, direct export of raw silk, tea and cotton thread, and some reduction in export tax'.[63] In other words, the party had begun to reveal an attitude of total agreement with the industrial and military expansion policies of the Government. The *Jiyūtō*, however, had not entirely abandoned its policies of tax reduction as can be seen in the statement that 'land tax reduction and land assessment revision remain our policy as hitherto'.[64] Even here, though, some change had clearly taken place. According, for instance, to Itagaki: 'Although we haven't seen the Government's reform as a whole, it is clear that we should agree to at least this part of the reforms',[65] while in the opinion of Hoshi: 'The *Jiyūtō* believes that if it is possible to put our ideas into effect even in small part, this should be done, and we deny that if the whole programme cannot be accomplished then nothing should be done.'[66] The attitude emerges clearly from these statements that taxes ought to be reduced within the limits which the Government would permit. Hoshi subsequently developed this point more specifically:

> The people are not saying that the land tax must be reduced by 0.5 per cent, nor that land assessment should be cut by ¥150,000,000, and so if action were definitely taken to reduce the land tax by 0.3 per cent, or to cut the total value of assessed land to about ¥100,000,000, we the people would welcome this as a first step in the process of reform.[67]

As we have seen, the dilemma which the tax reform advocates had got into in the second and third Diet sessions resulted from a number of factors: first, the achievement of land tax reduction and tax assessment revision was impossible because of the opposition to it of the House of Peers; second, if it were a case of *either* the State taking over the financing of the prisons *or* land tax assessment revision, the Government was prepared to go along with it, so passage through the House of Peers was possible, which meant that the achievement of some degree of tax cutting was out of the question; and third, even within the popular parties there were quite a number of sympathizers with the Government's policies of military expansion and industrial development. Thus the purpose of the change of direction undertaken by the *Jiyūtō* was to try to resolve all these problems at the same time. In other words the party was expressing support for the Government over the problem of 'national interest', and was using the Government's expansionist policies to bring the waverers into line. It was seeking to persuade the land assessment revision supporters by preaching gradualism and revisionism in relation to tax reduction, and in relation to the land tax reduction problem they tried to prevail upon the land tax reduction faction by applying gradualism and promising a 0.3 per cent reduction. Moreover, as is clear from Hoshi Tōru's remarks, the *Jiyūtō* was creating the impression of a party that gets things done, by implying that 'action' would 'definitely be taken' to reduce taxation, even if it were only a partial reduction. The fact that the *Jiyūtō*, which was the largest of the majority parties within the popular party alliance, should have officially changed course in this way, led inevitably to the collapse of that alliance.

Immediately before the frontal conflict during the fourth session of the Diet between the Itō Cabinet and the popular party alliance, Hoshi Tōru said: 'I loathe the words "popular parties"', and made a public announcement to the effect that 'the *Jiyūtō* and the *Kaishintō* should act separately, and so long as they claim the title of "party" they should each pursue their respective ideas.'[68] According to a *Jiyūtō* Diet members' report, 'Our party has hitherto presented bills in co-operation with other parties, but in this session of the Diet we have come to feel the disadvantages of doing so, and we have decided to act independently.'[69] It could indeed be said that the *Jiyūtō* had resolved to tread the path towards dissolution of the popular party alliance. What, then, following the break-up of that alliance, was the direction in which the *Jiyūtō* was likely to proceed? What it was in fact aiming at was a vertical coalition with the *hanbatsu* Government, and the status of an independent majority party. Takeuchi Tsuna, of the *Jiyūtō*, subsequently recalled that at the time of the inauguration of the second Itō Government, he had planned an alliance between Itō and Itagaki.[70] Moreover, within the party there were those whose expectations of the Itō Government were that 'if things go badly in the present Cabinet, there will be nothing for it but to abandon for the time being any hope for constitutional politics for Japan'.[71] Even when the first Matsukata Cabinet was still in existence, Kōno Hironaka told Suematsu Kenchō, who was close to Itō: 'our problem is that the place is full of old fogies, and it is difficult for us as yet to take over using the popular parties, and so we are placing our expectations upon you who are in an intermediate position between the popular parties and these old fogies; if people with some sense emerge in high places we shall support them from the outside.'[72] When we come to Hoshi Tōru, from before the second Diet session he was already expressing the opinion that 'if those of Sat-Chō [Satsuma-Chōshū] *genrō* rank are prepared to abandon their factional spirit and enter into reasonable and sincere discussions with the popular parties on matters of national moment, the popular parties will not stand in their way, but must participate in such discussions'.[73] This notion of a vertical alliance whereby the forces of the popular parties would enter into an alliance with some elements among Itō's following, did not emerge suddenly after the Sino-Japanese War. If the *Jiyūtō* was considering leaving the popular party alliance and teaming up with bureaucrats of Itō's faction, it was essential for it to obtain an absolute and independent majority in the House of Representatives. After Hoshi Tōru had argued that the popular party alliance was of no use, in March 1893 he made a speech in which he said:

> The fact that the *Jiyūtō* does not have a majority of the Diet members is a result of interference in elections. Therefore even though it is a minority in the Diet, it must be said that it is a majority in the country as a whole. Therefore we must not rely on other parties. The *Jiyūtō* is the only party that we need. Let there be only the *Jiyūtō*![74]

The party believed that if it entered into an alliance with the Itō Cabinet it would benefit thereby and would not be adversely affected by electoral interference. The idea that they might become an independent majority party in the Diet was no mere dream.

Thus the *Jiyūtō*, which sought to emerge from the dilemma of its tax reduction position by moving towards expansionist policies, took a large step away from attempting to overthrow the *hanbatsu* government through a popular party alliance, and moved rather towards a 'vertical alliance strategy' whereby it aimed to become the majority party on its own in alliance with one wing of the *hanbatsu*. The fourth session of the Diet, however, betrayed the expectations of both sides and raised the curtain on a monumental clash between the Itō Cabinet and the *Jiyūtō*. The change of front undertaken by the *Jiyūtō* did not develop according to the plan of the party leadership.

At the beginning of the fourth Diet session, the Itō Cabinet submitted an expenditure budget of ¥83,750,000, which included a revision of the land assessment as its only concession, but increased expenditure on two ironclads, one cruiser, one communications vessel, and also on riparian works. The policy was to make up the revenue loss resulting from land reassessment by increasing taxes on *sake* and cigarettes, as well as increasing income tax. Because the Itō Cabinet had not conceded administrative retrenchment, supplementing its loss of revenue as a result of land reassessment by increasing other taxes and directing surplus revenues into naval expenditure, the *Jiyūtō*, reflecting its groping for a change of direction, failed immediately to respond. Moreover, even in relation to its sole concession – land reassessment – the Government proposed to operate a contingency policy in case the House of Representatives should reject the increased expenditure on naval construction: 'Firstly, the House of Peers should in that case reject land assessment revision; secondly, if the House of Peers proves not to be reliable, the Government must immediately withdraw the revision bill'.[75]

The policy, however, seems to have expected too much of the change of front on the part of the *Jiyūtō*. It was no surprise after all when the House of Representatives, as it had done all along, attacked the budget by cutting civil servants' salaries and departmental expenses, rejected the item of expenditure relating to the construction of two ironclads, and dealt with the revenue bill still passing the land assessment revision proposal but rejected the tax increases on *sake* and cigarettes which had been proposed to make up the resultant shortfall. The change of direction which the *Jiyūtō* had been insisting on since well before the fourth Diet Session had been propounded in the form of 'expansionist and retrenchment policies running together', and therefore it was even more essential than before for it to stick to its policies of administrative retrenchment. To achieve both military and industrial expansion and the cutting of taxation at one and the same time, meant that even if some surplus revenues were available it would still be necessary to cut a swathe through administrative expenditure. Moreover, as we have seen, the reality of the

Government's expansionist policies was practically synonymous with expansion of the armed forces, and the 'Powerful Army', created with such singlemindedness, had weakened the financial resources of the 'Rich Country'. Another factor was that although since 1890 there had been a rising trend in rice prices, nearly ten years of consistently low prices for rice were still engraved in the memories of landlords and farmers, so that it was not yet possible to ignore demands for reduction in the land tax. The *Tōkyō Nichinichi Shinbun*, which was under the influence of Itō Miyoji, thus criticized the *Jiyūtō* for the incompleteness of its change of front:

> All 'progressive' policies and expansionist projects necessarily require a considerable financial input, and therefore if the *Jiyūtō* sincerely wants to undertake such projects it must first think of the expenditure required, and only then start calling for tax cuts. But if the *Jiyūtō* says on the contrary that tax cuts must come first, then however carefully these projects are evaluated, any such evaluation will be quite meaningless.[76]

The leaders of the *Jiyūtō* did not need the *Tōkyō Nichinichi Shinbun* to point out to them that if expansionist policies and administrative retrenchment were both pursued together, then it would become difficult to combine expansionism with reductions in taxation. Political parties, however, which unlike government officials always had to consider the next general election, could not change direction overnight. The *Jiyūtō* could not support the budget policy of the Itō Cabinet, which rejected administrative retrenchment, in return for its sole concession of revising land assessment insisted on increasing the taxes on *sake* and tobacco, and demanded acceptance of naval construction.

After its frontal clash with the Government over the budget in the fourth Diet session, the *Jiyūtō* only just managed to support the Government when it issued an imperial edict which amounted to a kind of administrative retrenchment. The *Jiyūtō* took the Itō Government's promise of administrative reform made in accordance with the proclamation of the Imperial edict as a fulfilment of its own demands for administrative retrenchment, and thus planned to move in the direction of development policies. This can be seen from the following passage:

> This reform on the part of the Itō Cabinet in fact takes over the policies of our Party by moving in the direction of restraint, and therefore may amount to a means of avoiding the divisions

between the popular and Government parties. *If these reforms by the Cabinet prove to be satisfactory, it should be possible to avoid conflict over policies of restraint between popular and Government policies....* Since last year our Party has been trying hard to support the Government's policies of development, and we cannot really reject the most pressing of these projects simply because we do not trust the Government. *And therefore now that the problems of policies of restraint are going to be solved, we must put all our efforts into achieving industrialization.*[77]

According to this the *Jiyūtō* seems to have interpreted 'policies of restraint' simply to mean administrative retrenchment, and then it was just left with 'achieving industrialization'. This shows just how sudden was the conversion of the *Jiyūtō* to the support for policies of industralization. The policies of restraint, however, which the popular parties had been advocating since the early Diet sessions did not consist solely of administrative retrenchment, but focused rather on tax reductions which would stem from administrative retrenchment. But the administrative reforms promised by the Itō Cabinet were intended wholly to raise expenditure for the construction of battle-ships, and were in no way meant to finance tax reductions. Therefore it was quite unreasonable of the *Jiyūtō* to regard the administrative reform as the complete accomplishment of 'policies of restraint'. This was why even in the fifth session of the Diet the *Jiyūtō* had to continue to advocate the simultaneous accomplishment of adminis-trative retrenchment and reduction of taxation. The *Jiyūtō* Diet Members' report, published during the suspension of the fifth Diet session said: 'Our Party on its own initiative has made financial calculations and as a result supports tax reduction and tax exemption and also advocates projects of industrialization.'[78] Thus, as before, it was promoting policies of industrialization along with policies of restraint.

When the coalition of the *Jiyūtō* and the Itō Cabinet became official after the fourth Diet, the *Kaishintō* attacked the *Jiyūtō*, saying that 'the *Jiyūtō* is in cahoots with the Government,'[79] and thus began to call itself the sole survivor of the popular parties. Nevertheless the abandonment by the *Jiyūtō* of its support for a tax reduction position and for easing of land assessment, as well as its complete conversion to policies of industrialization, occurred after the great turning-point of the Sino-Japanese War.

FROM EXPANSIONIST POLICIES TO HARD-LINE ANTI-FOREIGNISM: THE *KOKUMIN KYŌKAI*

From the first Matsukata Cabinet, support for the Government's industrialization policies was transmitted from the *Taiseikai* through the *Chūō Kōshōbu* [Central Club] to the *Kokumin Kyōkai*. When the second session of the Diet was dissolved the *Taiseikai* criticized the popular parties in the following terms:

> The purpose of the Army and the Navy is to be the nation's bastion, while the purpose of industry is to enrich the nation's strength. The nation will be strong only when she is militarily prepared, will be prosperous only when her industries are developed.... This is why we have adopted this policy. If you look, however, at the record of those political parties, they vainly refuse to trust the Government, and though they talk about military expansion and industrial development, in fact they reject it all out of hand.[80]

Criticism from this group of the administrative retrenchment–tax cutting policies of the popular parties was based on their belief in military and industrial expansion. This attitude was conveyed through the *Chūō Kōshōbu* and inherited by the *Kokumin Kyōkai*. The *Kokumin Kyōkai*, which was founded on 22 June 1892, advocated in its platform development of the armed forces, expansion of national power, promotion of industry and no reduction in taxation,[81] the central tenet being expansionist policies.[82] The bills proposed or supported by the *Kokumin Kyōkai* during the fourth session of the Diet included those for the State financing of prisons, the Hokkaidō colonization plan, [the plan to settle Japan's large and sparsely inhabited northern island, which the Meiji Government had embarked upon] expansion of sea lanes, revising the railway construction law, riparian works on four great rivers, and so on.[83] Thus its position was practically identical to the expansionism of the Matsukata Cabinet. The *Chūō Shinbun*, run by Ōoka Ikuzō, demonstrating that it was virtually an organ of the *Kokumin Kyōkai*, announced: 'We accept the viewpoint of the industrialists and we aim to support the development of national strength'; in concrete terms it promised to work hard for bills to 'abolish export tax, abolish tax on cakes, control and regulate pawnshops and secondhand shops, and encourage production of raw silk'.[84]

It was not surprising, therefore, that for the *Kokumin Kyōkai*, which in domestic politics advocated expansionism and almost without deviation supported the *hanbatsu* Government, the change of front by the *Jiyūtō* had a significance that was impossible to ignore. The *Chūō Shinbun*, organ of the *Kokumin Kyōkai*, wrote of the change in the *Jiyūtō* thus:

> 'What our friends are concerned with is the adoption of expansionist policies. We therefore eschew that radical party gang which in its attempts to overthrow the Government, or embarrass the Government, perpetuates extreme notions of developmental restraint. The radical parties, however, are getting back to the question of national interest and popular welfare, which can in no way be guaranteed by policies of restraint, and perceiving that they are in danger of losing popular support, are gradually turning to policies of expansion. The *Jiyūtō* is the most conspicuous example. Look at the speeches of Count Itagaki, or the arguments used on their election tours. Look at the recent actions of the *Jiyūtō*. At any rate they are amending their past errors and returning to the true path of military and industrial expansion. If one accepts their usual logic, they have virtually come over to our side. Now our policies of industrial and military expansion are the hope of our nation and people. Such policies are bound to prevail in the end. Why should we not shout this doctrine from the rooftops, serve the national interest and the happiness of the people, expand our national power and thus accomplish the principles of constitutionalism?'[85]

As this passage expressed it, the change of front by the *Jiyūtō* could be seen as 'virtually coming over to our side', or in other words was proclaimed as a victory for the *Kokumin Kyōkai*. At the same time, however, this involved the possibility of a loss of its individuality by the *Kokumin Kyōkai*, and for the *hanbatsu* Government it could mean that the *Kokumin Kyōkai* would lose its *raison d'être*. In the words of one of the principal leaders of the *Kokumin Kyōkai*, Sasa Tomofusa:

> At present the popular parties are being influenced by the trends of the time and are gradually abandoning their policies of restraint in favour of policies of expansion. If we are complacent and simply maintain our traditional attitudes, though the expansionary policies may be led by the *Kokumin Kyōkai*, the *Jiyūtō* will reap their fruits.[86]

Sasa recognized that the fact of the policies of the *Jiyūtō* becoming similar to those of the *Kokumin Kyōkai* represented a danger for the latter. If the policies were to become identical, the *Kokumin Kyōkai*, a minority party, would naturally pale in the shadow of the majority party, the *Jiyūtō*. The *Kokumin Kyōkai* would have to differentiate itself from the *Jiyūtō* by presenting policies which differed, to some extent at least, from those of its rival.

There was also another reason why the *Kokumin Kyōkai* was under pressure to change direction, namely that the second Itō Cabinet which replaced the first Matsukata Cabinet (the original parent of the *Kokumin Kyōkai*), had strengthened its own ties with the *Jiyūtō*. In the words of Miyake Setsurei: 'The *Kokumin Kyōkai*, which was a government party, has been banished by the Government, and is like a child cast out.'[87] Although the term 'government party' entered into the parlance of the popular parties, the 'transcendentalism' proclaimed by the Government at the time of the inauguration of the Diet meant that there could be no single government party which could be supported by the *hanbatsu* Government as a united group. As we have already seen, the power of the *Taiseikai* (a government party) had been reduced by internal cleavage before the second session of the Diet, the reason being that one section of the *Taiseikai* had aligned itself with the Government and begun activities conflicting with both the *Kaishintō* and the *Jiyūtō*, while the other, dissatisfied with this stance, set itself up as a 'neutral' group.[88] The 'neutrals', corresponding to the transcendentalism of the Government, were the stronger of the two.

The establishment of the *Kokumin Kyōkai* went beyond such neutrality and was designed to create an overtly pro-Government party. The electoral interference conducted by the Matsukata Cabinet was aimed at producing the expectation among pro-Government leaders that a government party would be formed, but the *Chūō Kōshōbu*, which was formed as an intra-parliamentary body as a result of the election interference found it difficult to maintain its cohesion. In the view of one of the *Chūō Kōshōbu* leaders:

> In the pro-Government faction there are two factions.... Faction A helps the Government only because its beliefs and strategies are similar. Faction B is virtually subordinate to the Government. Faction A, if the policy of the Government is inconsistent or breaks down, may well alter its resolve to assist the Government in its policies. Faction B is generally subordinate to the Government, but if Cabinet decisions are inconsistent, or if the Ministers or influential politicians upon whom they are dependent should face

the breakdown of their policies, then the Party might well split. *Thus unity or division for this pro-Government party really depends upon the Government's will.*[89]

The personal composition of factions A and B is not known, but we can say that both factions demanded clear support from the Government. The document goes on to argue that if Cabinet leaders 'maintain strong and united policies, vigorously confront the Diet, avoid being influenced by others and pursue the same line when the Diet is dissolved, then Government and parties will co-ordinate their activities, put forward similar policies and help each other with expenses'.[90] This was a call for the abandonment of transcendentalism based on 'neutrality', and for the creation of an openly *'hanbatsu'* party. Wholehearted support for military expansion, the unification of the Cabinet under the 'militaristic faction' represented by the Navy Minister Kabayama and the former Home Affairs Minister, Shinagawa, who had dissolved the Diet and then engaged in electoral interference, and reorganization of pro-Government Diet members with the wholehearted support of the Government, was the essence of the plan to form the *Kokumin Kyōkai.* This party, which took as its president Saigō Tsugumichi, one of the Satsuma faction *genrō* who had been particularly influential during the Matsukata Cabinet, and as its vice-president Shingawa Yojirō, who had resigned as Home Minister because he had been in charge of interference with elections, was launched on 22 June 1892.

Only a month or so after the foundation of the *Kokumin Kyōkai* the first Matsukata Cabinet collapsed, and in its stead Itō Hirobumi, who had been critical of the Matsukata Cabinet, and especially of its 'militant faction', ever since the elections had been interfered with, organized a new Cabinet. As is clear from a letter sent by one of Itō's confidants, the Chief Secretary of the Privy Council, Itō Miyoji, when the *Kokumin Kyōkai* was formed, it is clear that officials close to Itō were from the outset anything but happy about the foundation of the *Kokumin Kyōkai.* The letter read in part as follows: 'Although Shinagawa has left the Government he is still determined to interfere in elections, and if we fail to make clear that we have no connection with him, we shall be blamed for other people's failures and dishonour.'[91] The fact that Itō had come to form a cabinet placed the *Kokumin Kyōkai,* which had been founded on the express expectation of full backing from the Cabinet, into a terrible quandary.

Nevertheless, just as relations between the Itō Cabinet and the *Jiyūtō* up to the end of the fourth Diet session remained conflict-ridden as before, so up to the end of the fourth session of the Diet no conflict made itself manifest between the Itō Cabinet and the *Kokumin Kyōkai*. Sasa Tomofusa wrote before the fourth Diet:

> The Cabinet's policies ought to be ambiguous and not provocative. They should not, however, incline towards the popular parties. Counts Itō and Inoue are in a difficult situation in that if they favour the popular parties, then Yamagata and others may not agree, therefore by hurting the feelings of the *Kokumin Kyōkai* they will certainly induce a split in the ranks of the Cabinet. On the other hand if they come too close to the *Kokumin Kyōkai* they are likely to invite the anger of the popular parties, and thus I do not think that for the time being they should deviate from our path of cautious policies.'[92]

The *Kokumin Kyōkai* could not expect wholehearted support from the Itō Cabinet, but neither was it regarded with unmitigated hostility. One may read as an indication of the attitude that Sasa expected the *Kokumin Kyōkai* to adopt in the fourth Diet session, his statement that:

> irrespective of the measures that the Government will carry out in future we hope that it will not inflexibly follow its policies of industrial and military development; our party should avoid the kind of excessive hostility to Government leaders evinced by the popular parties, which have rejected industrial and military development policies simply with a view to taking power. We should also avoid similar errors in our approach to national planning.[93]

From this it seems clear that a break between the Cabinet and the *Kokumin Kyōkai* was hardly a remote possibility.

After the end of the fourth Diet session, when the *Jiyūtō* and the Itō Cabinet became more and more openly allied, the *Kokumin Kyōkai* came by comparison to assume an increasingly opposition party colouring. Itō Miyoji reported to Itō (the Prime Minister) that the *Kumamoto Kokkentō* and other leaders of the *Kokumin Kyōkai*, such as Motoda Hajime and Ōoka Ikuzō, 'conspiring with the *Kaishintō*', were with increasing openness adopting a line opposed to the Itō Cabinet.[94] What is particularly significant is that the *Kumamoto Kokkentō*, which was a central element in the *Kokumin Kyōkai*, rethought before the fifth session of the Diet the support for the policies of the Itō Cabinet which it had given during the fourth session, and moved to an increasingly anti-Government position. This is shown in the following quotation:

> Hitherto our party has always supported or opposed the Government according to its policies. It has never attacked simply for the sake of attacking like an opposition party, nor has it given uncritical support, like a Government party. All we have been seeking to do is to give positive criticism. Although this has been a reasonable course of action, *when we look back we see that frequently we have had no influence on the Government but we ourselves have been influenced by it.* Rather than correct the Government's mistakes, it seems that we have made them worse. This is because, firstly, our party has not been particularly strong, and secondly, because if one compares the Government and the opposition parties, it is the Government that has really been correct, and the fierceness of our attacks upon the opposition parties has weakened the force of our attacks upon the Government. Even so, *our policies have lacked clarity and penetration. There is no reason why the hanbatsu Government should continue for ever.* Its fall may not be far distant. The evils of this Government have become pervasive, people have lost patience with it and are unanimously opposing it. If there are people who wish to share the fortunes of the Government, they must also be prepared to share its misfortunes. They are like those who threw in their lot with the shogunate and went down with it.... Its fortunes have been declining and it has long been abandoned by all. *Now is the time to make up our minds whether to support the Government or to oppose it,* with due consideration to the present state of political affairs.'[95]

It seems strange to read such critical opinions from the *Kumamoto Kokkentō* about the 'hanbatsu Government', but this becomes comprehensible if one substitutes 'Itō' for 'hanbatsu'. The *Kokumin Kyōkai*, which argued during the fourth Diet that 'irrespective of the measures that the Government will carry out in future we hope that it will not inflexibly follow its policies of industrial and military development', was saying before the fifth Diet that its policies 'frequently have had no influence on the Government but we ourselves have been influenced by it', and thus made it clear that it was opposing the Itō Cabinet. The *Kokumin Kyōkai*, in deciding to change front, was obviously conscious of the fact that the Jiyūtō had entered into close relations with the Government. This can be seen in the following:

Although it is disadvantageous for us to permit the opposition parties to ally themselves with the Government, if we fail to do so, how shall we be able to establish the permanent identity and dynamism of our movement? Who indeed can say which course of action we should choose? To allow the opposition parties to rely upon the Government would be disadvantageous to us only in the short term. If we did so we should create a furore in the political world and *overturn the status quo*, but in so doing we should be creating long-term advantages for our party.[96]

Naturally the opportunity to 'overturn the status quo' would be the possibility of an alliance with the hard-line foreign policy faction between the fifth and sixth Diet sessions. The statement of Shiga Shigetaka when the *Shinpotō* party was formed later, that in the movement towards an alliance of hard-line foreign policy factions in 1893 and 1894, 'the promoter of an alliance of hard-line foreign policy factions was Sasa Tomofusa of the *Kokumin Kyōkai*',[97] serves to confirm this point. The *Kokumin Kyōkai*, which had lost a powerful source of support with the collapse of the Matsukata Cabinet, and had forfeited its policy independence with the political change on the part of the *Jiyūtō*, was now in the process of losing its position of pro-Government party because of the *de facto* alliance between the Itō Cabinet and the *Jiyūtō*. Therefore, whether it liked it or not, it was being forced to make a radical reassessment of its position.

The *Kokumin Kyōkai* demanded a radical reassessment in the direction of insistence on enhancement of national prestige, which was one of its basic policy planks along with industrial and military development. From July 1893 a movement was gradually building up towards the formation of the *Dai Nippon Kyōkai* [Greater Japan Association], as shown in the following newspaper account: 'The *Kokumin Kyōkai* and the *Tōyō Jiyūtō*, having also brought over to their side Members of the House of Peers, are in effect a single Presence within a Trinity, and are appealing to the populace for the formation of a big political party which would operate under the slogan of forbidding residence to foreigners except in designated areas'.[98] The Government's treaty revision negotiations recognized the principle of freedom of residence for foreigners as a concession in order to obtain treaty revision, but against the notion that foreigners should be granted freedom to engage in commercial and industrial activities the argument had been heard ever since the Inoue and Ōkuma Treaty revision talks that such a move in favour of foreigners was premature because Japanese commerce, industry and agriculture would – it was feared – suffer a serious blow.[99] While, however, revision negotiations were proceeding secretly under the Foreign Minister, Mutsu, emphasizing the principle of equality, the only argument concerning the Treaty revision that could be thrown into the political ring was the argument that it was premature to grant freedom of residence to foreigners. As such, it quickly came to attract a great deal of attention. Considering that points of conflict over policy between the Government and the popular parties had been relatively lacking since the change of line on the part of the *Jiyūtō* (which had espoused the principles of administrative retrenchment and tax reduction since the early Diets), this was the only slogan which was capable of creating a new issue between the parties and the Government. Also, the *Kumamoto Kokkentō* (the core of the *Kokumin Kyōkai*) found, in contrast with its allies, that the idea of forming an alliance with the popular parties over treaty revision had already been tested out in the movement against Ōkuma's treaty revision negotiations [in 1889]. One journal commented: 'When the struggle between Government and Opposition was over, a new struggle over treaty revision began between conservatives and progressives.'[100] At this point the *Kokumin Kyōkai* adopted as the first plank of its platform, in terms of 'the great cause of enhancing national prestige', the argument that it was premature to permit foreigners freedom of residence within Japan. This was a way of expanding the party's strength because it would easily 'appeal to high and low throughout the land'. Therefore it chose to confront the Itō Cabinet by using the *Kumamoto Kokkentō* as a 'link' with the *Dai Nippon Kyōkai* and becoming the nucleus of the hard-line anti-foreign movement.[101]

FROM RETRENCHMENT POLICIES TO A HARD-LINE ANTI-FOREIGN POSITION: THE *KAISHINTŌ*

It was the *Kaishintō* which 'fought vigorously and indeed vehemently in the Budget Committee on behalf of a bill to make a thorough scrutiny of the budget'.[102] The party's policy since the 'Great Imperial Edict' [10 February 1893] was 'to force the Government to concede a role for the parties in matters not connected with the Imperial Edict'.[103] In other words, it broadly accepted the Government proposals on items concerning salaries of officials and on expenditure relating to battleships, but it sought to make the Government accept the scrutiny bill on other matters falling under article 67.[104] In the period from then until just before the fifth Diet session the *Kaishintō* was able to have a monopoly of the administrative retrenchment and tax reduction policies which had been the main plank in the platform of the popular party alliance ever since the first Diet. Indeed the view was heard that 'the *Jiyūtō* had now become like the *Kaishintō*, and the *Kaishintō* has become like the *Jiyūtō*, so that their positions have been reversed',[105] and 'it seems that the honourable title "popular party" now adheres only to the *Kaishintō*'.[106] Even in anticipation of the fifth Diet the *Kaishintō* had still decided on a policy of budget scrutiny on the grounds that the Government's administrative re-organization and naval reform were quite insufficient, as can be seen from this statement: 'Through our policy of budget scrutiny which we have held for many years, we aim to produce a budget reduction and create a surplus of at least 10 million yen, which can be used for the purposes of tax reduction'.[107]

When we read the following statement of the *Kaishintō*, put out before the fifth Diet session, we find a clear indication of the attitudes of the party:

> Among the three popular parties some members of the *Jiyūtō* have broken their alliance with the three factions [the *Kaishintō*, *Dōshi* Club and *Dōmei* Club] during this Diet. This means a situation of squabbling among friends, in which the Government will walk away with the catch – a circumstance to be much regretted. We can, however, do nothing about the present situation. But our *Kaishintō*, irrespective of what other factions may do, must independently cleave to its moral position, must maintain its previous policies and must boldly progress in pursuit of its present goals. We believe that if we continue to work for our present policies, since the world is wide and our friends are many, even if the *Jiyūtō* should depart from our side, a majority throughout the nation will follow us in our successes and tribulations.[108]

Despite all this, when it came to the inauguration of the fifth session of the Diet, the only point of confrontation with the Government on the part of the *Kaishintō* was its support for the existing treaties [see p. 76], and it sent not a single member to the Budget Committee. A report by the *Kaishintō* on the fifth Diet session explained this in the following terms:

> In the fifth Diet the *Jiyūtō* abandoned its mission of cleansing the *hanbatsu* and broke its alliance with the popular parties. We are acutely aware that if we entered the committee as a minority, we

should have no chance of making the arguments prevail which we have held since the first Diet, and so we did not contest the committee election. This is why both we and the *Dōmei Club* failed to send any members to the Committee.[109]

The fact, however, that the *Kaishintō*, which from the fourth Diet session to the fifth had monopolized the slogan of administrative retrenchment and had alone enjoyed the name of 'popular party', should now have boycotted the Budget Committee, can only be seen as indicating a change of line by the *Kaishintō*. According to a spokesman for the party: 'The scrutiny bill, which has been the banner of the popular parties and enjoys so much trust among the people, has been placed in serious jeopardy by the withdrawal of the *Kaishintō*. Seeing this, our party feels the weight of its responsibility, and we must endeavour to do our duty for the nation.'[110]

This statement, on the other hand, seems to have been little more than an electoral ploy. The *Jiyūtō* attacked it in the following terms: 'The *Kaishintō* together with the *Dōmei Club* has intentionally avoided taking responsibility over the budget.'[111] 'The *Kaishintō* in a difficult situation has avoided its responsibility, but the *Jiyūtō* knows its responsibility.'[112] What is clear from the exchange of abuse, which the *Jiyūtō* and the *Kaishintō* engaged in for electoral purposes, is that however the issues may have shifted in the Diet, once an election loomed both parties had to return to their role of 'popular parties'. Even so, it is difficult to escape the conclusion from the above analysis that in the fifth Diet the *Kaishintō* had also abandoned its demands for administrative retrenchment.

Even on the matter of supporting the existing treaties – a policy which it was utilizing as an alternative weapon with which to attack the Government in place of the budget issue – the attitude of the *Kaishintō* lacked consistency. Previously, the party had urged the Government to revise the treaties. In particular, at the time of the Okuma treaty revision negotiations in 1889, it had been attacked by the hard-line foreign policy faction. Immediately before the fifth Diet session the Party urged treaty revision on the Government in the following terms: 'Why should the Government not engage in revision of the treaties in matters concerning the fortunes of our nation's prestige and the honour of our national independence?'[113]

Moreover, the *Kaishintō* argued against the position taken by the *Dai Nippon Kyōkai* and others that freedom of residence for foreigners was still premature. For instance; 'Those who put this view are untutored and unqualified, know nothing of foreign policy and are blindly following a trend,'[114] and again: 'The vagaries of the view of this conservative faction that foreigners should not have freedom of residence are beyond the realm of rational discussion.'[115] Clearly then, the *Kaishintō* was opposed to the 'hard-line anti-foreign' faction. Suddenly, however, during the fifth Diet, it came out in favour of maintaining the existing treaties and against the Government's treaty revision negotiations. The party proposed an unlikely alliance with the supporters of the present treaties, in the following words: 'Among those who want to retain the present treaties are those who think that freedom of residence for foreigners is premature, and those who want to exclude foreigners altogether. We, however, unreservedly propose retention of the present treaties on the principle of absolute equality.'[116] Previously, when the party's leader, Ōkuma, was Foreign Minister, the *Kaishintō* had proposed the retention of the present treaties as a weapon in the revision negotiations. Mutsu's draft, however, was a development of the revision proposals of Ōkuma, and so the proposal to participate in the movement to retain the existing treaties in order to criticize Mutsu's draft clearly meant that the party had changed its foreign policy. The policy which the popular parties had adhered to since the first Diet, of administrative retrenchment and tax reduction, had reached a deadlock, and the fact that 'readiness to hoist a second banner of unity'[117] was being demanded, put the *Kaishintō* in the same situation as the *Jiyūtō.*

As we have already argued, the object of retrenchment in the administrative retrenchment position of the *Kaishintō* was 'unproductive spending', but there were 'many circumstances in which the maintenance of productive spending would help lighten the people's burdens'.[118] For this reason when the *Kaishintō* was asked by the proponents of industrial and military development whether they thought that the building of a steelworks was unnecessary, they needed to reply: 'A steelworks is necessary both for military and economic purposes ... but why should the Diet outlay vast quantities of public funds on a project which has been poorly researched, poorly planned and from which it is difficult to be confident about future results'[119] When they were asked whether it was unnecessary to expand the Navy and build battleships, they had to reply: 'It is not so that the construction of battleships is unnecessary. Since, however, the blueprint is not yet fully worked out and there are many defects yet to be eliminated, it is not yet the time to proceed with such a huge project'.[120] In sum, when they were asked whether they were opposed to expansionist policies, they replied: 'We are people who want to carry out plans of development when we come to power, and we expect to bring them to fruition by our own hands. We are naturally too proud to entrust this project to others, especially those who do not enjoy our trust'.[121] Apart from the grounds of poor policy preparation and mistrust of those in charge of policy, the *Kaishintō* had no rationale for directly opposing the policies of industrial and military development.

Strange though it may seem at first sight, it had been the case, ever since the controversy over whether to subdue Korea [which divided the Government in 1873 after the Korean Government had rejected Japanese overtures for the commercial opening of Korea] that the slogan used to oppose the *hanbatsu* Government in its policies of industrial and military development had to be either 'tax reduction' or a 'hard anti-foreign' line. The fact that at this time the *Kaishintō* linked itself with the hard-line anti-foreign faction was similar to the circumstances in which the *Jiyūtō* had earlier entered into an alliance with the anti-foreign hard-liners, and formed the *Daidō Danketsu* movement. Just at that time the *Dai Nippon Kyōkai* movement was gradually attracting general attention. The mass media said either that 'simple arguments are easy to understand',[122] or that 'this movement is likely to develop far beyond our expectations',[123] thus predicting expansion outside the Diet. Within the Diet too, the *Kokumin Kyōkai*, after the fourth session of the Diet, instead of acting as a Government party proposing policies of industrial and military development, had begun to behave as an opposition party propounding a hard-line anti-foreign policy. The *Kaishintō*, by allying itself with the *Kokumin Kyōkai*, was able to obtain 110 seats, which surpassed the 94 seats of the *Jiyūtō*. Thus if one includes small factions such as the *Dōmei Club* and the *Tōyō Jiyūtō*, the alliance of anti-foreign hard-liners was not incapable of mustering a majority in the House of Representatives. Moreover, since the hard-line anti-foreign faction was opposed to the *hanbatsu* Government in the shape of the Itō Cabinet, the *Kaishintō* could still, as before, be called a popular party in that it was anti-*hanbatsu*. Thus the *Kaishintō* in the fifth Diet abandoned its tax reduction policies and took up the argument for maintaining the existing treaties as they were, so that in alliance with the *Kokumin Kyōkai* it ended up opposed to the Itō Cabinet and the *Jiyūtō*.

It may be a trifle harsh on the *Kaishintō* to explain its conversion to the hard-line anti-foreign position in terms simply of its problems with the tax reduction argument and majority faction machinations within the Diet. Between the fifth and sixth Diets the movement composed of the six 'hard' factions (as Hattori Shisō has pointed out) became more of a 'popular movement'[124] opposed to the *hanbatsu*. If we were to reverse the positions of the *Jiyūtō* and the *Kaishintō*, we could speak of the rebirth of the five-group alliance in the movement opposed to Ōkuma's treaty revision in 1889. This is shown symbolically by the fact that the slogans of the movement changed from 'too early to permit freedom of residence for foreigners' to 'support for the treaties as they stand', and to 'independent foreign policy' and 'responsible Cabinets'. In particular the fact that the Newspaper Journalists League, composed of seventy-six newspapers and journals, participated in the hard-line anti-foreign movement, not only changed the nature of the movement, but also enhanced its effectiveness as an anti-Government force.

We can well appreciate the strength of the Newspaper Journalists League from the letter written by the Chief Cabinet Secretary, Itō Miyoji, to the Prime Minister, Itō Hirobumi, in which he expressed the following view:

> It is clear that the League of Newspaper Journalists, which is a gathering of parties opposed to the Government, is helping the six factions, and if we neglect this League, it will easily have a harmful effect in the elections to be held in the localities. We should therefore quickly order its dissolution. We should take resolute action, using the Political Organizations Law, employing the clause concerning 'dissolution for the purpose of preserving public order'.[125]

The foundation of the Newspaper Journalists League took place immediately following the third general election after the dissolution of the fifth Diet. On 28 March 1893, journalists from ten Tokyo prefecture newspapers (*Nippon, Niroku, Hōchi, Chūō, Yomiuri, Mainichi, Kokumin, Kokkai, Kokumin no Tomo*, and *Shin Chōya*) met together in the *Kyōzon Dōshū* Club, and adopted the slogan 'A Responsible Cabinet, an Independent Foreign Policy'.[126] As a clear from the organization's statement of aims, the Newspaper League was clearly in support of leaving the treaties as they were. The statement read as follows:

> The maintenance of the existing treaties is the best method of abolishing a foreign policy based on restraint, promoting the achievement of treaty revision and inculcating a spirit of self-reliance among the people. Therefore the movement in the House of Representatives at the end of last year was not an anti-foreign exclusivist movement, but is a movement of national self-reliance.

Those who expressed sympathy for the movement of national self-reliance in the Diet which has just been dissolved, must not relax their determination to demonstrate their support.[127]

It can, however, be seen from the first half of this statement of aims that they were attempting to eliminate an exclusive anti-foreign colouring from the movement in support of the existing treaties:

The prime duty of our nation today is to demonstrate the principle of cabinet responsibility, thus overcoming the evils of the *han-batsu*, and to lay the foundations of a constitutional regime. The greatest desire of our people over many years has been to undertake the task of revising the treaties and thus to restore our national rights of independence and self-reliance, and establish the principle of an open and progressive nation.[128]

Concerning the role played by the Newspaper League in the change of slogans from 'support the existing treaties' to 'responsible cabinet, self-reliant foreign policy', Tokutomi Sohō of the *Kokumin Shinbun* reflected as follows:

At that period I was a supporter of freedom of residence for foreigners. At the same time I was not opposing the adoption of Roman script.... Therefore my opinion differed from those of my friends who were adopting a hard anti-foreign line, and who were opposing freedom of residence for foreigners. At this time I was anxious about becoming to involved with those friends who were propounding a hard-line anti-foreigner policy, and I tried to establish the slogan of self-reliant foreign policy. I myself, however, being excessively busy, entrusted the task to another, and had a small volume called 'Self-Reliant Foreign Policy' published by *Miyūsha* which is the *Kokumin Shinbunsha* under another name.[129]

The principal participants at the meeting of 28 March were Kuga Minoru (*Nippon*), Tokutomi Iichirō [Sohō] and Takegoshi Yosaburō (*Kokumin*), Suehiro Shigetaka (*Kokkai*), Ozaki Yukio (*Hōchi*), Ichijima Kenkichi (*Yomiuri*), Hizuka Tatsu (*Mainichi*) and others. It can easily be imagined that the Newspaper League, which was an alliance of Ozaki, Ichijima and Hizuka of the *Kaishintō*, Kuga of the Nationalists, and Tokutomi of the Commoners' Movement, helped to avoid some of the anti-foreign exclusivist colouring which derived from the movement opposed to freedom of residence for foreigners which originated with the *Dai Nippon Kyōkai*.

The journalists' alliance spread continuously from April to June. On 7 April it sent to all newspapers an invitation to join; on 13 April it appointed Shiga Shigetaka of the Journal *Nihonjin* as its standing representative, on 1 May it set up an office in the Tokyo Hotel; and on 2 May it accepted the invitation of the six hard-line factions and sent Shiga as its official representative. Then on the day after the inauguration of the sixth Diet, on 13 May, it held a general 'social gathering' of journalists from all over the country, and bringing together 176 representatives of 76 newspapers and journals, expressed support in the strongest terms for the alliance of hard-line factions in the sixth Diet. Among its resolutions is the following: 'We express our firm support of the Diet Members who have suffered dissolution of the Diet in their attempt to put into practice the previously mentioned aims of journalists from newspapers and journals throughout the nation, and we seek the re-election of those members.' Thus, just as the Chief Secretary, Itō Miyoji, had warned, the League took upon itself the task of playing a crucial role in the elections.[130]

This Newspaper League movement proposed to the Kaishintō the possibility of moving to form a *Dai Nippon Mintō* [Great Japan People's Party], opposed to the *hanbatsu*, which is like the *Daidō Danketsu* movement before it would absorb nationalist energies. The hard-line anti-foreign movement found satisfaction in its foreign policy because of the outbreak of the Sino-Japanese War,[131] but in domestic policy, it remained a movement in the tradition of the popular parties. The *Kaishintō* had a positive motive for amalgamating with the hard-line anti-foreign faction. In fact, the formation of the *Shinpotō* in 1896 was an extension of the hard-line anti-foreign faction, and the *Shinpotō* (which became the *Kenseihontō*), after the Sino-Japanese War had more of a popular-party quality about it than the *Jiyūtō*. On the other hand, in the alliance movement at the time the *Kokken* faction (absorbed, apart from the *Kokumin Kyōkai* element, by the *Kaishintō*) was around 1897 more of a 'popular party' than the leadership of the *Shinpotō*.

As we have already seen, the conflict between the expansionist policies of the *hanbatsu* Government and the retrenchment policies of the popular party alliance had almost disappeared from the political stage between the fourth and fifth Diets. This does not mean, however, that the conflict had entirely and absolutely disappeared. Even for the *Jiyūtō*, if the focus had remained entirely on the domestic aspects of expansionist and retrenchment policies, it could probably not have continued to support the Itō Cabinet without serious internal divisions. Whether the hard-line anti-foreign faction movement over the treaty revision question in 1893 and 1894 was reflecting the approaching signs of the Sino-Japanese War, or whether the relationship between it and the war was coincidental, is far from clear, but with the rise of this movement and with the Sino-Japanese War, the conflict between military-industrial development and tax reduction was dimmed and retired from centre stage. When the Sino-Japanese War resolved the foreign policy problems including the question of Treaty revision, the conflict between military–industrial development and tax reduction reappeared in the form of expansionist policies versus retrenchment policies, but in place of the land tax reduction controversy, the argument was now about increasing the land tax, and this showed just how drastically the situation had changed from that in the early Diets. We shall investigate this in Part II.

Part II

Political conflict after the Sino-Japanese War

3 Post-war reconstruction and the reactions of various political forces

Just after the Sino-Japanese War had ended in 1895 the Finance Minister, Matsukata Masayoshi, presented a statement of opinion to Itō, the Prime Minister, entitled 'Proposal Concerning Future Financial Planning', which laid down the substance of financial planning for the years following the war:

> As a result of the Sino-Japanese encounter Japan has suddenly become one of the Powers. We shall therefore become an object of increasing jealousy from all nations, and we shall require armed forces capable of responding to this. We shall also need armed forces to defend the territory we have newly acquired. We shall need armed forces against Chinese retaliation. To make such military preparations, however, will require from three to five years at least. The European Powers have already begun to alter their foreign policy towards Japan, and are making amendments to the Triple Alliance. [An alliance of France, Germany and Russia, which conspired to deprive Japan of some of her fruits of victory in the Sino-Japanese war. The actions of the Triple Alliance caused great resentment in Japan, and fanned the flames of nationalism.] The situation is such that we must embark upon the construction of armoured battleships to cruise in the Pacific. The completion of the great Siberian railway is expected within five years. We cannot delay a single day in expanding our military preparations. According to advice which the ministers have received from the authorities concerning the amount of expenditure involved, the Navy should have another 200,000 tons, the army should have new gun emplacements and modernized weapons, and the size of the Army should be virtually doubled. I endorse this advice.[1]

The extremely rapid build-up of the Army and Navy in order to handle the expected advance into East Asia by the Great Powers following the Sino-Japanese War, was the most crucial postwar issue for Japan. The abandonment by Japan of the Liaotung Peninsula brought about by interference on the part of the three nations [Russia, France and Germany], which in turn preceded specific encroachments by the Powers on areas of Chinese jurisdiction, was particularly important in building up a feeling of crisis. This becomes fairly clear in a draft of General Staff Headquarters, entitled 'Reasons for an Army Build-up'. The Army proposal called for a doubling of the existing seven divisions to fourteen, being based on the sense of crisis at the advance of the powers into China, and on the notion of a change from defence to offence, rationalized in terms of the aphorism that 'attack is the best form of defence'. The draft reads as follows:

As a result of our victory over China, the Powers have focused their sights on the East, and the day of reckoning for the East is rapidly moving closer. Our Empire, which has to deal with the situation, must be the guarantor of peace in the region. The only way to accomplish this task, however, is to frustrate those ambitious to violate our national sovereignty. In other words, we must build up sufficient strength to overcome their ambitions. Although it may not bear repeating too often that the principal object of national military preparedness lies fundamentally in defence and not in attack, if we wish to prevent foreign aggression, we must be prepared to deal out punishment. This is why contemporary strategic doctrine has abandoned the notion of a defensive posture and emphasizes attack, so that 'attack as the best form of defence' is a thoroughly respectable doctrine. Therefore our Empire from now on must stand on its own feet, must not remain contented merely with internal defence, but in order to handle external aggression it must develop sufficient capacity to be able to act swiftly to repel the aggressor. Consequently, it is necessary for the Imperial Army to develop a capacity in excess of fourteen divisions, apart from the armed strength it maintains in Taiwan.[2]

Victory in the Sino-Japanese War, on the one hand gave birth to a sense of crisis about the carving up of China by the Great Powers, and on the other created great self-confidence in the Japanese armed forces. Both these things together focused the attention of the *hanbatsu* Government on the necessity for a crash programme of military expansion which would be able to support the change from 'defence' to 'attack'. The fact that military expenditure which up to 1895 had been around ¥20 million, jumped in 1896 to ¥70 million and in 1897 to about ¥100 million shows this most graphically.

As is clear from the fact that this rapid military expansion could be sustained only by an increase in taxation, the plan of the Finance Minister, Matsukata, at the same time spoke of 'development of national strength' – a programme that would require augmented taxation. As he put it: 'We must take steps to bring about development of the national strength along with increases in taxation. While there may be many measures to be taken, principal among them are the improvement of transport, and the building up of agriculture, commerce and industry, the creation of industrial banks and the promotion of capital investment. These are our most pressing tasks.'[3]

The Itō Cabinet presented this plan for military expansion and industrial development to the ninth session of the Diet. Extraordinary expenditures can be divided into the plan for Army and Navy expansion, financed largely through Chinese reparations, and the plan for industrial development, including railway improvements and expansion of telegraph and telephone facilities, financed largely by loans. Expenditure on army expansion, for the building of barracks, weapons manufacture, the construction of gun batteries and so on, amounted to about ¥90 million over eight years, while spending on naval expansion, including warships, weapons, torpedoes and the Admiralty building, amounted to a ¥187 million over ten years. Adding to this ¥4 million for the establishment of a steelworks makes a huge grand total of ¥280 million. It was planned to finance all this military expansion with ¥270 million from the ¥330 million (including interest) received as reparations as a result of the Sino-Japanese War, and to make up the ¥10 million shortfall out of general revenue.

The plan for industrial development envisaged ¥26 million being spent on the upgrading of railways, ¥12 million on expansion of telephone communications, and ¥1 million on railways to open up Hokkaidō, totalling ¥40 million over a seven-year period. This was to be financed by the raising of loans, the interest on which was to be repaid out of the profits which the enterprises were to make. Apart from this a further ¥10 million out of reparations was to be used to supplement the capital of the Agricultural Bank (which was established as the Agriculture and Industry Bank) at the rate of two million yen per annum over a five-year period. Thus ¥280 million on military expansion, plus ¥50 million on industrial development was to be spent with reparations and loans as the principal sources of finance. This was the essence of 'postwar reconstruction'.[4]

Obviously, however, not all that was spent on Army and Navy

expansion came out of extraordinary expenditures. Weapons, ammunition, barracks, etc., necessary for the expansion of Army divisions, were taken care of by extraordinary expenditures which were no longer needed once the plan was fulfilled, but the pay for an increased number of men, as well as clothing, food, etc., necessary for their maintenance, had to come out of running costs. The same was the case for the Navy. Thus the working-out of the plan for military expansion was clearly accompanied by an enormous increase in running costs within the total costs for the Army and Navy. Matsukata forecast that running costs would be ¥10 million per annum for the Army and ¥8 million per annum for the Navy,[5] while Watanabe Kunitake, who succeeded Matsukata after his resignation as Finance Minister, forecast a ¥20 million increase in the total running costs of the Army and Navy.[6] His calculation was that while in the first year of the plan (1896) the combined running costs for the Army and the Navy would only amount to ¥3,490,000, it would gradually rise until in 1905 it would be ¥21,600,000.[7] Moreover, to the increase in running costs for the Army and Navy should be added running costs 'resulting from the outcome of the Sino-Japanese War', such as interest repayments on military loans, pensions, annuities for meritorious service, costs for fortifying Weihaiwei and supplementation of expenditures for Taiwan. These were expected to amount to ¥19 million in 1896 but ¥33 million in 1905.[8]

Whereas extraordinary expenditures were taken care of by reparations and loans, running costs such as these could be financed only by extra taxation. A plan for increased taxation was presented to the ninth Diet session, which was the first following the Sino-Japanese War, and is set out in Table 3.1. It can be seen that no raising of the land tax was proposed. Matsukata made clear that he had no intention of increasing the land tax when he said: 'Land tax is the easiest tax to collect, but it is not advantageous for the national economy to increase the burdens placed upon the farmers. Moreover the burdens on Japanese farmers are already heavy, and since the Meiji Restoration we have always been attempting to reduce the land tax. Therefore we must not increase it.'[9] Certainly as a starting point for 'postwar reconstruction' this had an important political significance. The victory in the Sino-Japanese War and the Triple Intervention had the effect of strengthening a militaristic mood among the people, but if at this stage an increase in the land tax had been proposed, it would have encountered strong opposition in the House of Representatives just at the point when the Government was embarking upon its policies of 'postwar reconstruction'. Therefore from a political point of view it is quite understandable that the first tax increase plan did not include a rise in land tax. From the viewpoint, however, of the financial authorities, it is unlikely that Matsukata and Watanabe really thought that the land tax ought not to be increased. First of all, the increase in running expenses over a ten-year period, which principally included increases for the Army and Navy, could naturally be expected to go beyond the initial planned estimates as the plan was carried out. Secondly, even in the initial plan there was a shortfall of ¥7 million between the planned tax increases of ¥26 million and the cost increases of ¥33 million. Watanabe argued that this shortfall could be covered by a natural increase in revenue from 1897 onwards,[10] and that this natural increase would be absorbed by an increase in administrative costs. In fact, however, the expectations of Matsukata and Watanabe were that this would happen only if general administrative expenses did not further increase, running costs for the Army and Navy in no sense exceeded expectations, and the increase in revenue from income tax, registration tax and liquor tax, as well as from the tobacco monopoly, in no way fell below expectations. It is difficult to believe that the officials of the Ministry of Finance really thought that all these uncertain elements would turn out right, and that the tax increase plan would be the last word on the subject. The postwar reconstruction plan, which was presented at the same time as the 1896 budget, did not contain a single certainty among its complicated calculations of revenue and expenditure, and yet if any one of its forecasts had

Table 3.1 The first post-war period tax increase plan (in 1,000s)

A. Contribution of business tax to national taxes	7,500
Newly established registration tax	7,200
Increase in *sake* production tax	10,100
Revenue from leaf tobacco monopoly	10,310
Total	35,110
B. Contribution of ship tax, vehicle tax and tax on sweets to local taxes	6,900
Expenses for collecting these taxes	1,400
A − B	26,810

Source: Hisho ruisan zaisei shiryō, vol. 2, pp. 105–6

proved substantially inaccurate, this would have meant a shortfall in revenue. In fact, as we shall see later, not one of the plan's assumptions turned out right, and a mere two years later it became necessary to take steps to increase the land tax, which had hitherto been avoided, in order to make up a shortfall in revenue. Thus the closing of ranks between the *hanbatsu* and the parties, which had been maintained since the outbreak of the Sino-Japanese War, broke down under the impact of the land tax increase question. We should not, however, seek to explain this in terms of the inaccuracy of planning assumptions on the part of the financial authorities. It was clear to the financial authorities that an increase in the land tax would be necessary to fulfil the postwar reconstruction plan, but they thought it politically desirable to postpone it as long as possible.

In the ninth Diet session, which was the starting-point for this massive plan of military expansion and industrial development, the parties almost entirely gave their support to the plan. In March 1896 the President of the *Jiyūtō*, Itagaki Taisuke, spoke as follows at a party meeting:

> This is a crucial session of the Diet which has the responsibility of post-war reconstruction. If we consider Japan's position in the Far Eastern situation as a whole, military expansion is absolutely indispensable. Therefore increased national expenditure is absolutely indispensable. This means that the calculations of national revenue are also absolutely indispensable. So an increase in taxation is absolutely indispensable. We must dispense with the negative tax reduction policies of days gone by, we must take a stand for development and create prosperous industries, and thus we must create a people that is both prosperous and prepared to spend money.[11]

It is difficult to find any point of difference between this speech of Itagaki and the previously cited memorandum of Matsukata. Itagaki admitted that the Far Eastern situation meant that military expansion should be given first priority, and so he accepted taxation rises. As we have already seen in the last chapter, the *Jiyūtō* after the fourth Diet put forward a policy of 'combining expansionist and retrenchment policies', which meant supporting the *hanbatsu* Government on the 'national interest question', which included the question of national defence, but it was not until the new situation following the Sino-Japanese War that the party officially came out in complete support of the Government's policies of military and industrial development. It was the experience of the Sino-Japanese War – a war on a scale not seen since the days of the *Bakumatsu* [*c.* 1853–1868] and the Meiji Restoration – and the bitter pill of the Triple Intervention, which showed the extent of the power gap still remaining between Japan and the Great Powers, that permitted a change of front that had been impossible until the war. The *Tōkyō Keizai Zasshi* [Tokyo Economic Journal] wrote at the beginning of 1896: 'When it was generally accepted that the land tax should be reduced, no arguments could be found to oppose this, but with the outbreak of the Sino-Japanese War there was a sudden change of view, and the notion that there should be military and industrial expansion became the normal consensus, so that those not accepting the view have come to be looked upon as scarcely human: so great has been the change in public opinion.'[12] This shows graphically the impact of the war.

It was not only, however, a recognition of the international situation and its problems, nor was it simply an atmosphere of national militarism caused by the war, that determined the direction of political forces within Japan. Matters of pragmatic interest ought also not to be neglected. As is clearly demonstrated by Matsukata saying that there must be no increase in land tax, whereas Itagaki urged that tax increases were 'absolutely indispensable', the fact that the Government's tax increase bill did not include any increase in land tax made possible co-operation between the Itō Cabinet and the *Jiyūtō*. However strong the militaristic atmosphere had become as a result of the war, if a land tax increase bill had been presented to the ninth Diet session, the *Jiyūtō*, which had always been proposing a reduction in the land tax, would probably have found it difficult to accept, and this would have obstructed the smooth development of the post-war reconstruction plan. Moreover it must not be forgotten that party support for post-war reconstruction was obtained at the cost of many concessions on the part of the *hanbatsu* Government.

In the middle of the ninth Diet the *Jiyūtō* presented the Prime Minister, Itō, with the following demands, which indicate that its support for post-war reconstruction was not unconditional:

> If the post-war reconstruction bills are to pass the Diet in completely unamended form the Government must act to establish some measure of freedom of speech and assembly.
>
> As a logical extension of his present strategy the Prime Minister ought to join the *Jiyūtō* ... and those Cabinet Ministers not agreeing with this should leave the Cabinet.[13]

In contrast to the clear change of front by the *Jiyūtō*, there were two sides to the attitudes of the *Shinpotō*. The two-sidedness of the

Matsukata-Ōkuma Cabinet (the second Matsukata Cabinet), which replaced the second Itō Cabinet, shows this accurately. As we shall see later, the Matsukata Cabinet presented a second military expansion plan supplementary to the first such plan, and after following the previous Government's industrial development plan, allowed its total costs to rise to ¥240 million, three times what they were before the war. In contrast, however, there were quite a number of people in the Cabinet who expected military retrenchment and financial restraint. Tani Tateki even took his hopes for military and financial restraint to the point of writing: 'I believe that the new Cabinet should risk everything for the sake of military retrenchment, and those who think as I do would unhesitatingly face death just to help the new Cabinet in this regard.'[14] The view that 'the emergence of the Matsukata Cabinet raises hopes of financial restraint'[15] was certainly one aspect of the situation. Thus while it is true that the *Shinpotō* was in effect a government party giving full support to the military and industrial development plans of the second Matsukata Cabinet, it nevertheless managed to leave a distinct popular-party image when compared with the *Jiyūtō*.

A new situation which had emerged after the Sino-Japanese War was that independent movements based on commercial and industrial interests had begun to intervene in the political conflict which hinged on the earlier confrontation between governmental policies of expansion and the pressure from landlords and farmers to reduce taxes. With the start of post-war reconstruction the Government was trying to gain party support by avoiding land tax increases and was proposing instead to make corporation tax a nationally administered levy; but this provided the opportunity for the emergence of political activity on the part of commerce and industry. It is possible to trace back the movement to organize local chambers of commerce and industry, and to unify commercial and industrial demands nationally, to the first National Conference of Chambers of Commerce and Industry in 1892, but it was not until after the third Conference in 1894 that the Tokyo Chamber joined, and it became a genuinely national association.[16] The levying of corporation tax nationally gave the National Conference of Chambers of Commerce and Industry the chance for real activity. In February 1896 the Ōsaka Chamber petitioned the Government to 'reduce the level of taxation', since 'the proposed new corporation tax law is certainly a great blow for the commercial world, and it will necessarily exert a considerable influence on how businessmen and industrialists conduct their activities'.[17] Subsequently the Yokkaichi Chamber demanded tax reduction through a revision of taxation methods.[18] By November 1896 seventeen separate chambers of commerce and industry had presented statements concerning corporation tax law revision to the Conference, and on 19 November an extraordinary general meeting of the National Conference was held in Tokyo to formulate a view on the corporation tax law. Since corporation tax was aimed at large and small concerns, company organizations and one-man enterprises, there were naturally some difficulties in achieving unity of view, but ultimately a proposal was directed to the Minister of Finance and the Imperial Diet, arguing that the calculation of individual corporation tax should be shifted from a capital basis to an income basis, that taking company enterprises separately taxation should be calculated on profits rather than capital, and that the rate of taxation should be reduced.[19]

If we think of it by comparison with the attitudes of governments since the Meiji Restoration, which in placing the burden on landlords and farmers had protected and fostered businessmen and industrialists, the imposition of a ¥7.5 million national corporation tax was a severe blow to commerce and industry. Since at that time land tax revenue was less than ¥40 million, if the new corporation tax had been imposed before the war it would have been possible to answer the popular parties' demands for a land tax reduction of 0.5 per cent without touching military expenditure. Moreover, at the cost of repeated severe conflict between Government and Diet the land tax was eventually increased during the thirteenth Diet, and this brought an increased revenue of ¥8,420,000. From all this, the shock felt by commerce and industry by the imposition of national corporation tax can well be imagined. The local chambers of commerce and industry throughout the nation called for reduction or abolition of corporation tax, and for land tax to be increased, while they also began to criticize the postwar reconstruction plan. Indeed the Ōsaka Chamber, in its petition cited above, called unambiguously for an increase in land tax as a means of reducing corporation tax:

> Is this new tax really fair and equitable which allows farmers alone to avoid the burdens and duties of providing for increased national expenditure? Surely if we look at the present condition of the farmers, particularly in terms of a comparison between the legal and actual price of land, of the low price of land and the high price of rice, and of the general level of profits, not only can they well support some increase in the land tax, but the prosperity and profitability of certain Government enterprises suggests that they

too could bear increased taxation, as indeed could farmers, rather than placing the burden on commercial and industrial interests alone. This is why this Chamber, taking into account various circumstances, believes and advocates that corporation tax should be reduced, and that the resultant shortfall should be made up by increasing the land tax.[20]

Again, a resolution of the National Conference of Chambers of Commerce and Industry, dated November 1896, appealed for an increase in land tax in the following words: 'Excessive increases in taxation of commerce and industry, on the grounds that they are required by postwar needs, is in no sense a balanced policy.'[21] In an extraordinary conference held in 1897, there were many who felt that the corporation tax should be completely abolished and that land tax should be increased.[22] Thus the opposition among chambers of commerce and industry to the Government's new corporation tax, which was connected with its post war reconstruction plans, tended to become a movement of commerce and industry in favour of *increasing* the land tax.

On the other hand we must not overlook the fact that the movement among chambers of commerce and industry at that time also involved criticism of the Government's postwar reconstruction plan itself. In contrast to the political parties, which while criticizing increases in the land tax were quite happy with the reconstruction plan, the chambers of commerce and industry were advocating an increase in the land tax but were criticizing the reconstruction plan. The plan was criticized, for instance, in a letter sent to the Prime Minister, Itō, by the Tokyo Chamber of Commerce and Industry in February 1896. This letter, on the grounds that the expansion of the budget was too rapid, merely expressed the hope that 'a cautious policy should be adopted of avoiding over-rapid expansion and of carefully calculating national resources and the wealth of the people'.[23] A 'proposal for financial retrenchment', presented to the Extraordinary Conference of the Chambers of Commerce and Industry in 1897, clearly criticized 'unproductive military expansion'.[24] It read in part as follows:

If we ask why our national expenditure should be so rapidly expanding, the answer lies entirely in the area of military expansion. Even though fundamentally military expansion is necessary, we must distinguish between what is essential and what can be postponed. The first step towards post-war reconstruction lies in the recovery of national strength which has been sapped by the war, whereas the expansion of the armed forces should be seen as a secondary task. Unfortunately, however, our Government is putting the cart before the horse. If we put all the money that we have received in reparations into unproductive military expansion, when shall we be able to achieve national recovery?[25]

From this it can be seen that the movement of Chambers of Commerce and Industry against the imposition of a new national corporation tax was tending towards a position of opposing military expansion as the central issue of postwar reconstruction.

It is immediately evident, however, that the simultaneous support by the Chambers of Commerce and Industry for reduction of military expenditure and augmentation of the land tax was contradictory. If what they wanted was reduction in military expenditure, they could have proposed abolition of corporation tax without proposing any increase in the land tax. If 10 per cent had been subtracted from the military expenditures for 1896 of ¥73 million, then probably the corporation tax would not have been necessary at all. If, on the other hand, because of the post-war international situation they had gone along with military expansion, then opposition to corporation tax would have had to be coupled with a proposal to increase land tax. This was diametrically opposed to the support given by the *Jiyūtō* and the *Shinpotō* for the military expansion plan and for the imposition of corporation tax as a means specifically to avoid increasing land tax. It is very clear that the conflict which rapidly emerged after the Sino-Japanese War between town and country, bourgeoisie and farmers, arose from the fact that neither side firmly opposed the Government's plans for military expansion. Criticism of military expansion by the Tokyo Chamber of Commerce and Industry failed to be adopted by the National Conference because of strong opposition from Takahashi Korekiyo of the Yokohama Chamber. As this shows, opposition to corporation tax, which involved both cutting military costs and increasing land tax, gradually came to focus on land tax and to neglect the military cost question. The deepening post-war depression between 1897 and 1898 gave momentum to this trend. The call to strengthen the national financial position by raising land tax and thus to save the economic world from disaster gradually became louder. Indeed, the louder came the call to increase land tax, the fainter grew the argument that military expenditure should be reduced.

Taguchi Ukichi, of the *Tōkyō Keizai Zasshi*, and Shimada Saburō, of the *Mainichi Shinbun*, developed clear arguments of the kind used by businessmen and industrialists to criticize the post-war reconstruction. In arguing that 'on the one hand land tax should be increased, and on the other hand the expansion of the army should be halved'[26] they were adopting just the same position as the previously cited document of the Tokyo Chamber of Commerce and Industry. They were, however, different in the thoroughness of their criticism of military expansion, and in the fact that they argued that the interests of tenants and poor people lay with commerce and industry, from which they developed an attack on landlords and political parties. Taguchi – as the basis of his argument for increasing land tax – wrote: 'Even if land tax is increased, the tenants will not pay tax, and even if it is reduced, they will not reap the benefit'.[27] When the first Ōkuma Cabinet was established [1898], he wrote: 'Although a party cabinet has been inaugurated without difficulty, the prosperity of the poor is going to decline, and the reason for this is the continual increases in consumption tax'.[28] In this way he maintained that while the parties wanted to avoid increasing the land tax, in fact if this were done it would actually increase the burdens on the peasants and the poor. Taguchi, who later clashed with Kanai Noburu and others who denied the necessity for social policies,[29] was acting as spokesman, not only for businessmen and industrialists but also for workers and tenants. Shimada Saburō, who was, it is true, arguing from the standpoint of labour–management co-operation, was on the same lines as Taguchi when he wrote: 'There is a basic necessity for labour solidarity and labour unions'.[30] Their argument was thus diametrically opposed to the campaigns during the early Diet sessions to 'lighten the people's burdens' [meaning to reduce taxation], and when they advocated increasing land tax, they were in fact calling for 'lightening the people's burdens' in a certain sense.

There were a number of people who were criticizing military expansion and post-war reconstruction from the standpoint of tax reduction for landlords and peasants. These included Tani Tateki and Soga Sukenori of the *Sanyōkai* and the *Konwakai* group in the House of Peers. As we saw in the previous chapter, Tani Tateki had supported the popular parties over administrative retrenchment, but had opposed them over tax reduction. In fact, Tani's advocacy of administrative retrenchment and military build-up lay midway between the military and industrial development position of the *hanbatsu* Government and the tax reduction position of the popular parties. After the war, however, the political parties had come to support the expansionist policies of the Government, but Tani and his group, in contrast, moved closer to the position which the parties had held during the early Diet sessions, and became one of the centres of the movement for slowing the military build-up and for not increasing the land tax. Taguchi Ukichi criticized the movement of Tani and his friends as aiming to support small farmers but ending up benefiting the large landlords,[31] but as Tani said to Kōtoku Shūsui, 'German socialism aims at land redistribution for the small farmer,'[32] and Tani certainly did not intend to benefit the large landlord. As we shall discover in Chapter 6, in the anti-land tax increase movement of 1899 Tani, unmindful of the embarrassment within the *Kenseihontō* which this caused, criticized military expansion while at the same time opposing a land tax increase.

Among those who through Tani's introduction had developed close connections with the House of Peers group (mentioned above) and who had developed criticisms of the 'post-war reconstruction party',[33] were the 'hard-line foreign policy' faction centred on the journal *Nippon*, including Kuga Minoru, Fukumoto Makoto, Kunitomo Shigeaki and others. That they too were criticizing excessive military expansion following the war is demonstrated by the following passage written by Fukumoto:

> The State is not merely an organ of military expansion, the prosperity of the people is not to be brought about merely by military expansion, but rather, if a military programme is uncontrolled and undiscriminating, it may even rob the people of its prosperity and weaken national power.[34]

That they were also, like Taguchi and his friends, representing the standpoint of the poor, is shown by the fact that Kunitomo lamented that economic liberalism made harsh the gap between rich and poor, that land tenancy was causing the ruin of middle and small farmers, and that observing Western European state socialism one could see that it was founded in the same principles of 'universal benevolence' as Japan's ancient monarchical politics.[35] The same attitude is revealed in what Fukumoto wrote about the Ashio mine pollution incident:

> If the present Government, like its predecessor, is fearful to act in relation to the present incident, it should remember that we also stand at the head of two thousand people, or rather we stand at the head of millions from Gumma, Tochigi, Saitama and Ibaragi prefectures, and the Government should not doubt this message which we shall drum into them.[36]

In this way the Tokyo Chamber of Commerce and Industry, Taguchi,

Shimada and their friends, on the one hand, and the *Sanyōkai* and *Konwakai* groups in the House of Peers, as well as Kuga, Fukumoto, Kunitomo, etc., on the other, all let loose their shafts of criticism at the Government's policies of post-war reconstruction, and especially of military expansion. When, however, the land tax increase issue arose, the views of the two groups were anything but united. Dividing them was the conflict between town and country, as is evident from the following comment by Kuga Minoru on increasing the land tax:

> The proposed increase in the land tax arises from the hopes of commerce and industry, but is detrimental to the interests of agriculture. In recent times our industry and commerce have been accustomed to claim that they are short of money and to demand increasing subsidies to bail them out. If land tax is raised and Government revenue increases, it will give a respite to Government finances, and as a result the value of bonds and shares will rise. This will provide a breathing space for commerce and industry. Considering this, the controversy about land tax comes down to a clash between the interests of town and country.[37]

Thus among the critics of the Government's postwar reconstruction plans were to be found both those who wanted tax reductions for the cities and those who wanted them for the countryside, so that the surfacing of the land tax increase question made it impossible for them to cooperate with each other.[38]

As we have seen, the Sino-Japanese war brought about a big change in the nature of political conflict when compared with that which occurred during the early Diet sessions. The *hanbatsu* Government, which had taken on as its basic task the plan for military and industrial expansion, was having to change its attitude to the political parties if it was to carry out the plan successfully. This was because a rapid expansion of the budget was not possible by relying on the Government's power of carrying on with the budget of the previous year, while tax increases and new taxes required the concurrence of the House of Representatives. Secondly, the militaristic atmosphere engendered by victory in the Sino-Japanese War and the new anti-foreign feeling caused by the Triple Intervention had already made possible for the political parties a change in direction towards which they had been groping before the war. It was becoming quite possible that the political parties might attain power, as a result of their becoming sympathetic with the Government's expansionist policies, since the Government needed their co-operation in order to carry out its post-war reconstruction policies. 'Vertical coalitions' had already come into being, as for instance in the coalition between the second Itō Cabinet and the *Jiyūtō*, and in that between the second Matsukata Cabinet and the *Shinpotō*. The *hanbatsu* were sacrificing their monopoly of power, while the political parties were sacrificing their tax reduction arguments.

Coalition cabinets, however, between the *hanbatsu* and the political parties suffered from two dilemmas. Firstly, the partial concession of political power made by the *hanbatsu* Government was a rude shock to the bureaucrats and to a majority of the House of Peers who had been the chief prop of the *hanbatsu* Government up to that time, and made them regroup their forces, not under the banner of the *hanbatsu* Government as a whole, but under the leadership of those in their ranks most opposed to the political parties. The clique of bureaucrats and members of the House of Peers called the Yamagata faction was an example of this. The fact that when the *genrō* Itō Hirobumi succeeded with difficulty in achieving the support of the *Jiyūtō* he was forced to encounter opposition from the Yamagata faction graphically demonstrates this dilemma. The second dilemma was that even though the coalition between the *hanbatsu* and the political parties was based on the principle of not tackling the problem of increasing the land tax, nevertheless it was impossible to carry out the post-war reconstruction plan without doing precisely that. This was why it proved impossible for the second Matsukata Cabinet to continue its alliance with the *Shinpotō* once it had decided to present a bill to increase the land tax, why following this there were constant clashes between the *hanbatsu* and the political parties, and why, with the first Ōkuma Cabinet, for the first time a party Cabinet was installed, for however short a period. In the following chapter we shall examine the first question, namely the nature and significance of the Yamagata faction, and from Chapter 5 onwards we shall investigate the rise and fall of party conflict over the emergence of the land tax increase issue.

4 The formation of the Yamagata faction

As we saw in the last chapter, post-war reconstruction required a huge budget increase, and not only did more tax need to be levied for this purpose, but the *hanbatsu* Government had become weaker in relation to the House of Representatives than it was before the Sino-Japanese War. In the early Diets, when the conceding of tax reductions could be avoided but it was not necessary to increase taxation, the main concern of the Government was to have the budget passed by the House of Representatives. Since, however, the House of Peers could be relied upon to reject tax reduction demands (including demands for the reduction of land tax), the Government did not really need any policy on the matter. Certainly to get the budget through the Lower House was extremely problematical, and we have already seen in the previous chapter that the protection given to the Government by the Imperial Constitution whereby it was possible to carry on with the budget of the previous year was not as effective as is generally imagined. On the other hand, in the period up to the Sino-Japanese War, when the level of national expenditures was fairly restricted, the ability to carry on with the budget of the previous year guaranteed the Government at least minimum implementation of its policies. After the war, which had resulted in a sudden doubling and even tripling of the budget, the ability to carry on with the budget of the previous year lost absolutely all meaning from the Government's point of view. Execution of the previous year's budget would have meant the immediate abandonment of 'post-war reconstruction'. Moreover the characteristic of the Constitution which had worked so well for the Government during the early Diet sessions – that 'law has precedence over a budget, which has no power to change a law'[1] – came after the war to have the reverse effect of tying the hands of the Government. Before the war, because of this relationship between the budget and laws, even when the

Government was forced to accept demands from the popular parties to cut expenditures, it was possible to get the House of Peers to reject the tax reduction bill as a separate issue from this. After the war, however, it was the *hanbatsu* Government itself which had to present bills for increases in taxation and steer them through both houses of the Diet, and it only needed the House of Representatives, (as it had previously only needed the House of Peers), to reject a bill for it to lapse. Even if the House of Representatives accepted the expenditure budget, it still had the power to decide which items of taxation should be increased in order to raise the revenue required. Thus after the war the Government was forced to allow the political parties some degree of participation in power if it was to get them to accept the budget and increases in taxation. Thus, following the end of the ninth Diet session the *Jiyūtō* President, Itagaki Taisuke, entered the second Itō Cabinet as Home Minister, and after the end of the tenth Diet session many members from the *Shinpotō* were sworn in as vice-ministers and heads of bureaux.

Although it was for the purpose of carrying through the post-war reconstruction, the appointment of so many party members to important bureaucratic positions created a serious threat to the existing class of officials. Given that a considerable part of the bureaucratic class adhered to the ideas of 'transcendental government' discussed in Chapter 1, the entry into cabinet and high bureaucratic office of party members not only affected the personal interests of the bureaucratic class, but also conflicted with their personal ideology.

The fact that in order to carry out post-war reconstruction the Government required the cooperation of the parties in the Lower House both in a policy sense and in terms of their participation in power, resulted in a reduction in the political importance of the House of Peers, and earned the strong antipathy of that House. As we have seen, the ability of the *hanbatsu* Government to control the vociferous demands of the popular parties for tax reduction during the early Diet sessions was wholly due to the House of Peers. After the war, however, the Government and the parties came closer together, and in the ninth and tenth Diets the parties practically accepted the Government's budget, while the Government showed it was prepared to make concessions to party demands on issues unconnected with reduction, such as election law revision, revision of the local district system and revision of newspaper regulations. The *raison d'être* of the House of Peers for the Government had clearly begun to decline. Moreover party members were rapidly coming to

occupy the important posts of cabinet minister, vice-minister, prefectural governor, etc., to which Members of the House of Peers had
no slight aspirations. The House of Peers was losing its capacity to
remain for ever a dependable bulwark for the government of the day.

The fact that in the ninth and tenth Diets the *Jiyūtō* and the
Shinpotō, which in the early Diets had vigorously confronted the
hanbatsu Government as 'popular parties', had now come round to a
position of support for the *hanbatsu*, made things particularly difficult
for the *Kokumin Kyōkai*, which had been a 'pro-Government' party
in the early Diet sessions. For the *Kokumin Kyōkai*, which had seen
its own significance as lying in its opposition to the tax reduction
policies of the popular parties and support for the Government
policies of military and industrial expansion, the total acceptance by
the *Jiyūtō* and *Shinpotō*, during the ninth and tenth Diets, of
enormous budgets designed to promote just such policies of development was a matter which clearly affected its own *raison d'être*. We
have already examined in the previous chapter how this sense of crisis
for the *Kokumin Kyōkai* already existed in embryonic form about the
time of the fourth Diet, but the new situation following the war was
that not only were the *Jiyūtō* and the *Shinpotō* co-operating with
Government in a policy sense, but that by participating in Cabinet
they had turned themselves into part of the policy implementation
apparatus. The *Kokumin Kyōkai* was in danger of being completely
excluded from the changing trend of the times.

Thus the bureaucratic class, Members of the House of Peers, and
the *Kokumin Kyōkai*, which had been the principal support for the
hanbatsu Government in the early Diet sessions, were coming to be
excluded for the time being as a result of the reconciliation which had
taken place between the Government and the former popular parties.
Of course complete agreement between the Government and the
parties over the land tax increase problem was still short of realization
– indeed was still only temporary and patchy – but at the same time it
showed the way towards the developments of the near future. Since
research into the political history of the period hitherto has focused
mainly on the foundation of the *Rikken Seiyūkai*,[2] the attitudes of the
bureaucrats, members of the House of Peers and the *Kokumin
Kyōkai* referred to above have not yet been sufficiently clarified.[3]
Without, however, analysing the attitudes of these groups at that
period, it is probably impossible to explain why it was that no party
Cabinet was able to emerge until 1918. If the Yamagata faction,
which brought together in one body the three elements of bureaucrats, the greater part of the House of Peers and a minority of the

House of Representatives, namely the 'pro-Government parties' (the names changed from *Kokumin Kyōkai* to *Teikokutō* to *Daidō* Club to *Chūō* Club, but the reality remained practically the same), had not existed, the political parties might well have become the principal element in the power structure without going through the detour of the Katsura-Saionji period. [1905–12] Even after the formation in 1913 of the *Rikken Dōshikai* by part of the Yamagata faction under Katsura (following the formation of Itō's *Rikken Seiyūkai*), the Yamagata faction in the House of Peers retained, as previously, a fierce sense of its own independence.[4] Until Hara Kei partially succeeded in bringing the House of Peers under his control, the Yamagata faction continued to maintain – as it had before – power equal to the majority party in the House of Representatives.[5] Now the manifest consolidation of the Yamagata faction as a separate entity took place in the process of opposing the emergence of party forces following the Sino-Japanese War, as we shall discuss below. With these considerations in mind we shall in this chapter examine the attitudes of bureaucrats sympathetic to Yamagata, of the House of Peers and of the *Kokumin Kyōkai*, in the period before the inauguration of the first Ōkuma Cabinet in 1898.

THE SECOND ITŌ CABINET AND THE YAMAGATA FACTION

As we saw in the previous chapter, reconciliation of the *Jiyūtō* with the Itō Cabinet was attempted before the fourth Diet session, and in the fifth and sixth Diets the *Jiyūtō* acted in effect as a party taking the side of the Itō Cabinet. In November 1895 the *Jiyūtō* issued the following statement: 'The policies of our party are moving in the same direction as those of the Government, and by cooperating with them we shall be performing our national duty, and shall be contributing to the development of Japan.'[6] Preparations for the alliance took place from June of that year between Hayashi Yūzō, Kōno Hironaka, and Matsuda Masahisa of the *Jiyūtō* and the Chief Cabinet Secretary, Itō Miyoji. The *Jiyūtō*, from the beginning of the negotiations for coalition, demanded that Itagaki be admitted into the Cabinet after the end of the ninth Diet. According to a letter from Itō Miyoji to Itō Hirobumi (the Prime Minister) dated 6 November 1895, the same morning Hayashi Yūzō had visited him and had 'repeatedly requested that if the Diet session were successfully completed, Itagaki be admitted to the Cabinet after the end of the Diet session.' He had replied to Hayashi that since 'the Prime Minister was keeping this in mind', Hayashi should not 'demand a specific promise from him'.[7] Thus, the *Jiyūtō* was demanding the appointment of Itagaki as Home Affairs Minister as a reward for its support of the Government in the ninth Diet, support which derived from the post-war reconstruction question, and the Government was generally going along with this. And so, on 14 April 1896, the President of the *Jiyūtō*, Itagaki Taisuke, was appointed Minister of Home Affairs.

The appointment caused a great shock within the class of bureaucrats, and especially among prefectural governors, who were under the aegis of the Home Minister, but within the Home Ministry there had already been some dismissals of anti-*Jiyūtō* and anti-party officials. The dismissals in February 1896 of Nomura, the Home Minister, Egi, the Prefectural Bureau Chief, and Tsuzuki, the Public Works Bureau Chief, were in this category. The fact that a Cabinet allied with the *Jiyūtō* was incompatible with Tsuzuki Keiroku stemmed naturally enough from his 'transcendentalist' point of view, which we examined in Part I. Concerning the cases of Nomura Yasushi and Egi Kazuyuki, the Kyōto Governor Yamada Nobumichi wrote: 'Nomura has been dismissed and Egi has been re-posted; reflecting on this we can see that the pro-*Jiyūtō* bureaucrats Itō Miyoji and Suematsu Kenchō have won, while the anti-coalition faction has lost. If this is the case, the danger is that the Government may be devoured by the *Jiyūtō*.'[8] From this it is clear that it was people opposed to the coalition who were re-deployed. The origin of the problem lay in a conflict between the Home Ministry and the *Jiyūtō* over the issue of revising the system of local government. The Itō Cabinet, as a reward to the *Jiyūtō* for collaborating with it in the ninth Diet, agreed to the longstanding *Jiyūtō* demand for abolition of special cities and of large-scale landlord membership of district assemblies. The Ministry of Home Affairs was totally opposed to the former, and on the latter did not relent in its insistence that instead of abolishing the provision for large landlords to be members of district assemblies, a system of weighted voting should be adopted for elections to district assemblies.[9] This was why the differences of attitude between the Cabinet and the Home Ministry came into the open in committee hearings of the House of Representatives, forced the Home Minister, Nomura, into a position where he had to eat his words, and ultimately led to his resignation. The tough attitude on the part of the Home Ministry was principally the work of Tsuzuki and Egi; and Tsuzuki in particular, however much he had to testify before the committee of the Lower House as a Government committee member, was never prepared to change his views.[10] Thus it was that following the resignation of Nomura as Minister of Home Affairs, things came to the point that Tsuzuki and Egi were relieved of their bureau headships. Yoshikawa, who was Nomura's successor, summoned Tsuzuki and Egi, and initiated their transfer to prefectural governorships. Egi accepted his demotion to the governorship of Ibaragi Prefecture, but Tsuzuki refused to accept demotion and resigned.[11] The fact that this conflict between the Cabinet and the Home Ministry even reached the plenary session of the Diet in replies by Government committee members is demonstrated in the following reply to the plenary session of the House of Councillors concerning the local government system revision bill, by Soga Sukenori of the *Konwakai*:

> When I asked the Government committee members at the beginning of questioning whether they supported this bill enthusiastically or supported it unenthusiastically, they replied that they were neither enthusiastic nor unenthusiastic. The Government committee members have been replying to every question in this neither enthusiastic nor unenthusiastic fashion. Does the Government mean that it is doing its duty by public opinion and doesn't mind if the bill is passed, or is it saying that it doesn't mind if it isn't passed? ... I understand the general situation to be that the Government without supporting it enthusiastically would be happy with it, that the Government's *pro forma* support means it is generally happy with it. This is why I feel inconclusively about the matter.[12]

It was said of the bureau heads Tsuzuki and Egi, that 'the spirit of the Home Ministry is to be found in Tsuzuki and Egi, whereas ministers and vice-ministers are merely men of straw',[13] and that 'when Tsuzuki Keiroku, Head of the Public Works Bureau, and Egi Kazuyuki, Head of the Prefectural Government Bureau, call prefectural governors fools, those governors listen with bated breath'.[14] When men such as these were suddenly demoted, the shock to the bureaucracy can readily be imagined.

When Itagaki was appointed Minister of Home Affairs, the sense of crisis and antipathy within the bureaucracy grew even sharper. On 14 April, the day when the appointment was made, the Governor of Kyōto Prefecture, Yamada Nobumichi, wrote to Sasa Tomofusa of the *Kokumin Kyōkai*:

> Now that Itagaki is to occupy the position of Home Minister, we shall have to confer about the resignation of our colleagues, and

with Ōura coming to Tokyo we shall have to discuss the procedures with Shirane, Kiyoura and Matsudaira. Then we will have to submit our resignation. I shall let you know about this.[15]

Kiyoura Keigo, at the same period, reported to Yamagata who was overseas that 'a secret conference' had taken place 'to consider retirement if it is not possible to overcome the subordination to a Home Affairs Minister who is a member of the *Jiyūtō* of prefectural governors such as Yamada, Utsumi, Matsudaira, Ōura and Komatsubara', and that a definite decision had not been reached because 'in your absence we did not wish to make up our minds prematurely'.[16] At the same time Shirane Senichi was Minister of Transport, Kiyoura was Vice-Minister of Justice, Matsudaira Masamichi was Governor of Kumamoto Prefecture, Ōura Kanetake was Governor of Yamaguchi Prefecture, Komatsubara Eitarō was Governor of Shizuoka Prefecture, and Utsumi Tadakatsu was Governor of Ōsaka Prefecture. We can see, therefore, how a group of bureaucrats centred on prefectural governors was coalescing under the patronage of the *genrō* Yamagata Aritomo. In the second Yamagata Cabinet, which was formed two and a half years later, of this group of bureaucrats Kiyoura was made Minister of Justice, Matsudaira was made Vice-Minister of Home Affairs, Tsuzuki was appointed Vice-Minister of Foreign Affairs and Ōura was appointed Director-General of Police. From this too it can be appreciated that the group of officials centred on the Home Ministry, formed around the time that Itagaki became a Cabinet minister, were the nucleus of what came to be called the 'Yamagata bureaucrats'.[17]

The group in the House of Representatives which had the closest relationship with the Yamagata bureaucrats was the *Kokumin Kyōkai*. This relationship was established right from the start through the good offices of Shinagawa Yojirō and of the *Kumamoto Kokkentō*. Itō Miyoji reported that 'two or three governors clearly have a relationship with the *Kokumin Kyōkai*',[18] and from about the time that Itagaki entered the Cabinet these relations became considerably closer. When the second Itō Cabinet allied itself with the *Jiyūtō*, the *Kokumin Kyōkai* called the *genro* Itō Hirobumi 'Itō the President of the *Jiyūtō*',[19] and in order to oppose this combination, its policy was to 'consult the opinion of the Transport Minister, Shirane Senichi' and to 'foster latent forces'.[20] The *Kokumin Kyōkai* took on the task of faithfully putting into practice the pet scheme of Yamagata Aritomo for a triangular relationship between the three parties. The three-party scheme, however, was really an idea thought up by bureaucrats, and even though the *Kokumin Kyōkai* was only a small party of about thirty Diet members, it was indeed a political party, having interests not necessarily identical with those of the bureaucratic class. Within the *Kokumin Kyōkai* there was extreme disquiet, not so much in the immediate aftermath of Itagaki being made a Cabinet minister, but once Itō began talks with Ōkuma of the *Shinpotō*, with a view to having him in the Cabinet also. The party began to voice demands that it too should be represented in Cabinet, as can be seen in the following extract from a letter written by Motoda Hajime, one of the *Kokumin Kyōkai* leaders, to Sasa Tomofusa:

> Events regarding the Cabinet in recent days have given rise to concern, and since it seems likely from what Count Inoue says that counts Matsukata and Ōkuma may become Cabinet ministers, we of the *Kokumin Kyōkai* must make sure we do not remain mere passive spectators of such a massive change in the political situation.... The *Kokumin Kyōkai* for the most part contains men who are strongly pro-Government, so we must take mature consideration of the complexity of the relationships surrounding us, and if Count Ōkuma also should enter the Cabinet we shall have to reconsider our position. Ōoka is also of the same opinion and I should like to request your reconsideration in advance.[21]

Even despite this circumlocutionary language it is possible to detect the anxiety felt by the *Kokumin Kyōkai* at participation by the *Jiyūtō* and the *Shimpotō* in a power structure from which they themselves were likely to be excluded. In devising a three-party triangular system, the Yamagata bureaucrats planned to manipulate the two major parties by bringing the *Kokumin Kyōkai* under their own control. Now the *Kokumin Kyōkai* was the smallest of the three parties, but held the casting vote between the *Jiyūtō* and *Shinpotō* – the two major parties, neither of which claimed an absolute majority. Therefore the bureaucrats preferred a national unity Cabinet in which not only Itagaki but also Ōkuma was in the Cabinet, rather than a Cabinet joined only by Itagaki. This is clear from a letter sent to Inoue Kaoru by one of the Yamagata bureaucrats, Ōura Kanetake:

> The event of which I secretly informed you before my departure has now taken place, and I was lucky enough to arrive in Tokyo on the day of Count Itagaki's appointment to Cabinet. I quickly went to Itō's residence and was at pains to express my views on whether or not the *great gate should be opened* [i.e. whether Ōkuma should

also be let into the Cabinet], but since the policy intention is to open the great gate, and he is determined on this course of action, Viscount Takashima supports the entry of Itagaki into the Cabinet, on the condition of the opening of the great gate, and for this reason Kabayama and Matsukata are of the same opinion'.[22]

The second Itō Cabinet in the end had to resign because it was unable to obtain the agreement of the *Jiyūtō* to the entry into Cabinet of Matsukata and Ōkuma, but what we shall be concerned with here is the attitude to this of the *Kokumin Kyōkai*. It is clear from the letter of Motoda Hajime, cited above, that Motoda Hajime, Ōoka Ikuzō and others believed that the *Kokumin Kyōkai* should also be represented in the second Itō Cabinet, but Sasa Tomofusa seems to have been opposed to this.[23] The fact that Motoda and Ōoka, who were later to participate in Itō's *Seiyūkai* party, should have proposed their own membership of Itō's Cabinet, whereas Sasa, who was to remain in Yamagata's *Teikokutō*, should have opposed it, shows that there was a contradiction between the triangular party scheme of the Yamagata bureaucrats, and the *Kokumin Kyōkai*. Once the alliance of the second Itō Cabinet and the *Jiyūtō* had been replaced by an alliance of the second Matsukata Cabinet and the *Shinpotō*, instability within the *Kokumin Kyōkai* became considerably more severe. It was only that part of the *Kokumin Kyōkai* which consistently opposed any kind of party-type cabinet that linked up with the *Teikokutō*, the *Daidō* Club and the *Chūō* Club to form what became more like a discrete force of Yamagata bureaucrats within the House of Representatives.

The Cabinet which had entered into an alliance with the *Jiyūtō* met a changing response from the House of Peers. Relations between the Itō Cabinet and the House of Peers had temporarily worsened just before the Sino-Japanese War during the fifth and sixth Diets. At that time, however, the *Sanyōkai* of Konoe Atsumaro, Nijō Motohiro and others, with the *Konwakai* of Tani Tateki, Soga Sukenori and others, joined forces with the six hard-line anti-foreign factions on a platform manifestly hostile to the Itō Cabinet. Meanwhile, however, the *Kenkyūkai*, the largest party-cum-faction in the House of Peers, ultimately would not go along. At first, Senge Takanori, Okabe Nagamoto and others from the *Kenkyūkai* were signatories to the 'Report' of the group of thirty-eight members of the House of Peers, opposing dissolution of the fifth Diet, but at a meeting on 22 January 1894 they cancelled their participation.[24] Considering that Senge had been appointed Governor of Saitama Prefecture two days before, and that attempts were made through Itō Miyoji to influence the *Kenkyū-kai* secretaries Torii Tadafumi, Ōkōchi Masachika, Hotta Masayoshi, Madenokōji Michifusa, Okabe Nagamoto and others, the Government's efforts in respect of the *Kenkyūkai* appear to have been crowned with success.[25] The House of Peers, after Tani Tateki's 'diligence and military spirit' proposal in the second Diet, up until the Sino-Japanese War, remained in a state described as one in which 'the popular parties consist of the *Sanyōkai* (meaning Prince Konoe) and the 'Diligence and Military Spirit' group (meaning Tani and Miura), while the pro-Government parties consist of the *Kenkyūkai* members (Senge, Nakayama); their respective memberships are about equal'.[26] During the twenties of Meiji [1887–97] the House of Peers was not as monolithic as is frequently assumed. Even, however, the *Sanyōkai* and the *Konwakai*, called the 'popular parties of the House of Peers' by Kaneko, advocated, as we have seen, the 'diligence and military spirit' approach, while up until the Sino-Japanese War they supported expansion of armaments and opposed land tax reduction; only in their support for administrative retrenchment did they seem like 'popular parties'. Their function, therefore, as a bulwark against the tax reduction arguments of the popular parties was fulfilled adequately even in the case of the *Sanyōkai* and the *Konwakai*.

After the Sino-Japanese War, however, the *Sanyōkai* and the *Konwakai* became more critical of armaments expansion, and began to express open opposition to the Government's post-war reconstruction plan. On the other hand the *Kenkyūkai*, which had consistently been a loyal supporter of the *hanbatsu* Government, also began to change its attitude when the Itō Cabinet went into an alliance with the *Jiyūtō*. Concerning the activities of the *Kenkyūkai* in the ninth Diet, Itō Miyoji reported:

'The session will close tomorrow, and an avalanche of Government bills has been passed, but the bills for revision of the local government system and the electoral system, which the *Jiyūtō* hoped would get through, have been killed in the House of Peers'; moreover the centre of this activity is 'the *Kenkyūkai*, which we thought of as the instrument of government' and 'its prime movers have connections with Vice-Minister Kiyoura Keigo and the former Home Minister Nomura, while many of their sympathizers are bureaucratic members of the House of Peers.'[27]

Again, Kiyoura Keigo, whom Itō reported to be the power behind the scenes of the *Kenkyūkai*, wrote to Yamagata Aritomo that:

the House of Peers rejected unanimously the local government revision bill at the end of the ninth Diet, because the Government had agreed to the bill in order to appease the *Jiyūtō*.[28]

In fact, the committee set up to deal with the local government revision bill in the House of Peers was led by Senge Takanori, the boss of the *Kenkyūkai*, and Kiyoura Keigo as deputy chairman under the chairmanship of Tokugawa Iesato, and the committee discussing the election law revision bill in the House of Representatives was led by Ogimachi Michimasa of the *Kenkyūkai* as chairman, while the members included Hirata Tōsuke, an appointed member from the Yamagata faction.[29] The *Jiyūtō* attacked these moves in the House of Peers saying they had been 'deceived by the Government's scheming',[30] whereas in fact the *Kenkyūkai* had broken away from Itō's control and had lined up with the Yamagata faction bureaucrats. From a different point of view the *Sanyōkai* and the *Konwakai* were opposing the Cabinet coalition of Itō and the *Jiyūtō*, and we shall take another look at the nature of this group in the context of the second Matsukata Cabinet in the following pages.

THE SECOND MATSUKATA CABINET AND THE YAMAGATA FACTION

After the failure of the second Itō Cabinet over the question of the entry into the Cabinet of Matsukata and Ōkuma, and its consequent resignation, the movement to install Yamagata as Prime Minister began to get off the ground. The Kyōto Governor, Yamada Nobumichi, related its structure to Sasa Tomofusa of the *Kokumin Kyōkai* in the following words:

> The political situation is coming to a head, and so since Yamagata and Matsukata are here at the present time, I tried at first to strengthen Yamagata's resolve, but he did not seem to be active on the question; Count Matsukata tried to advise him along the same lines, but because he was ill he refused to do anything about it. Matsukata and I then discussed it among ourselves, and we decided that if Yamagata was not prepared to become Prime Minister then I would tell him that Matsukata would refuse to enter the Cabinet. When I told him this, he was very embarrassed. I think that he is now seventy to eighty per cent decided, and if he is also pressured by Matsukata and persuaded by the people in Tokyo, I think he will make up his mind. If he does become Prime Minister, Kabayama will have to be Home Minister – or failing

him, Shirane. Perhaps Saigō should return to the Army and Kabayama should be appointed to the Navy, or if not him, Shirane. I think Shinagawa should take Agriculture and Commerce or Education. It has already been decided that if Shirane takes Home Affairs, then Matsudaira should be Vice-Minister, and if that happens we shall have to select some suitable person for Governor of Kumamoto Prefecture. Even if Ōura is suitable, I think he should be Chief Inspector of Police, and if we consider Komatsubara, he will have to be Chief Cabinet Secretary, and a successor is under consideration.[31]

Thus the Cabinet was to comprise Yamagata Aritomo as Prime Minister, Saigō Tsugumichi as Army Minister, Kabayama as Navy Minister, Shirane Senichi as Home Minister, Shinagawa Yajirō as Minister of Agriculture and Commerce (or Education), Matsudaira Masanao as Vice-Minister of Home Affairs, Ōura Kanetake as Chief Inspector of Police, and Komatsubara Eitarō as Chief Cabinet Secretary. It is evident why this group of bureaucrats placed their hopes upon a Yamagata Cabinet.

At this juncture, however, no Yamagata Cabinet materialized, and when the second Matsukata Cabinet was formed with the support of the *Shimpotō*, the position of the Yamagata bureaucrats became quite delicate. As is clear from Yamada's letter, the Yamagata bureaucrats were in a fairly intimate relationship with Matsukata, Saigo, Kabayama and others of the 'Satsuma faction'. The appointment of Kabayama as Home Minister in the second Matsukata Cabinet was even a partial fulfilment of their scheme. Yamada even wrote that 'Kabayama has received the post of Home Minister, and I must say that this is the best choice'.[32] The fact that Kiyoura and Nomura both entered the Cabinet, Kiyoura as Minister of Justice and Nomura as Minister of Communications, made it difficult for the Yamagata faction to criticize the Matsukata Cabinet. On the other hand the appointment of Ōkuma Shigenobu, of the *Shinpotō*, as Foreign Minister in the second Matsukata Cabinet meant that in place of an 'Itō-Itagaki Cabinet' there was a 'Matsukata-Ōkuma Cabinet', and since they were opposed to party cabinets the Yamagata bureaucrats were in a position where they could hardly avoid criticizing the Cabinet. Yamada Nobumichi also wrote: 'If Ōkuma has joined the Cabinet without sacrificing his principles; I think it will be time to discuss whether to advance or retreat'.[33]

With their own representatives, Nomura, Kiyoura and Kabayama, in the Cabinet, but having to contend with the success of the political party forces (since Ōkuma was a Cabinet minister and the Government was in coalition with the *Shinpotō*), the Yamagata bureaucrats were not able to react so clearly to the Cabinet as they could towards its predecessor. The second armaments expansion plan, undertaken by the Matsukata Cabinet, which we shall examine later, may have been one of the reasons why it was difficult for them to come out in direct opposition to the Cabinet. In the event the Yamagata bureaucrats had no choice but to persuade themselves of the unconvincing proposition that it was a non-party Cabinet. They reasoned that 'the conditions for the coalition look as through they will naturally dissolve, so that the first impression is one of relief',[34] and 'When I visited Kabayama, Matsukata and Takashima, I [Yamada Nobumichi] was reassured to find that there is absolutely no reason to worry since the Cabinet's thinking is firmly centred on the Emperor'.[35] Ōura Kanetake wrote, at the end of the second Matsukata Cabinet: 'I did not like the Itō-Itagaki Cabinet, nor do I like the present Matsukata-Ōkuma Cabinet ... but there is nothing for it but to reconcile ourselves to the fact that a Cabinet congenial to us cannot materialize.'[36] As this indicates, the Yamagata bureaucrats, and especially the local officials' group which was their nucleus, were in a state of disappointment at the time. It was precisely at this time of 'tribulations' that the solidarity of this group of bureaucrats grew stronger, and the Yamagata faction, which continued over such a long period to act as a bulwark against the political parties, was being created.

The *Kokumin Kyōkai*, however, faced a crisis with the emergence of the second Matsukata Cabinet. As we have seen, even at the end of the second Itō Cabinet there was anxiety within the *Kokumin Kyōkai* at its having been excluded from a cabinet in which the *hanbatsu* and party forces were in coalition. When the Matsukata-Ōkuma Cabinet was formed, this anxiety deepened somewhat. The *Yomiuri Shinbun* of 4 November 1896 reported what was happening in the *Kokumin Kyōkai* as follows:

> It is widely known that while claiming to be impartial the newspaper of the *Kokumin Kyōkai* has been rudely attacking the new Cabinet, but recently seems to have changed the force of its argument. According to information that we have obtained, this is because the Kumamoto *Kokken* faction, which is a central part of the *Kyōkai*, has unanimously decided to support the present Cabinet. Apparently when the Cabinet was first formed the Kumamoto *Kokken* faction had not made up its mind, and Sasa

Tomofusa had not made his view clear, but now several officials including senior members of the Kumamoto group, such as Ariyoshi and Yasuba, have all decided to help the present Cabinet. Since the nationalist faction thinks that this might precipitate a split in its ranks, it is calling for strict adherence to this decision, and since Sasa, who could not bear to provoke a split in such a stable group as this by opposing the decision, has come round to the same view, this has meant a shift in the position of the *Kokumin Kyōkai* as a whole.[37]

Shinagawa Yojirō sent this article from the *Yomiuri Shimbun* to Sasa Tomofusa, and wrote that 'Yasuba and the others are in a very great hurry'. In other words, apart from what it said about Sasa, the article was close to the truth. Shinagawa and Sasa were defenders of the 'three-party triangle' notion,[38] and 'intended that the *Kokumin Kyōkai* should distinguish itself by occupying a special position in between the *Jiyūtō* and the *Shinpotō*,[39] but nevertheless the idea of participating in the Matsukata Cabinet and sharing power alongside the *Shimpotō* gradually gained strength within the party. The unrest in the Kumamoto *Kokkentō* was most conspicuous, and Adachi Kenzō reflected about it in the following way:

The President of the *Kokumin Kyōkai*, Viscount Shinagawa, has from the beginning maintained a policy of opposing the Matsukata Cabinet, and he continued to stick to this position even after the Matsukata Cabinet became independent [of the *Shimpotō*]. Sasa, however, is on an overseas trip, while Kiyoura and Yamada, the two senior local leaders, have been promoted to important positions in the Cabinet, and therefore Shinagawa is very worried about the trouble which may be caused within the Kumamoto faction, and is wondering whether that faction may not in the end be pulled into the Cabinet also'.[40]

Within the Government there was a plan to re-post Ōura Kanetake and to find a governorship for Yasuba Yasukazu, a senior leader of the Kumamoto *Kokken* faction, which had been advocating participation in the Matsukata Cabinet.[41] A little later, they were scheming to obtain the support of the Kumamoto *Kokken* faction by the appointment as Minister of Agriculture and Commerce of either Yasuba or Yamada Nobumichi, the Governor of Kyōto Prefecture who was another senior leader of the Kumamoto group.[42] Also, the overseas trip of Sasa Tomofusa, referred to in Adachi Kenzō's reflections, seems to have been a means of heading off a conflict inside the Kumamoto *Kokken* faction between the coalitionist and the anti-coalitionists.[43]

We have already described how a Cabinet including *Shinpotō* participation succeeded one which had *Jiyūtō* participation, and how the hopes of the *Kokumin Kyōkai* for a Yamagata Cabinet were not satisfied, and so the position of the *Kokumin Kyōkai*, like that of the local bureaucrats' group, was becoming more difficult. At the end of the second Matsukata Cabinet, when there was already a strong expectation that an Itō Cabinet would emerge, Ōura, one of the members of the local bureaucrats' group, wrote, as we have seen, that 'there is nothing for it but to reconcile ourselves to the fact that a Cabinet congenial to us can never materialize',[44] but at exactly the same time Shinagawa Yajirō, head of the *Kokumin Kyōkai*, sadly reflected that 'if the Itō Cabinet is formed, the *Kyōkai* will split'.[45] Nevertheless, although they were suffering from the same kind of problem, the respective capacities of the bureaucrats and the political parties to counteract such a development were quite different. While the bureaucrats had the chance gradually to build up solidarity, the problem for a political party like the *Kokumin Kyōkai* was that all it could do was to witness a decline in the number of Diet Members affiliated with it. The *Kokumin Kyōkai*, which had sixty-eight Diet Members at the time of its foundation, by the end of the eleventh Diet was reduced to twenty-three affiliated Diet Members. With 23 seats out of a total of 300, the prospect of holding the casting vote was problematical. All that the Yamagata faction could hope to achieve in the House of Representatives was the pro forma title of a pro-Government group.

In contrast, the Yamagata faction in the House of Peers was rapidly increasing in strength over the period of the second Matsu-kata Cabinet. Certainly, at the beginning of the Matsukata Cabinet, the Yamagata faction in the House of Peers was in the same kind of difficulty as the local bureaucrats' group and the *Kokumin Kyōkai*. This was because the *Sanyōkai* and the *Konwakai*, which were rivals of the *Kenkyūkai*, were from the beginning of the second Matsukata Cabinet behaving as the Cabinet's supporters. Ever since the hard-line anti-foreign league movement [i.e. the six hard-line factions referred to on p. 108] which immediately preceded the Sino-Japanese War, the *Sanyōkai* and the *Konwakai* had been on close and friendly terms with the *Shinpotō*. This was why the Cabinet through Ōkuma, the Foreign Minister, had sought to prevail upon Konoe Atsumaro, the leader of the *Sanyōkai*, to enter the Cabinet as Minister of Education. According to the *Konoe Diary*, on 17 September 1896 he was sounded out by Matsukata the Prime Minister, through the offices of Tanaka Gentarō[46] and on 22 September Takada Sanae, acting as Ōkuma's messenger, invited him to join the Cabinet.[47] Takada, who visited him again the next day, demanded that he join the Cabinet, giving him the message from Ōkuma that:

> The policy of this Cabinet is not different from what the Prince has been advocating, and so he should not be forced to make unwilling compromises even if he enters the Cabinet, and even if his commitments at the Peers' School make it very difficult for him on a personal level, it is desirable that he become a Cabinet Minister right away, and it would be pleasing if he were able to combine his presidency of the Peers' School with the position of Minister of Education.[48]

When Konoe refused the offer of a Cabinet position, Matsukata and Okuma pressed him to become President of the House of Peers, and on 3 October they achieved their aim.[49] The Matsukata Cabinet would attempt through Konoe to obtain the support of the *Sanyōkai* and the *Konwakai*. Tani Tateki of the *Konwakai* also said: 'I believe Konoe ought to be Education Minister',[50] and, 'Many times have I supported the resignation of the Itō Cabinet, many times have I backed Matsukata and Ōkuma, and I believe this to be wholly in the national interest,'[51] thus placing high hopes on the Matsukata Cabinet. Table 4.1 indicates the balance of power in the House of Peers at the time.

By obtaining complete support from the *Sanyōkai* and the *Konwakai* it would have been possible to control the House of Peers to a certain extent. For the Cabinet, however, these two groups could not be relied on to behave as pro-Government parties. As Tani Tateki wrote in his diary: 'I hear that Matsukata has taken the position of Prime Minister with the aim of halting the expansion of armaments. Can this be believed? If it can, then it is happy for the nation.'[52] As this indicates, their support for the second Matsukata Cabinet was premised on armaments reduction and financial stringency. As we shall see, Matsukata himself made many statements criticizing post-war armaments expansion, and there is a sense in which 'reduction of armaments was an official promise of the Matsukata Cabinet'.[53] On the other hand, as we saw in the previous section, the draft post-war reconstruction plan was drawn up by Matsukata himself, and the Matsukata Cabinet subsequently took upon itself the task of carrying out the supplementary plan. Thus from the start there was a certain contradiction over armaments expansion between the Cabinet on the

Table 4.1 Numbers of members affiliated with groups and factions in the House of Peers

Kenkyūkai	65
Sawakai	22
Independents aligned with the above groups	51
Total	138
Konwakai	64
Sanyōkai	20
Independents aligned with the above groups	38
Total	122
Members of the Imperial Family	12
Members normally absent	18
Speaker and Vice-President	2
Total	32
Grand total	292

Source: 'Kizokuin tōhabetsu ichiranhyō' in *Makino Nobuaki bunsho*. The table relates to about the end of 1895 and the beginning of 1896. See also Appendix 4.

one hand and the *Sanyōkai* and the *Konwakai* which constituted the pro-Government party group in the House of Peers. Soon after the Cabinet was organized Tani jotted down the following critical opinion:

> In recent newspapers Ōkuma is reported as making a speech in which he expressed the opinion that there should be no cutting down of military preparations, but this seems to be a makeshift policy devised because he was afraid of the wrath of the military, and I am quite incapable of expressing the same opinion. If we do not reduce military preparations in the present financial circumstances, we shall be forced to the following measures:
> 1 raise the land tax by 0.5 per cent;
> 2 raise the tax on *sake*.
> If this is not done, then this is what will have to be done:
> 1 reduce the salaries of officials and reduce the running expenses of each ministry;
> 2 overcome the temporary emergency by raising foreign loans;
> 3 increase the production of banknotes.

Whatever fancy ideas people may have, there is no other course open ... I believe, and we must not worry about annoying the military. Our argument may sound simple, but we must cut the Army down to an increase of two divisions, and the Navy to 150,000 tons, and we should give priority to financial cut-backs. If things are done according to Ōkuma's speech, we shall solve a problem in the short term but shall be storing up trouble in the long term. If the Government proposes to increase land tax, the present Cabinet will risk destruction. The same is true of tax on *sake*.[54]

Tani's predictions were quite correct. As we shall see in the next section, the Matsukata Cabinet, which had inherited the armaments expansion plan, was forced to resort to increasing the land tax, and for that reason was pushed into resigning. He was more far-sighted than the *Shinpotō*, which supported the Matsukata Cabinet's plans for armaments expansion on the grounds that 'by making full military preparations we shall be able to secure peace and security, and shall positively contribute to the development of production',[55] but yet opposed increasing the land tax.

During the budget deliberations in the House of Peers the *Sanyōkai* and the *Konwakai* sought to press this point home. In the budget committee of the House of Peers on 5 March, Members of both Houses decided on an Army and Navy budget reduction of ¥30 million and negotiated with the Government to this end, but the Government was not in agreement with this reduction, saying that 'since this budget was drawn up on the basis of last year's plans, it is not possible to change it'.[56] Subsequently, with both sides still in conflict on the issue, the Budget Committee, which had the *Sanyōkai* and the *Konwakai* as its main stream, presented to the plenary session on 16 March an amendment bill which included reduced expenditure on armaments. Because of opposition, however, from the *Kenkyūkai*, the only result was some reduction in expenditure of the Ministry of Home Affairs and the Ministry of Commerce.[57] This was a total defeat for the *Sanyōkai* and the *Konwakai*.

This confrontation over expansion of armaments between the Matsukata Cabinet and the *Sanyōkai* and *Konwakai* caused a change of attitude on the part of the *Kenkyūkai*. When the Matsukata Cabinet was first installed, the *Kenkyūkai* made clear that it was not 'disposed to line up with a government based on parties and factions'.[58] But over the course of the confrontation between the Government and the *Sanyōkai* and *Konwakai* concerning the budget, the *Kenkyūkai* came to change its attitude to the Government. Speculating on the attitude of the *Kenkyūkai*, Konoe Atsumaro of the *Sanyōkai* wrote as follows:

> The *Kenkyūkai* will support any Cabinet. Therefore they think they will follow the present Cabinet, yet as they see the *Sanyōkai* and *Konwakai*, which have always been opposed to the Government, coming to have close and friendly relations with it, they do not want to show loyalty to a Cabinet in which these parties are leading them by the nose; but they also find it difficult to oppose the Cabinet. Concerning Soga's bill to revise the budget, might not the Government use it as an excuse to reduce expenditure, given the fact that there are difficulties involved in rapid increases in expenditure? If so, might not the *Sanyōkai* and the *Konwakai* use this as a reason for joining the Cabinet? If the Government were of the opinion that it was difficult to reduce expenditure straightaway, it would be a good chance for us to create a split between the Government and these two parties. We know about their swinging from the left to the right from a conversation between Okabe and others and the Prime Minister.[59]

Therefore Konoe Atsumaro, leader of the *Kenkyūkai*, tried to stop the movement of Soga Sukenori against armaments expansion with the words 'They are jumping onto Itō Miyoji's bandwagon.'[60] Even Tani Tateki moved to a position of compromise, arguing that 'it is clear from the Budget Committee that since armaments expansion has already begun last year, it is impossible to reduce expenditure, and enormous budget expansion is not the fault of the present Government but of the previous one. It is too much now to blame the present Government for this ... and if we attack them for this we shall be demanding the impossible'.[61] The famous petition to the Throne for armaments reduction presented to the tenth Diet by Tani Tateki and others, instead of stopping budget reduction at that Diet session, was a compromise policy which did not go beyond 'the fact that it reached the ear of the Emperor by petition that there was a demand to Cabinet to seek financial restraint by the next Diet session'.[62] Nevertheless, Soga Sukenori, Tomita Tetsunosuke, Kubota Yuzuru and Nishimura Ryōkichi, of the *Konwakai*, disagreed with it.[63] In the *Sanyōkai*, Honda Masanori, Matsudaira Norisuke and Shimazu Tadasuke, who had become Budget Committee members, rejected Konoe's persuasion, saying, 'Because we are members of the committee, we do not wish to have our activities restricted';[64] and thus the budget question produced a head-on confrontation with the

Government. Incidentally, although it was put forward as a compromise proposal, the petition to the Throne by Tani and others for armaments reduction is important for understanding the character of the *Sanyōkai* and the *Konwakai*. It read as follows:

> We have already for a long time concentrated on perfecting our national defence; indeed now, on the strength of our victory in the war, we are levying new taxes and raising loans, and we are going to spend the greater part of the money we raise on the expansion of armaments. It looks, however, as if the amount remaining to be spent on education, industry, transport and a host of other purposes will be very little. Indeed, does not this policy of post-war reconstruction militate against the Emperor's desire for the maintenance of peace and the furtherance of the national destiny? If, on the grounds that military preparedness was as yet insufficient, we were to impoverish the nation, the responsibility would not merely rest with cabinet ministers ... We earnestly petition Your Majesty to warn your ministers to revise this precipitate armaments expansion, to promote the development of private industry and strengthen the financial base, thus stabilizing the nation.[65]

The fact that such direct criticism of post-war reconstruction came, not from the *Jiyūtō* or the *Shinpotō*, but from a group in the House of Peers, is quite ironic. A breakdown of the sixty-nine supporters of the petition to the Throne according to groups and factions is given in Table 4.2.

We can see, therefore, that at this period the House of Peers was a particularly disagreeable entity from the standpoint of the *hanbatsu* Government. If the Government proposed to carry out post-war reconstruction in conjunction with the *Jiyūtō* and the *Shinpotō*, then the *Kenkyūkai* was opposed because it believed in transcendental government, whereas the *Sanyōkai* and *Konwakai*, though they were quite happy for the Government to be in coalition with a political party (and particularly with the *Shinpotō*), were critical of the post-war reconstruction plan itself. What put an end to this complex situation in the House of Peers was the general selection of members holding peerages (counts, viscounts and barons) in July 1897. The changes in party strength among the viscounts (the most important category of peers) is shown in Table 4.3.[66]

This was an overwhelming victory for the *Kenkyūkai*, and a total defeat for the *Sanyōkai* and *Konwakai*. As a result, the House of Peers came to be controlled almost completely by the *Kenkyūkai*,

Table 4.2 Supporters of the petition to the Throne against armaments expansion, according to groups and factions

Factional group	No. of supporters of the petition
Konwakai	34
Sanyōkai	10
Pro-*Konwakai* Independents	10
Sawakai	6
Kenkyūkai	4
Pro-*Kenkyūkai* and pro-*Sawakai* Independents	4
Unclear	2
Total	70

Source: *Nippon*, 16 March 1897, p.4; *Makino Nobuaki bunsho*, table entitled: 'Kizokuin giin tōhabetsu ichiranhyō'.
The 'tōhabetsu ichiranhyō', in the *Makino bunsho* was probably drawn up between November 1895 and January 1896. Therefore there is likely to have been some shift in affiliations between then and the 'Petition to the Throne' resolution in March 1897. The two Members listed as 'unclear' in the table are so because of the time difference between the two sources. Moreover, although 69 supported the petition, the total number in the table is 70. No doubt there is a mistake in the *Nippon* article, but since it is not clear where the mistake lies, the figure has been left as 70. Also there were some among the 47 Members who supported and signed the petition when it was presented, who are not included in the 70 in this table. The implications of this will be discussed later.

which while bringing its thinking into line with that of the *hanbatsu* Government on the matter of post-war reconstruction, was, in spite of that Government, opposed to a Government coalition with political parties. To this was added in the following year (1898) the Independent Club composed of those Members nominated by the Emperor,[67] founded in reaction against the formation of the first Ōkuma Cabinet (which was also the first political party cabinet), and from July 1897 to the middle of 1898 the control of the House of Peers by the Yamagata faction was practically complete.

As we can see, therefore, when the *hanbatsu* Government, in order to carry out its policies of post-war reconstruction, had to accept participation in power by the former popular parties, notably the *Jiyūtō* and the *Shinpotō*, such a coalition with political parties was opposed by precisely those groups which had formed the backbone of the Government's support – namely the bureaucrats, the *Kokumin Kyōkai*, the *Kenkyūkai* of the House of Peers and so on. They began to form a discrete group under one of the *genrō*,

Table 4.3 Factional allegiance of viscounts who were Members of the House of Peers

Factional group	January 1896	July 1897
Kenkyūkai	21	45
Sawakai	1	1
Pro-*Kenkyūkai* or pro-*Sawakai* Independents	9	5
Total	37	51
Konwakai	11	5
Sanyōkai	13	8
Pro-*Konwakai* and pro-*Sanyōkai* Independents	6	6
Total	30	19
Others	3	–
Grand total	70	70

Yamagata Aritomo. Although it is true that in the House of Representatives the *Kokumin Kyōkai* failed in its attempt to operate as the Yamagata faction, control of the House of Peers by that faction became rapidly more effective. Subsequently, when the question of increasing the land tax for the sake of post-war reconstruction became a further pressing issue, the policy of coalition between *hanbatsu* and political parties crumbled, and out of the clash between them emerged Japan's first-ever party Cabinet, the first Ōkuma Cabinet. This was the time, however, when the parties were made to understand the significance of the Yamagata faction which had come into being in the preceding period.

5 The question of increasing the land tax

We have already seen that the coalition of the *hanbatsu* and political parties in the ninth and tenth Diets was established on the condition that there would be no increase in land tax. Despite the fact that the post-war reconstruction plan supported by the parties would obviously soon require such an increase, the parties continued to support post-war reconstruction while opposing a rise in land tax. This was why, when the second Matsukata Cabinet resolved to present a land tax increase bill to the eleventh Diet, the prospect of forming coalition cabinets between the *hanbatsu* and parties was dimmed, and a situation developed similar to that of the early Diets, in which the *hanbatsu* were in direct confrontation with an alliance of parties.

It is true that there was severe inflation in the price of rice following the Sino-Japanese War, and that since for the landlords – many of whom had already become parasitical – the inflation did not involve increases in the costs of production, the land tax burden had in practice been lightened considerably, and a land tax increase would not be so burdensome for them as might have been imagined. It is also true that for political parties which had wholeheartedly backed post-war reconstruction the grounds for opposing land tax increases were extremely weak. Policy conflict between the *hanbatsu* Government and the parties in fact existed only within narrowly defined limits. This, however, had the contrary effect of exacerbating their superficial conflict. Unlike the situation in the early Diets, the Government was faced with the responsibility of actually introducing a bill to amend the land tax regulations, and therefore the strength of the parties had doubled. The parties now had no need to aim to have a bill passed, only to have one rejected. The Government, which had to bear the 'burden of proof', found the parties, even though they had become far more development-minded and co-operative than they were in the early sessions of the Diet, far more of a nuisance than they previously had been. For the parties, on the other hand, in spite of the logical contradiction in lauding policies of industrial and military expansion while refusing to raise revenue for them, it was possible, if they opposed increases in land tax, to force open even further that door to power which had already opened for them to a certain extent. This was why the clash between the *hanbatsu* and the parties over the land tax question emerged for both of them as something approaching a life and death struggle. This was demonstrated in an extreme form when the transcendentalist third Itō Cabinet failed in its attempt to increase the land tax, and had to hand over power – admittedly on a temporary basis – to the parties. We shall go to see how the *hanbatsu* Government, encountering opposition from the parties in its attempt to bring about a land tax increase, had to go so far as to divest themselves of power for a while.

THE SECOND MATSUKATA CABINET AND THE LAND TAX INCREASE QUESTION

We saw in Chapter 1 how at the launching of the post-war reconstruction plan Matsukata, the Minister of Finance, affirmed that land tax would not be increased. When we reach the eleventh Diet, however, two years later, the same Matsukata resolved to increase the land tax, and as a result lost the confidence of the House of Representatives and was forced to tender the resignation of his Cabinet. He gave the following reasons for having to move on the land tax issue:[1]

1 unexpected increases in extraordinary costs of Army and Navy expansion;
2 unexpected increases in costs for Taiwan;
3 a sixfold increase in financial assistance to shipping;
4 a shortfall in revenue from corporation tax, registration tax, leaf tobacco revenue, etc.

Since expenditure had exceeded the estimates, and revenue had fallen short of the estimates, there was naturally a deficit. Matsukata outlined three proposals:

1 reduction of the armaments expansion plan;
2 further raising of loans;
3 increases in taxation.

He rejected (1) and (2), but insisted on (3). He argued that cutting back on the planned armaments expansion was impossible, and laid the responsibility on the Itō Cabinet, which had proposed the plan during the ninth Diet, and on the political parties which had supported it:

> Should we alter the post-war plan which was approved almost unanimously in the ninth Diet, and change to a policy of 'armaments reduction'? Well, we should think very hard indeed before the ninth Diet endorses the armaments expansion plan. Indeed, if today we were to amend a basic national policy of this kind, not only would it affect confidence at home and abroad, but indications concerning the Great Powers do not permit it. Indeed, even if we were to adopt a policy of reduction, since the greater part of the plan has already been put into effect, the amount of savings that could be made would be quite minimal.[2]

Similarly, he rejected the floating of new public loans, on the following grounds:

> On the question of how to make up the imbalance of revenue and expenditure, either we could rely on the short-term expedient of extending the period for payment of military outlays or loan repayments, or we could last out for a while by the issuing of new loans. Neither course, however, would meet with the approval of anyone having the long-term national interest genuinely at heart. Above all, a policy of making up a shortfall in revenue by reliance on loans would gradually accentuate the cause of the illness, or even if it granted temporary respite from pain, there would be no way of avoiding a recurrence at a later stage. Indeed, if we examine the present situation at home and abroad, the outlook for loan raising is extremely poor. We should have practically no chance of attracting subscribers unless we appealed to the market with a price that was cheap but if we were to mop up capital in this way, we should risk causing at least a general collapse of the stock market, and this could seriously worsen the difficult circumstances into which many businessmen have now fallen.[3]

In other words, from consideration of 'sound finance', and from anxiety about the condition of depressed entrepreneurs, the option of raising finance by either floating loans or postponing loan repayments was rejected. If the armaments expansion plan could not be altered, and neither could loan repayments be delayed nor new loans be floated, then naturally, 'it goes without saying that the only possible policy is to increase taxation'.[4] Moreover, since as a result of establishing various new forms of taxation and planning for increases during the early period of increasing taxation, the tax yield was in each case less than expected and a revenue shortfall resulted, it was also natural for Matsukata to reach the conclusion that 'the proliferation of categories of taxation yielding little revenue is merely troublesome and unprofitable to both Government and people'.[5] Thus an increase in the land tax was mooted on the grounds that 'there is a case for some increase in the land tax today, not only because it is the prime source of revenue in the country, but with the change in the unit of currency the price of rice may be expected to be about ten yen per *koku*'.

As we have already seen, however, there was in the financial policies of the Matsukata Cabinet a big gap between image and reality. We found in the previous chapter that there were not a few who expected the Cabinet to cut back the plan for arms expansion. It is true that in the passage cited above Matsukata wrote that 'we should think very hard indeed before the ninth Diet endorses the armaments expansion plan', and in September 1897 he wrote as follows:

> Among those who wish to reduce expenditure are those who fear that military spending will not serve the development of the national economy, but will rather do it harm. Although their patriotic spirit must be acknowledged, if they wish to make changes now to the plan they will have to change the whole of it ... The time for argument is before implementation, but now implementation is under way.[7]

In January 1898 he wrote that 'on the size of the armaments plan, anyone can see that it is indeed enormous'.[8] Indeed at first glance one might conclude that he was not entirely happy about the armaments expansion plan. In these statements, however, the blame is placed on the Itō Cabinet as the originator of the plan, and he was saying that in practice it was impossible to alter it. Even more to the point, the postwar reconstruction plan which Matsukata was now criticizing was, as we saw in Chapter 3, inherited almost intact from the one drawn up while Matsukata was in office. Later on, he presented to the tenth Diet a second armaments expansion plan, encompassing ¥38,350,000 for the Army and ¥118,320,000 for the Navy.[9] It was from a misunderstanding about the Matsukata Cabinet, which was pursuing policies of arms expansion while criticizing arms expansion, that the 'petition to the Throne for arms restriction' and similar exercises were initiated, as we saw in Chapter 3, by the *Sanyōkai* and the *Konwakai* in the House of Peers.

Matsukata also criticized the Itō Cabinet for excesses in its industrialization plan:

> My departure from the Cabinet in 1895 was brought about by the fact that, although fearing the consequences of the plan to increase taxation, I had urged that an extraordinary Diet session be summoned; my consent was nevertheless not given to the plan. For this reason the 1896 budget was a patched-up budget; moreover, it included additional costs for river repairs, railway construction, telegraph and telephone installation, and other items. The plan was for most of the revenue shortfall to be covered by loans, but the market certainly would not bear such an annual call on its resources.[10]

This is why it was said that 'when the Matsukata Cabinet was formed, public opinion expected it to reorganize finance'.[11] If we read it carefully, however, the Matsukata Cabinet's 'reorganization of finance' did not involve the reduction of planned construction, but rather pointed in the direction of increases in taxation. If we also take into account the previously mentioned principle of not relying upon public loans, it is possible to understand the general outline of the Matsukata Cabinet's finance policy. In the later stages of the Cabinet, the post-war depression had already begun to make itself felt, and industrial circles not only were refusing to take up the loans, but were even beginning to propose that the loans they already had should be paid back by the import of foreign capital.[12] It was to satisfy the demands of the industrial world that Matsukata determined not to float loans. When Matsukata said that 'my financial policy aims to strengthen the base',[13] this meant maintaining the balance between revenue and expenditure by increasing taxation, and did not mean reducing either planned military expansion or industrial development. Tani Tateki felt that his expectation of a reduction in the armaments expansion plan and no increases in taxation had been betrayed. His criticism therefore supports this point:

> The Government says to 'strengthen the financial base, strengthen the financial base, strengthen the financial base', but all this means is that taxes will rise year by year and the financial base will never be strengthened.[14]

Naturally, if the armaments expansion plan could not be put back, if the burdens of industrialists could not be increased, and if it was necessary to cover the shortfall in revenue, then there was nothing for it but to increase the land tax.

After his resignation, however, Matsukata put it like this: 'I knew well that with the Diet hastening towards a general election, and for various other reasons, it was unprofitable to propose an increase in land tax at that time.'[15] As this indicates, a land tax increase bill would have had no chance of passing the House of Representatives. The *Jiyūtō* and the *Shinpotō* had come to give wholehearted support to the post-war reconstruction plan, but on the land tax question, where they had hitherto been demanding a *reduction*, it was impossible to expect them to execute a sudden change of direction and give their support to an *increase*. As Matsukata pointed out, however, three full years had passed since the fourth general election in September 1894, and irrespective of whether or not there was a dissolution, the fifth general election would have to be held during 1898. It is self-evident that with a general election in prospect, the parties could not be expected to agree to an increase in land tax, which would be unpopular with landlords and farmers. In the Cabinet only Ōkuma, the Foreign Minister, voiced strong opposition to increasing the land tax, and subsequently on 6 November, resigned.[16] Previously the *Shinpotō* had refused to collaborate with the Cabinet because of its lack of unity concerning finance policy and the composition of the Cabinet.[17] After the refusal of the *Shinpotō*, the attempt by the Army Minister, Takashima, to bring the *Jiyūtō* into a coalition was officially rejected by the Council of the *Jiyūtō* on 18 November,[18] and the Cabinet was therefore completely isolated in the House of Representatives. The fact that he was in a position where, however hard he tried, he could not secure the passage of a land tax increase bill, was clear to Matsukata himself. The *hanbatsu* Government side, however, came to realize that it was impossible to carry on with the implementation of its post-war reconstruction if it avoided the issue of land tax increases. This will be important to our examination of subsequent political changes.

THE ESTABLISHMENT OF THE THIRD ITŌ CABINET

Developments from the end of the second Matsukata Cabinet to the establishment of the third Itō Cabinet were characterized by various attempts at coalition between the *hanbatsu* and the parties, but these all failed because of the existence of the land tax increase problem, and attempts to stabilize power and carry out post-war reconstruction on the basis of a *hanbatsu*-party coalition strategy came up against a brick wall. It was particularly noticeable that in the various coalition strategies (Itō–*Jiyūtō*, Itō–*Shinpotō*, Satsuma faction–*Jiyūtō*) the

Yamagata faction was not included. The criticism, on the part of the Yamagata faction, against the strategy of *hanbatsu*-party coalition for the sake of carrying out post-war reconstruction (discussed in the previous chapter), was now being expressed by actions rather than by words. As was already clear in the refusal of the *Shinpotō* to enter into a coalition with the second Matsukata Cabinet, so long as the land tax increase problem remained, it was extremely difficult to create a coalition with political parties, and it was even more difficult for a 'transcendental' Cabinet, which did not have party support, to pass a land tax increase bill through the House of Representatives, and this was why so many different coalition strategies were attempted. All these attempts failed, and when the third Itō Cabinet had to face the twelfth Diet as a transcendental Cabinet, the outcome of the land tax increase bill could also be predicted.

The precise reason why the third Itō Cabinet had to be transcendental was that the *Shinpotō* demanded, as conditions for their entry into the Cabinet, that Ōkuma be made Minister for Home Affairs and that the party also be given three other ministerial posts, while the *Jiyūtō* demanded the post of Home Minister for Itagaki; however, Itō refused their respective demands.[19] Itō dreamed of forming a 'Cabinet of national unity' including both the *Jiyūtō* and the *Shinpotō*, but since he was faced by general elections following the dissolution of the eleventh Diet, he was hesitant to give the post of Home Minister to either of the two parties.[20] For exactly the same reason, however, both those parties held out for the Home Ministerial post. It is hardly necessary to go over the reasons why it was advantageous to hold the post of Minister for Home Affairs with a general election in the offing. Itō's notion of a Cabinet of national unity was designed to secure the support of the House of Representatives for the pending land tax increase bill, but what made him judge that it was possible was not unconnected with the fact that since the later stages of the second Matsukata Cabinet, the *Shinpotō* and the *Jiyūtō* had begun to think in terms of breaking the deadlock by entering into a coalition with Itō. It was not only the *hanbatsu* Government that had been pushed into a corner by the land tax increase problem. Both the *Jiyūtō* and the *Shinpotō*, unless they could think of some way of breaking the deadlock, would find that their participation in power, secured after the end of the war, was crumbling, and they would be forced to return to the position of parties entirely in opposition.

Even before its conflict with the Matsukata Cabinet surfaced, the *Shimpotō* was insistently demanding – and a similarly strong demand came from Iwasaki Yanosuke of the Mitsubishi company – the formation of a powerful Cabinet with Itō as Prime Minister, Matsukata as Minister of Finance and Ōkuma as Minister of Foreign Affairs. In June 1897 Itō Miyoji wrote to Itō Hirobumi as follows:

> The other day when Ōishi paid us a visit, he said that it would not be at all difficult to run Itō and Ōkuma together, and that Matsukata would easily accept the post of Minister of Finance; also Iwasaki was doing his best in this regard ... According to a secret talk I had with Ōishi, Inukai was supporting this combination, not because of the influence of Ōishi, but because of the influence of Iwasaki.[21]

Later Itō Miyoji, as the result of a face-to-face meeting with Iwasaki, reported the following:

> He recalls that at the time of your departure he said that there was nothing for it but to organize a Cabinet based on yourself, Ōkuma and Matsukata, and that you did not reject this; therefore, when you return home he wants to construct a great alliance, and he believes that he himself will be the best person to persuade Matsukata.[22]

In other words, Oishi Masami, Inukai Tsuyoshi and others who were leaders of the *Shinpotō* – partly because of the strong wish of Iwasaki of Mitsubishi – were working actively to persuade Itō Hirobumi to make a coalition Cabinet centred on Itō himself, Ōkuma and Matsukata. Behind Iwasaki's enthusiasm lay probably the requirement on the part of business for a strong Cabinet, able to put business back on its feet and to give sustenance to the business world by raising the land tax. It seems that the *Shinpotō* was prepared to consider consolidating its participation in power by coming into line with an increase in the land tax.[23]

While Itō Miyoji was acting as a direct line of communication from the *Shinpotō* to Itō Hirobumi, he was also exerting himself to keep the *Jiyūtō* on Itō's side. He reported to Itō Hirobumi that 'when the chance comes, Itagaki and his followers will naturally be on your side, and I am doing my best to prevail upon them to this end'.[24] Itagaki Taisuke expressed to Itō Hirobumi his desire to take part in the Cabinet through a coalition, saying: 'The present Cabinet has run out of policies, is tired, and has reached the evening of its days. The time has come for you to replace it, materially improving the political situation.'[25] Thus the fact that the *Shinpotō* and the *Jiyūtō* were strongly in favour of participating in the next Cabinet in coalition with Itō strengthened his resolve to construct a Cabinet of national unity.

Gradually, however, the cracks in the coalition between the *Shinpotō* and the Matsukata Cabinet widened and a complete rift became merely a matter of time. When this happened, attempts were initiated within the Matsukata Cabinet to make an alliance with the *Jiyūtō*. An example of this was the coalition strategy which Takashima, the Minister for the Army, attempted through Matsuda Masahisa who represented the Satsuma faction within the *Jiyūtō*. Takashima asked Itō Miyoji to be his intermediary in his plan for an alliance with the *Jiyūtō*, but was refused,[26] while the coalition argument proposed by Matsuda and others within the *Jiyūtō* gradually attracted an increasing number of supporters, so that after opposition from Itagaki, Hayashi and others was overcome, the stage was set for formal negotiations.[27] In these negotiations the conditions which Matsuda Masahisa presented to Kabayama, the Minister for Home Affairs, were three in number: namely that the *Jiyūtō* should have two ministerial posts, that it should have more than five governorships and that its political views should be adopted. A provisional compromise was made on the basis of 'giving the Ministry of Justice to Hoshi, giving it one more position after the Diet session and helping with election expenses', and on 18 November 1897 this was put to the council meeting.[28] Of the Executive Board members of the *Jiyūtō*, Matsuda took a positive and Hayashi a negative attitude, while Itagaki flatly opposed the idea of coalition, saying: 'Even to attempt any sort of negotiations with the present Cabinet, which must be regarded as our political enemy, is a loss of face for our party'.[29] In the end at the party's council meeting of 18 November, a mere two out of thirty supported the proposals, a further seven supported them conditionally, and thus the coalition negotiations were rejected.[30]

Having seen the breakdown of the Matsukata Cabinet – *Shinpotō* coalition, and the failure of the scheme put forward by Takashima (the Army Minister), Kabayama (the Home Minister) and others for an approach to the *Jiyūtō*, Itō gradually came round to the previously mentioned idea of a Cabinet of national unity, which would include Ōkuma and Itagaki. Naturally, neither the *Shinpotō* nor the *Jiyūtō* were able, because of their internal circumstances, to put forward less onerous conditions for entering into a coalition than they had previously insisted on. When it became clear to Itagaki, of the *Jiyūtō*, that his appointment as Home Minister had been vetoed by Itō, and that no promise would be forthcoming in the near future, he opened up to Itō Miyoji in the following terms: 'It is difficult to maintain the support of local branches for our entry into a coalition, and not only must we distance ourselves form the coalition officially, but also we cannot become involved with it behind the scenes. Itō Miyoji sympathized with Itagaki's attitude, and reported to Itō Hirobumi:

> I have tested opinion within the *Jiyūtō*, and find that the bulk of party members are annoyed with the unreliability of Count Itagaki and others. Therefore there is an upsurge of ill-feeling towards you, and there is little prospect of bringing the party together in a satisfactory way. Hayashi is resigning, and it is difficult to gauge what attitude the party will take. Simply to speak of the Eastern Crisis [a term used to indicate the aggressive policies of the Western Powers towards China] and to call for a Cabinet of national unity will not solve the present crisis.[31]

In these terms he criticized the weakness of Itō's idea for a Cabinet of national unity.

On 8 January 1898, the day before Itō Miyoji wrote this letter, relations between Itō Hirobumi and the *Jiyūtō* came within a hair's breadth of complete breakdown at a meeting between Itō and the *Jiyūtō* executives at the Imperial Hotel. Perhaps it was because of the strong warning from Itō Miyoji, but on the 12th another meeting was held, as a result of which the *Jiyūtō* announced that 'agreement in spirit had been reached', thus suggesting there was hope for future progress. On 6 February Itō invited members of the *Jiyūtō* and thanked them for their co-operation. Total breakdown in relations between Itō and the *Jiyūtō* came at a general meeting of *Jiyūtō* Diet Members on 18 April following the general elections. At the Cabinet meeting on 13 April a fierce argument took place on the coalition question between Inoue (Minister of Finance), and Itō Miyoji (Minister of Agriculture and Commerce); on 15 April Itō, the Prime Minister, formally announced to the *Jiyūtō* his refusal to admit Itagaki into the Cabinet; and on the 18th the *Jiyūtō* officially decided to reject coalition.[32]

As we have seen earlier, the reason why the second Matsukata Cabinet had forfeited the support of the *Shinpotō* and had been forced to break off the coalition and to tender its resignation was that it had resolved to increase the land tax. In other words, it was doubtless clear both to the *Shinpotō* and to the *Jiyūtō* that the *hanbatsu* Government had taken increasing the land tax as its most crucial current task. If this is so, how do we explain that both the *Shinpotō* and the *Jiyūtō* were angling for a coalition with the third Itō Cabinet, and that the *Jiyūtō* in particular was making some continuing efforts towards coalition right up to the Diet members' general meeting on 18 April? The only plausible explanation is that both parties were prepared to accept an increase in land tax provided that the coalition conditions were satisfactory. In this sense, the various attempts to create a coalition, between the original proposal by the second Matsukata Cabinet for a land tax increase and the official rejection by the third Itō Cabinet of coalition with the *Jiyūtō*, were all an important part of the land tax increase campaign. The fact that the parties began to take the attitude that they might as well support a land tax increase, provided that the conditions for coalition were satisfactory to them, shows firstly   that the conflict over increasing the land tax was no longer a question of black and white, and secondly that for the political parties it was getting into power and obtaining political posts that assumed the greatest significance.

Thus it was that the third Itō Cabinet, which aspired to become a Cabinet of national unity, succeeded in forging a coalition neither with the *Jiyūtō* nor with the *Shinpotō*, and therefore emerged as a transcendental Cabinet. When the first transcendental Cabinet after the Sino-Japanese War appeared with increasing the land tax as its principal task, the parties were naturally forced to try a return to the popular party coalition strategy of the early Diets.

THE THIRD ITŌ CABINET AND THE LAND TAX INCREASE QUESTION

Inoue Kaoru, Minister of Finance in the third Itō Cabinet, which was established in January 1898 following the second Matsukata Cabinet, seems to have hesitated at first to present a land tax increase bill to the twelfth Diet. The Home Minister in the previous Cabinet, Kabayama Sukenori, reflected that 'the initial financial policy of the present Cabinet seemed to have a restrictive character, but when the Diet session began, the tax increase bill broke like a clap of thunder'.[33] Also Hirata Tōsuke, who was Secretary General of the Privy Council at that time, recalled that 'Inoue argued against presenting a tax increase bill *at the extraordinary Diet session* but Itō forced the issue and had it presented'.[34] Inoue himself, when he met representatives of the *Kokumin Kyōkai* on 28 April 1898, told them:

> If I had occupied the financial office two or three years ago, I should not have planned such a large budget, and I might well have pursued policies of retrenchment. *Today, however, when projects are already under way*, the basis for financial expansion

has already been laid. For instance, when you are building a house, however much you may think you can stop work half-way through, it is in fact impossible, so that genuine retrenchment is unattainable. Therefore I am planning to carry out the plans in full, and while it may be possible to trim back some expenditure, it is difficult now to cover the expenditures of the various ministries simply with normal revenues. So it is necessary to obtain revenue from somewhere, and it may be necessary to increase taxation *from 1899 onwards.*[35]

The expression 'to increase taxation from 1899 onwards' may have meant that a land tax increase bill would be presented to the ordinary session of the Diet during the winter, but it may be better to explain it as meaning that there was no plan to present a bill to the twelfth Diet, which was an extraordinary session. In the twelfth Diet Tokumasu Gentarō, of the *Jiyūtō*, criticized Inoue in the following way:

Earlier Inoue, the Minister of Finance, told the representative of the *Keizai Kenkyūkai* that important tax increases were not a matter to be presented to the short extraordinary Diet session. Therefore whatever may happen in the thirteenth session, I think the Minister will recall that he said clearly no tax increase bill would be presented in the extraordinary session.[36]

Tokumasa's statement is probably correct.

As can be seen in the hesitation of the Finance Minister, Inoue, it was especially difficult to present the land tax increase bill and have it accepted in the twelfth Diet, seeing that it was an extraordinary session. The reason was that since it was not possible to present the next year's budget to an extraordinary session (unlike the regular session), the Diet was required to accept increases in taxation without knowing what was in the budget. The natural order was for the Government to make clear what were the expenditure and revenue levels of the following year's budget, then to announce in precise terms the revenue shortfall, and finally to appeal to the need to increase taxation. It was not likely that the Diet would accept a tax increase bill if that was all that had been presented. But on the other hand this also shows that the overwhelming majority vote in the twelfth Diet against the proposed increase in the land tax ought not to be taken at its face value. Itagaki Taisuke said, about six months later, when the land tax increase bill was passed:

I hear that already at the time of the Matsukata Cabinet, a year and a half ago, Count Ōkuma thought that the land tax increase

bill ought to be presented in order to put our finances on a more
stable footing. Subsequently the Itō Cabinet presented it to last
year's twelfth Diet, but although I warned them that it was
inappropriate to present a land tax increase bill to the extraordinary Diet at a time when the expenditure budget was not
before it, the Cabinet did not accept my warning; as a result we
clashed and the Diet was dissolved, but I did not oppose it
absolutely.[37]

This in fact was not entirely a case of being wise after the event. In
other words, the fact that the land tax increase bill in the twelfth Diet
was rejected by an overwhelming majority of 247 against to 27 in
favour did not mean that the political parties were adopting a stance
of total opposition to it.

The same thing can be said about the question of revising the
assessed value of land. Before the voting on the land tax increase bill
in the House of Representatives of 10 June 1898, a preliminary
attempt was made by Bandō Kangorō and others to present a land
tax assessment revision proposal. It is clear from the text of this
proposal that its motive was to demand of the Government regional
tax reductions through revision of land tax assessment before deliberations took place on the land tax revision bill. The proposal read
as follows:

> The unbalanced nature of the present land tax and its unequal
> burdens upon the people is an obvious fact. The bill to revise the
> land tax regulations, presented by the Government at the plenary
> session, will not simply increase the rate of land tax, but will more
> and more increase its unequal balance, and the tax burdens will
> come to be felt more and more unequally. How can we sit back
> and ignore this? Therefore we hope the Government will aim to
> reduce the land tax on those regions which are most disadvan-
> taged, revise the basis for calculation of the tax, and present a bill
> aimed at revising the present land assessment formula within
> acceptable limits.[38]

Since the land tax was determined at 2.5 per cent of the assessed
value of the land as stated on the title deeds, local landlords whose
land assessment was reduced by a revision of the land assessment
regulations were likely to find that the amount by which their tax
increased would be substantially less.

In other words the move to discuss land assessment first suggested
the view that an increase in the land tax did not particularly matter so

long as land assessment were revised. This is clear from a statement of Wada Hikojirō (Hiroshima) of the *Kokumin Kyōkai*, a member of the land assessment revision group, in the committee discussing an increase in land tax: 'If we come to a decision without revising land assessment, we cannot help but oppose the bill which is only to increase land tax.'[39]

This pre-emptive move was ultimately defeated by 165 votes to 127 (a difference of 38), but it is significant that out of the 127 who voted for it 47 were *Jiyūtō* members. (See Table 5.1.) One of these, Suzuki Gizaemon from Chiba Prefecture, appealed to his electors, following the dissolution of the twelfth Diet, in the following terms:

How can the Opposition point to us and say that we are supporting the tax increase bill? This is a false allegation. How can they be so foolish as *to mistake our support for revision of land assessment for promotion of increased land tax?* Does anyone apart from supporters of the opposition candidate confuse the two things? Land assessment revision is our basic argument, and having supported it in the twelfth Diet we must give some explanation of our reasons to people. All knowledgeable people are well aware of the inequality of land assessment between different prefectures. Thus for several years the *Jiyūtō* has advocated it and the *Shinpotō* has supported it, and in 1883 the Government tabled a land assessment revision bill in Parliament. This, however, unfortunately lapsed because of the dissolution of the House of

Table 5.1 Supporters of the pre-emptive move for a proposal to revise land assessment in the twelfth Diet

	Supporters	Total seats
Jiyūtō	47	98
Yamashita Club*	38	48
Kokumin Kyōkai	24	26
Independent	12	23
Shinpotō	4	91
Dōshi Club	2	14
Total	127	300

*A businessmen's club in the House of Representatives.
Source: Drawn up from *Dai 11–12 teikoku gikai shūgiin giji sokkiroku*, pp.311–13, and *Gikai seido nanajūnenshi – seitō kaiha hen*, pp.311–15

Representatives. For the past five years it has been impossible to find a chance to effect land assessment revision because of the many affairs of State, and during the twelfth Diet session the Government presented the land tax increase bill. If land assessment rates are to be changed, irrespective of whether they are increased or not, the imbalance of land assessment, which is the root of the present rates, ought to be revised first. We believe in other words, that land assessement revision must be carried out whether or not the rates of tax are to increase. *The land assessment in Miyagi Prefecture, Yamaguchi Prefecture and the various prefectures of Tōhoku is a mere twelve yen per tan* [approximately 0.245 of an acre] *of agricultural land*, whereas Ōsaka and Hyōgo prefectures are *fifty-two yen*. Taking my prefecture of Chiba, the rate is *thirty-two yen*, which is far higher than the national average. If, however, one looks at *the actual amount harvested*, the land in Miyagi, valued at twelve yen, produces seven bales, whereas although the land in Chiba is valued at *thirty-two yen*, it yields on average only four bales. So far as tax is concerned, however, Chiba bears 2.8 times the burden borne by Miyagi and the various prefectures of Tōhoku. Apart from the one faction that opposes us, there is nobody who does not think that revision is overdue.[40]

Here the position of the land assessment revision faction within the *Jiyūtō* is clearly revealed. They were afraid that an insistence on land assessment revision would be taken to be part of an argument in favour of land tax increase. 'Whether or not the rates of tax are to increase', and 'irrespective of whether they are increased or not' – these were extreme examples of the argument that land assessment should be revised. It is hard to deny the fact, however, that land assessment revision became possible after the Sino-Japanese War as a result of the emergence of the land tax increase question.

The statement that 'if land assessment rates are to be changed ... it is the imbalance of land assessment, which is the basis of the present rates, that ought to be revised', appears not to deny that it was possible to argue, following the Sino-Japanese War, for land assessment revision as a substitute for land tax increase.[41] If, however, the figures cited are accurate, the 12 prefectures of Tōhoku yielded seven bales whereas the ¥32 Chiba Prefecture yielded a mere four bales, and thus the burden on landlords in Chiba was 4.6 times greater than that on the landlords in Tōhoku. Naturally, when the land tax increase question first arose, the land assessment revision faction thought that land must be reassessed before any tax increase was brought about. Obviously this faction did not want an increase in land tax, but if that were inevitable, then, in their desire that there should be a land assessment revision first, they tended to play a kind of auxiliary role in support of the land tax increase faction.

Not all, however, of the 127 supporters of the previously mentioned pre-emptive move were members of the land assessment revision faction. In contrast to those advocates of land assessment revision who had turned into positive supporters of a land tax increase in their pursuit of land assessment revision, there were also those who were on a level with the *hanbatsu* Government in supporting land assessment revision with the genuine aim of seeking an increase in the land tax. After the pre-emptive move to revise land assessment had been rejected, twenty-seven Members centred on the *Kokumin Kyōkai* supported the land tax increase, and this group falls into the above category. Ōura Kanetake, a Yamagata faction bureaucrat and Governor of Kumamoto prefecture, praised Sasa Tomofusa, of the *Kokumin Kyōkai*, who though isolated, had made a speech in favour of increasing the land tax, saying that he 'respected your most excellent argument'.[42] The behaviour of the *Kokumin Kyōkai* was thus identical with that of the Yamagata faction bureaucrats. Seven Members from Yamaguchi Prefecture, who could not expect their land assessment to be reduced if reassessment were carried out and thus could not hope for any profit from it, all nevertheless supported the pre-emptive resolution, and support for the land tax increase bill cannot be understood in party political terms. The *Kokumin Kyōkai* later actually got in before the second Yamagata Cabinet in tabling a land assessment revision bill in order to facilitate the passage of a land tax increase. In the same way it should be noted that thirty-eight members of the Yamashita Club, which was principally a businessmen's group within the Diet, supported the pre-emptive resolution. It is true that there were many land assessment revision supporters within the Yamashita Club, but we must not forget that many businessmen who were Diet Members hoped for land tax increases for the sake of a reduction in corporation tax and relief for the economic recession, and as a means to this end they desired a revision of land assessments.

We have already related how, apart from the *Kokumin Kyōkai* and the Yamashita Club, the party taking the most conciliatory attitude to the land tax increase question was the *Jiyūtō*. The fact, however, that it was an extraordinary Diet session, and the fact that the Itō Cabinet had prevented the simultaneous presentation of a land assessment revision bill, meant that it was impossible for the

Jiyūtō to change direction. As we have seen, the third Itō Cabinet was the first transcendental Cabinet since the end of the Sino-Japanese War. Thus a transcendental Cabinet which was not in coalition with political parties presented a land tax increase bill, unaccompanied by land assessment revision, to an extraordinary Diet session which could not deliberate upon the regular budget. It was unrealistic to expect the passage of the bill. Therefore, why and by what means did the Cabinet attempt this impossible feat?

The 'explanatory statement' on the land tax increase bill tabled by the Itō Cabinet in the twelfth Diet read as follows:

> The reason why there is a difference of more than ¥10,000,000 between the land tax increase bill tabled in the eleventh Diet and the bill tabled this time is that, considering the economic changes that have taken place since last year, and the present state of the nation's finances, it is necessary to repay public loans, and also it is necessary to budget for an increase in various regular expenditures as a result of price increases ... Perhaps because the 1898 budget tabled in the eleventh Diet session failed to pass, the revenue budgeted for 1898 fell short by a large margin, and it was necessary to arrange covering finance by using the special indemnity fund. If the land tax increase bill fails to pass once again, there will be a huge shortfall for 1899 as well. It is, however, calculated that in 1899 the surplus in the special indemnity fund will be exhausted, and the shortfall in revenue will be able to be covered only by further public loans. If we go on from year to year covering revenue shortfall by issuing loans, our financial base will weaken, confidence in the nation will be lost and the situation will become hopeless. Therefore it is urgently necessary to pass the land tax increase bill.[43]

Thus, perhaps because of the post-war recession, the Government quickly gave up its attitude – derived from post-war reconstruction – of maintaining equality of tax burdens between agriculture, commerce and industry and hastened the repayment of loans to business circles. If, however, the Government were to speed up its repayment of loans at a time when revenue shortfalls were accumulating, then naturally increases in taxation would gradually become indispensable.

Secondly, since the political parties after the war almost unanimously refused to contemplate a reduction in expenditure, and since the land tax increase bill had failed to pass the eleventh Diet, then however much the Government tried to carry on with the budget of the previous year, shortfalls of revenue would continue to accumulate; and since there was a limit to what could be financed out of the indemnity fund, if the *hanbatsu* Government could not increase the land tax, it would be forced to cut back on the post-war reconstruction plan itself. It was their need to carry out this plan and to counteract the economic recession that made the Itō Cabinet decide to submit the land tax increase bill in the extraordinary Diet session.

However important it was, there was no point in doing this unless they were able to succeed. What then were Itō's expectations when he submitted the bill? The Army Minister, Katsura, wrote in his autobiography:

> When Marquis Itō resolved to hold a general election and tabled the land tax increase bill again in the new Diet, there was no doubt that it would be passed.[44]

The Secretary-General of the Privy Council, Hirata Tōsuke, also noted that Itō:

> made clear to Members of Cabinet and to others, and stated officially in the Privy Council, that if the bill were not to pass, then repeated dissolutions of the Diet would become necessary and the Constitution would have to be partly suspended.[45]

Unless, as Katsura and Hirata believed, Itō thought that he should first dissolve the Diet and then, following dissolution, pressure the House of Representatives and so bring about the passage of the land tax increase bill, it is impossible to comprehend why he should have brought in the bill without being in coalition with the *Jiyūtō* or the *Shinpotō*, and without also tabling a land assessment revision bill in the extraordinary Diet session.

On 10 June the plenary session of the House of Representatives rejected the land tax bill by an overwhelmingly large majority of 247 to 27, and the Government immediately dissolved the House. About the time of the dissolution a movement towards union between the *Jiyūtō* and the *Shinpotō* suddenly gathered strength. It is clear that both the Matsukata and Itō cabinets were placed in extremely difficult circumstances by the urgency of the land tax increase question, and this gave self-confidence to members of political parties. On the other hand, when both cabinets took the extreme measure of cutting their links with the parties and dissolving the Diet, this caused resentment among party members, and with self-confidence and resentment coming in quick succession, the idea of seizing power by means of a party alliance gathered force.

Rejection of the land tax increase bill, dissolution of the Diet, and the re-emergence of a party alliance had, as we have seen, been fairly much expected by the Cabinet, but when these things actually happened the Government found it difficult to make up its mind what to do. Hirata Tōsuke recalls the reaction within the Government following the Diet dissolution in the following terms:

On 11 June Shibusawa Eiichi and Ōkura Kihachirō visited Itō, the Prime Minister, and said concerning the unification of the *Jiyūtō* and the *Shinpotō* and the consequent formation of the *Kenseitō*, that the Government had no choice but to form its own political party and that Shibusawa and Ōkura would finance such a party. Itō gladly accepted this and consulted with his Finance Minister, Inoue. Inoue disagreed, and put forward the argument that it would be preferable to yield the Cabinet to the parties and allow them to run the Government for a while. Consequently a clash took place between the two Ministers, which made Katsura and Sone anxious about it, so that they attempted to have Yamagata intervene. Some time before this Itō had consulted with Yamagata on the question of organizing a political party, and Yamagata had agreed with him. Yamagata, in accordance with the wishes of Katsura and others, told Inoue that a party was necessary, and Inoue eventually agreed with this for the sake of maintaining the unity of the Cabinet. At this point the Prime Minister outlined his plans to Cabinet at a Cabinet meeting held at his private residence on the morning of the 13th. The plan stated that an increase in taxation was essential, and that it was ridiculous for it to be rejected in the House of Representatives. In order to achieve such an increase, either a new party must be formed, or a compromise should be reached with the existing parties. The Cabinet Members, together with Yamagata, who in accordance with Itō's wishes was present also, considered these questions, and resolved to implement the first element of the plan, namely, to organize a Government party. Although Cabinet so resolved, it merely decided on a policy of organizing a political party sponsored by the Government, and no decision was taken at the time on the procedures and methods of organization. This evening, therefore, I went to Yamagata, and heard for the first time of the Cabinet resolution. I agreed that since, in present circumstances, the Government needed party support, it was necessary to go along with a policy dictated by the necessity of organizing a party with the same ideology as the Government itself, but if the Government were to add itself to a political party, it would mean that there would be a party Cabinet and the Prime Minister would be doubling as Prime Minister and party leader. I asked him if Cabinet had resolved this way or not, and he replied that in fact the Cabinet had only decided to organize a political party, but had not made up its mind about how to do so or what should be its order of procedure. He said that he was anxious to avoid later trouble on this point, and he asked that you should write him your views about it. This, then, was Yamagata's opinion. I went straight home and drafted this statement between eleven at night and two in the morning and sent it to Yamagata early in the morning of the following day. Yamagata, having read it, immediately went out see Inoue, and asked him to send it to the Prime Minister, after reading it quickly ... After I had checked out the opinion of the Prime Minister, it was clear that he thought he should himself become party leader, that he should bring Cabinet members into the Party, and that he should organize a pure party Cabinet. I approached Sasa Tomofusa and Shinagawa, and persuaded them that the Government should not organize a party Cabinet. I also discussed with them how to save the situation. On the other hand, despite the fact that Ōkura and Shibusawa were themselves working on the Prime Minister to persuade him to organize a party, this was frustrated by the opposition from Iwasaki Yanosuke. On the day of the meeting of the promoters of the scheme at the Imperial Hotel, they found an excuse not to come, and since the originators of the scheme did not turn up, other businessesmen were concerned not to be involved. Therefore, various groups and factions were suspicious and split up, and so the plan to form a political party failed completely.[46]

Hirata in these recollections appears to be a day late,[47] but they nevertheless contain some important points. Firstly, Inoue Kaoru, who was in charge of finance, at first opposed Itō's plan to organize a party, or rather thought that the Cabinet should be given to the political parties. About two months later Ōura Kanetake wrote to Inoue: 'Your idea will result in the collapse of the Government and will make people realize that a so-called party Cabinet will not work.'[48] Inoue, as financial manager, was acutely aware that so long as conflict with the parties persisted, an increase in land tax was likely to be postponed, with the attendant problems that this would involve. But he was also convinced that whoever was in power, there was almost no scope for choice in financial policies. Secondly, on the question of trying to achieve an increase in the land tax by organizing a political party and holding a general election in order to counter the popular party alliance, the more positive line was that being taken by Yamagata, Katsura and others rather than that of Inoue. On this point Yamagata himself wrote:

> Now that the *Shinpotō* and the *Jiyūtō* are co-operating in their attacks on the Government, we must either form our own party or else we shall no longer be able to maintain the national interest and defend the State as we have done since the Restoration. We have no choice but to organize ... an Imperial party by a resolution of Cabinet, and the task is urgent.[49]

Thirdly, those who were most strongly opposed to Itō's plan to form a Government party were not the upper-echelon members of the Yamagata faction, such as Yamagata himself and Katsura, but the lower level Yamagata bureaucrats and members of the *Kokumin Kyōkai*. Even in Hirata's reminiscences there is the sense that he went to Yamagata to protest, and at about the same time Ōura Kanetake, the Governor of Kumamoto Prefecture, wrote to Sasa Tomofusa of the *Kokumin Kyōkai* in the following terms:

> I have seen about the co-operation between the *Jiyūtō* and the *Shinpotō* in the telegram from Tokyo. Of course this is only a temporary expedient and will not last long, but it is like it was in 1891 and 1892. At the moment the Government is pursuing a consistent policy, and it may have to take a very strong line and *suspend the Constitution.* But, as I have said before, it is important to have an alliance of Yamagata, Itō, Inoue, Kabayama and Saigō. What do you think of this? *It cannot be helped if the issuing of an emergency ordinance to increase taxation leads to suspension of the Constitution.* I am very worried about how far the Government has gone in deciding this.[50]

If, as Ōura argued, an increase in the land tax were to be forced through by means of an emergency ordinance, there was no need to organize a Government party. All that was needed was for solidarity to be maintained within the *hanbatsu.* According to his reminiscences, when Hirata met Sasa and Shinagawa of the *Kokumin Kyōkai* and persuaded them to oppose the formation of a Government party, Sasa had just received this letter from Ōura. Since if those who wanted land assessment revision were all brought together and put into one big Government party, the *raison d'être* of the *Kokumin*

Kyōkai would gradually disappear, the *Kokumin Kyōkai* had good reason to listen to what Hirata and Ōura were saying.

Was it, though, in fact possible to force through a land tax increase by means of an 'emergency ordinance', as Ōura was arguing? Even the *Commentaries on the Constitution* declare respect for the powers of the Diet to deliberate on the imposition of taxes:

> It is one of the most beautiful features of constitutional government and a direct safeguard to the happiness of the subjects, that the consent of the Diet is required for the imposition of a new tax, and that such matters are not left to the arbitrary action of the Government. When a new tax is imposed over and above already existing ones, or when the rate of taxation is to be modified, it must be left to the opinion of the Diet what would be a proper degree of taxation. Were it not for this efficient constitutional safeguard, it would be impossible to insure to the subjects security for their resources.[51]

The forcing through of a land tax increase by means of the Emperor's emergency ordinance power, as established by article 8 of the Imperial Constitution,[52] would have been a difficult operation if the Constitution were to be strictly adhered to. Moreover, unless emergency ordinances were subsequently approved by the Diet in its next session, they became invalid. If an emergency ordinance whose necessity had been admitted in the name of the Emperor were then rejected by the Diet, this could affect the powers of the Emperor. Even so, since this concerned the power to discuss the imposition of taxation, which was the most important power possessed by the Diet, the Diet would not be able easily to make concessions. To increase taxation by means of an emergency ordinance was thus next to impossible.

The problem, then, of how to increase the land tax while the *Jiyūtō* and the *Shinpotō* were moving into an alliance, caused severe confusion in the ranks of the *hanbatsu*. Anyhow, although even Yamagata was prepared to accept that a Government party ought to be formed, it would do nothing to alleviate the situation even if a party were established that was rather larger than the existing *Kokumin Kyōkai*, and was not created by the Government itself but was close to the Government. As we have seen, to increase taxation by means of an emergency ordinance was out of the question. Moreover the plan, espoused to the end by Itō, for a single great political party combining those who wanted land assessment revision with industrialists, became a manifest impossibility about 19 June, both because the supporters of land assessment revision were worried about trends in the electorates, and because the industrialists retreated when they observed the opposition to the scheme by Iwasaki Yanosuke, President of the Bank of Japan.[53] The only way left was to hand over power at once to the parties and to leave financial management in their hands. On 24 June at the *genrō* conference Itō backed Ōkuma as his successor for the prime ministership, and although Yamagata and others vigorously opposed this, nobody was actually prepared to put an opposing motion. It is said that Itō later commented to Utsumi Tadakatsu, Governor of Kyōto Prefecture, as follows: '*Genrō* such as Inoue, Yamagata and Matsukata were acting like cowards, and because they were not prepared to take the responsibility I handed power over to Ōkuma and Itagaki.'[54] Thus it was that on 30 June 1898, the first Ōkuma Cabinet, the first party Cabinet in the history of Japan, came into being.

6 The collapse of the party Cabinet

The circumstances in which the *Kenseitō* Cabinet was set up were not such as to guarantee its stable existence. Feelings of antipathy to the emergence of the first-ever party Cabinet, on the part of *genrō*, bureaucrats, Members of the House of Peers and others, swirled around the new Cabinet, while on the other hand, inside the two parties which had joined forces, there was a welling up of enormous expectations towards a party Cabinet realized as a result of ten or twenty years of devotion to the cause. Right from its inception the Cabinet was buffeted by these completely contradictory forces.

EXTERNAL CAUSES: FORCES IN THE BUREAUCRACY AND THE HOUSE OF PEERS

Shortly after the Cabinet was inaugurated Fukuzawa Yukichi, in an editorial in *Jiji Shinpō*, wrote:

> Now that the *Kenseitō* has obtained a majority in the Diet and has taken over the Government, people might think that the party Cabinet can do anything it wants in order to fulfil its promises, but the reality is very different. First of all, the Navy and Army are retaining their Cabinet Ministers from before, and are not allowing party members to take any role, even on a temporary basis, so that they have hardly lost anything at all. They are like an excrescence on the surface of the Cabinet.[1]

Fukuzawa was here indicating the role as a check on the party Cabinet retained by the Army and Navy Ministers. At first the Yamagata faction bureaucrats, who were not pleased with the formation of a party Cabinet, attempted to prevent the establishment of the Cabinet by making the Army and Navy Ministers refuse to serve. Hirata Tōsuke, in a letter to Yamada Nobumichi, describes the situation thus:

Today the Emperor has informally ordered the Army and Navy Ministers to remain in their posts, and therefore there is no possibility for us to carry out our plan.[2]

Yamada Nobumichi went so far as to write, concerning the question of whether Saigō was to remain as Navy Minister: 'If Saigō remains, the people will think of him as Judas'.[3] Similarly the Chief of the General Staff, Kawakami Sōroku, is said to have tried to persuade Katsura and Saigō to stop the formation of a party Cabinet by preventing the Army and Navy Ministers from remaining in their posts.[4] In the end it was on the Emperor's orders that Katsura and Saigō remained in their respective positions of Army and Navy Minister, but the two Ministers, having stayed in their posts as a result of the above circumstances, were hardly likely to be co-operative towards the administration of the party Cabinet's policies. On both financial questions and questions of bureaucratic reform Katsura and Saigō hindered Cabinet policy making from within. On the financial question, Katsura and Saigō, from the beginning of the Cabinet's career, made the Prime Minister, Ōkuma, promise that he would not alter the plan for armaments expansion.[5] In the Cabinet meeting to discuss the budget of 1899, held on 15 and 16 October, they obstructed the demand of Matsuda, the Finance Minister, for a reduction in the budget, and therefore on the 15th the Cabinet meeting came close to total breakdown.[6] The opposition of the two Ministers to bureaucratic reform was also extreme. As we shall see later on, the plan developed by the Extraordinary Administrative Affairs Investigation Bureau of the Cabinet on bureaucratic reform, compared to the reform proposal put forward by the *Kenseitō* Investigation Committee separately from the Cabinet, took a very gradualist approach, and yet Katsura warned strongly against it in the following terms:

> In the report of the Administrative Affairs Investigation Committee (from which the Army and Navy were excluded), the Commitee wants to revise the rules on entry of officials to the service, and the rules governing Cabinet officials, and it proposes that Cabinet Ministers should be selected from the ranks of Diet Members. In other words I think that it seeks to lay the foundations for a party Cabinet. But however much they may argue and investigate among themselves, they cannot put this to the Throne without first going through Cabinet, and when it is presented to Cabinet, that is the time that we should criticize it.[7]

It is clear from this that the first Ōkuma Cabinet, as the first party Cabinet, because of the existence within it of *hanbatsu* forces in the form of the Army and Navy Ministers, found its freedom of action severely restricted. As we shall see, this first party Cabinet in our history was unable to lay a finger on the armaments expansion plan developed by the *hanbatsu* governments since the Sino-Japanese War, and they were unable to obtain substantive reforms of the bureaucratic system, despite the fact that party members had been awaiting such reform for a long time. It would, even so, be excessive to attribute the whole reason for this to a propensity for compromise on the part of the leaders of the two parties. If they had touched the armaments expansion plan of the Army and Navy, the Cabinet would have fallen more easily than did the second Saionji Cabinet in 1912. As the Army Minister, Katsura, himself boasted in his autobiography, on these grounds the *Kenseitō* Cabinet was a 'paralyzed Cabinet'.[8]

It was not only the pressure exerted from within by the Ministers of the Army and the Navy, but also the existence of a movement outside the Cabinet, devoted to its overthrow, among the Yamagata faction bureaucrats and in the House of Peers, that accounted for the fact that this was a 'paralyzed' Cabinet. We have seen how Tsuzuki Keiroku, who was a transcendentalist and one of the Yamagata faction bureaucrats, wrote an article called 'To Members of the House of Peers'[9] immediately after the *Kenseitō* Cabinet was formed, and argued that it was the duty of the House of Peers to overthrow the Cabinet. Tsuzuki, who had successfully climbed the bureaucratic ladders of the Ministry of Home Affairs and the Ministry of Foreign Affairs, has given us a means of understanding the mentality of the bureaucratic class concerning the emergence of Japan's first party Cabinet.

Tsuzuki held that the significance of the *Kenseitō* Cabinet lay not in the Cabinet's policies, nor in the personalities of its Members, but 'in the pros and cons of democratic politics represented by counts Ōkuma and Itagaki'.[10] When Tsuzuki said, 'The achievements of any Cabinet are more or less the same, so that small differences and occasional failures are not a life and death question for Members of the House of Peers',[11] this should be understood as indicating that the bureaucratic class did not regard the political parties as dangerous to the accomplishment of post-war reconstruction. If we examine his attack on the party Cabinet, it can be seen that in the sense of crisis felt by the bureaucrats concerning the emergence of a party Cabinet, there was an ideological element and an element involving bureaucratic interests. Tsuzuki starts by describing the essence of party Cabinets as democracy:

Counts Ōkuma and Itagaki have always called for party politics, they have praised responsible cabinets, they have pressed for the realization of democracy, they have demanded the revision of the system in the direction of equality, and they have attempted to place those of high rank under the power of the masses of the people. In other words they are both in power on a party-political base, and bureaucratic appointments are decided following on the decisions of the political parties. In addition, national policy is decided following party decisions, and responsibility for administration rests with party factions. They have completely neglected the role of the House of Peers, and in preaching equality they equate your cab drivers with you yourselves; they are aiming to destroy that very order which is the basis of the peerage system, and this is what the two of them believe.[12]

It is worth remembering, for the sake of the reputation of Japan's first party Cabinet, that despite the fact that in policy terms the *hanbatsu* Government and the party Cabinet had come close together, the image of the party Cabinet as pressing for 'the realization of democracy' and demanding 'revision of the system in the direction of equality' persisted. This, however, was not quite the main point of Tsuzuki's attack on the *Kenseitō* Cabinet. The principal reason for Tsuzuki's attack upon it was really that since the early Diets, in contrast to the gradual reduction of conflict over matters of *policy* between the *hanbatsu* Government and the parties, conflict between the bureaucracy and the parties over political *power* had actually worsened.

Although since the early Diets both camps have engaged in verbal conflict both in plenary session and in committees, and the Government has compromised on many points following exchanges of opinion and after studying explanations, the parties have also come to see that many of their arguments are not worth pressing to a conclusion. The force of many of their arguments has thus been blunted, and apart from things about which by force of circumstances they do not wish to compromise, there is not much difference between the positions of the Government and those of the parties. In addition, it happens every year that the Government is unable to pass the budget without obtaining the consent of the House of Representatives, and therefore its weak point is that it cannot achieve national growth. Even though there are many issues of national significance, the Government has to concede to the political parties on matters of controversy. Since the points at issue between them have been reduced in number, it has gradually become clear that the aims of the parties lie not in the fulfilment of their demands, but in their desire to obtain power. Their hitherto latent desire to capture political power is now blazoned on their banners. This is developing into a tacit mutual understanding between the Government and the *Jiyūtō*, into coalition, into Itagaki's elevation to the Cabinet, into appointment according to merit, eventually into the appointment of Count Ōkuma, and into the expansion of the limits of appointment according to merit ... At this point political statements by the parties completely disappear, and apart from the capture of power, they have no aims on the political stage. They are overtly arguing that there should be no Emperor, no Government, no House of Peers, but that the people should be controlled by the will of a majority of party members. They are arguing for a Cabinet responsible to the Diet, which makes decisions according to the orders of a majority of the House of Representatives. In the case of the *Kenseitō* and in the case of Hatoyama's speech [Author's note: this should read 'Ozaki's speech'], they put forward the slogan 'overthrow the *hanbatsu*', but in fact what they really want is to replace it in Government.[13]

We are not aware of a clearer analysis than this of the logic of conflict and compromise between *hanbatsu* and bureaucrats on the one side and parties on the other. The explanation that the *hanbatsu* Government was unable to put into practice its policies of industrial and military expansion unless it obtained the consent of the House of Representatives in budget deliberations, and that therefore the *hanbatsu* Government was forced to allow the parties to participate in power, is one of the central topics of this book. The reason, however, why we have quoted Tsuzuki at length, and the aims of Tsuzuki himself, do not lie here. The fact that policy differences had become less acute meant that the reason for a political monopoly by the *hanbatsu* forces had disappeared, and this threatened the established position of the bureaucracy. This was why Tsuzuki, as a bureaucrat, was so worried about the emergence of the *Kenseitō* Cabinet.

From Tsuzuki's standpoint, a party Cabinet was capable of being understood – and thus attacked – only as a manifestation of thirst for power on the part of party members:

Since they are intent on taking power, power is what satisfies them. They do not care whether their policy is carried out or not.

Somebody who takes power for the first time has to distribute power among other party members, or he will not be able to maintain party harmony. This is the significance of distribution power according to merit. The Government becomes a welfare agency for party members and the National Treasury becomes a plaything of party factions.[14]

Certainly the desire for office on the part of party members in the *Kenseitō* Cabinet was extreme. A list of officials apart from Ministers at the time of the fall of the *Kenseitō* Cabinet is given in Table 6.1. It is easy to understand from the table just how great was the impact on members of the bureaucratic class. Moreover, even this did not permit the demands of the party members to be satisfied. As we shall see, the demand to rescind the Civil Service Appointments Ordinance, and to appoint party members to central and local, high and low positions, was welling up within the party, and it was almost too much for the party Cabinet itself. In the eyes of Tsuzuki, who burned with all the self-confidence of a specialist bureaucrat, this may have been a case of national crisis rather than of personal crisis. What was, however, for Tsuzuki the bureaucrat a question of thirst for office, was for party members a question of 'appointment according to merit', while what for Tsuzuki the bureaucrat was management of the nation's affairs by specialist bureaucrats, was for party members appointment by the *hanbatsu* Government according to personal connections, and thus something to be got rid of. The logic of self-justification was present on both sides, but the basic factor was that the parties along with the bureaucracy were gradually obtaining the qualifications for the exercise of power.

Thus Tsuzuki, who felt that the entry of party members into the bureaucracy constituted a threat, argued for their exclusion from bureaucratic circles by a speedy revision of the official appointments ordinance. He wrote:

The basic distortion of party politics is that every time there is a change of Cabinet, one party is substituted for the previous one, and this disorganizes the whole administrative structure. The American people, at the time of Cleveland, set up an official appointments law in order to cope with this problem. Japan, however, has been absorbed in breaking the official appointments law. When officials are appointed and dismissed every time there is a change of government, it is naturally difficult for the administration to maintain a consistent policy, and in the end the nation's foreign policy and domestic administration inevitably come to be

Table 6.1 Party Members in office under the Kenseitō Cabinet (omitting Ministers)

Cabinet

Cabinet Secretary General	Taketomi Tokitoshi
Legislative Bureau Chairman	Kōmuchi Tomotsune
Private Secretary to the Prime Minister	Ōishi Kumakichi

Foreign Ministry

Vice-Minister	Hatoyama Kazuo
Councillor	Shiga Shigetaka
Chairman of the Executive Bureau	Hayakawa Tetsuji
Chairman of the Commerce Bureau	Shigeoka Kungorō

Home Ministry

Vice-Minister	Suzuki Atsumi
Chairman of the Police Bureau	Ogura Hisashi
Private Secretary	Saitō Keiji

Finance Ministry

Vice-Minister	Soeda Juichi
Councillor	Kurihara Ryōichi
Private Secretary	Sakurai Takashi

Justice Ministry

Vice-Minister	Nakamura Yaroku
Private Secretary	Miyawaki Gōzō

Education Ministry

Vice-Minister	Kashiwada Morifumi
Councillor	Takada Sanae
Private Secretary	Nakamura Tasuku

Agriculture and Commerce Ministry

Vice-Minister	Shiba Shirō
Chairman of the Agricultural Bureau	Kikuchi Kurō
Chairman of the Fisheries Bureau	Takeuchi Masashi
Chairman of the Forestry Bureau	Sasaki Shōzō

Communications Ministry

Vice-Minister	Minoura Katsundo
Chairman of the Railways Bureau	Itō Daihachi
Private Secretary	Matsumoto Gōkichi
Inspector-General of Police	Nishiyama Shichō

Head of the Hokkaidō Administration

	Sugita Teiichi
Secretary	Horiuchi Kenrō

Prefectural Governors

Tokyo	Kikuchi Kanji
Toyama	Kanao Ryōgen
Shizuoka	Katō Heishirō
Nagano	Sonoyama Isamu
Ishikawa	Shiba Sankurō
Tochigi	Ogino Samon
Gunma	Kusakari Chikaaki
Kagawa	Ono Ryūsuke

Source: 'Kaku shō genzaiin narabini seitō shusshin kanri', *Kenseishi hensankai shūshū monjo* (Hirata Tōsuke Kankei monjo) conducted in an uneven fashion. When it comes to this point, government officials find it difficult to conduct their business smoothly, and this unavoidably results in low morale because they will not regard their job as a permanent duty. It is therefore impossible for them to work devotedly for the national interest, and there is no guarantee that no-one will prepare for his retirement by abusing his administrative power.[15]

This was exactly the same point as was to be made within a year in the official appointments ordinance under the second Yamagata Cabinet:

> Officials, apart from ministers of state, must be tested and selected according to the official appointments ordinance. Officials should have tenure of position, and should not be dismissed because of changes in the political situation but only for failures and unlawful acts. However careful we may be in the selection of entrants, unless we guarantee their position against dismissal, how can we expect them to perform diligently and well?[16]

As we shall see, the *Kenseitō* vigorously demanded the abolition of the official appointments ordinance in respect of their Cabinet. The bureaucrats, on the other hand, most strongly opposed this, and demanded strict adherence to the ordinance.

The bureaucrats, who both ideologically and from the standpoint of their own interest as professional officials, were gripped by an acute sense of crisis by the emergence of a party Cabinet, recalled the fact that the Imperial Constitution provided for a two-chamber system. The hopes which the bureaucrats placed upon the House of Peers gradually strengthened after the emergence of *hanbatsu*–party coalition cabinets following the Sino-Japanese War, but the arrival of the *Kenseitō* Cabinet even further boosted these expectations. Tsuzuki called for the House of Peers to rise against the *Kenseitō* Cabinet:

> They do not take the House of Peers sufficiently into account, and they have created a *Kenseitō* Cabinet which involves only *Kenseitō* members. Their attitude is that the House of Representatives should entirely monopolize power. Not only are they reprehensible in relation to the House of Peers, but they are reprehensible in respect of the Constitution, which gives the House of Peers equal rights with the House of Representatives.[17]

What, then, was the reaction to the emergence of the party Cabinet by the House of Peers, which was expected by the bureaucrats to stand up against it? In the previously cited editorial in the *Jiji Shinpō*, Fukuzawa Yukichi wrote, concerning the direction being taken by the House of Peers:

> The new Government is said to have a majority in the Diet, but the House of Peers remains, as ever, hostile to political parties. The Members of the House of Peers are not supporters of the present Government. It is a great mistake to think that the House of Peers always supports the Government of the day. Whereas governments hitherto have laboured under the control of the House of Representatives, from now on they will play to the tune of the House of Peers.[18]

Fukuzawa's observation was quite accurate on this point. Within the House of Peers, two leading Yamagata bureaucrats, Hirata Tōsuke of the *Sawakai* and Kiyoura Keigo of the *Kenkyūkai*, were working hard to shorten the life of the party Cabinet. As we have already seen, the antipathy of the House of Peers to the coming to power of the party forces reached its height with the coalition of Itō and the *Jiyūtō* during the ninth Diet session. In the reselection of counts, viscounts and barons in July 1897, the *Kenkyūkai* was completely victorious, and since then the degree of control by the Yamagata faction over the House of Peers had rapidly increased. Nevertheless, as Hirato Tōsuke reflected, its organization seemed still to be incomplete. He wrote:

> The House of Peers has from the beginning been divided into many internal factions: leaving aside the *Konwakai* and the *Sanyōkai* (the *Sanyōkai* later amalgamated with the *Asahi Club*, and then in conjunction with the *Asahi Club* and the *Konwakai* became the *Doyōkai*), as well as Members of the House of Peers paying the highest taxation rates, all the other factions have been working under the aegis of the Government ever since the first Diet of 1890, and yet they have scarcely maintained firm solidarity. Those Diet Members co-opted by the nobility are generally weak and have no definite ideas, merely acting spinelessly in response to changing circumstances.[19]

Hirata and others attempted to make sure that the situation in the House of Peers 'should be brought under control, and we must do our duty by subduing the rampant power of those political party fellows, through the House of Peers'.[20] These attempts came to a head straight after the tax increase bill proposed by the third Itō

Cabinet had been overwhelmingly defeated in the House of Representatives by the *Jiyūtō* and the *Shinpotō*. Hirata thought that 'a difficult state of affairs has emerged from the rejection of the tax increase bill', and proposed that in order to cope with the situation 'a strong group should be formed in order to consolidate a majority in the House of Peers'[21] – a group headed by Inoue Kaoru to render help to Yamagata and Matsukata. On 22 June he is said to have visited Inoue and obtained his agreement. When, however, two days later at a conference with the Emperor it was decided to hand over the Cabinet to the *Kenseitō*, Inoue, perhaps out of some sense of obligation to Itō, left Tokyo and shut himself away, without a word of communication with Hirata and his friends. The latter thereupon sought to persuade Yamagata and Matsukata that the forces in the House of Peers should be consolidated around Yamagata, and having obtained the agreement of both men set about rallying their forces in the House of Peers. They are said to have gone so far as to have reached a 'decision to choose delegates from each faction, borrow the residence of Hayashi Yūkō, meet there secretly for deliberation, and finally, after holding a series of meetings, make a petition to the Throne for impeachment'.[22] Because of this vigorous activity by the Yamagata bureaucrats, the House of Peers gradually came round to the position that the party Cabinet should be got rid of. Even Takeuchi Koretada of the *Konwakai*, which had been friendly to the party Cabinet, wrote:

> The main reasons why the *Kenkyūkai* is opposed to the present Government are that the men in key Government positions have no experience whatsoever, that there are many who think of nothing but how to hang on to their present positions, and that there is nothing that can be done about it. If things continue as they are, not only will the progress of the nation be hindered, but in the end it will be impossible to prevent the national policy from being harmed. Therefore this is not the time to keep our silence. We must proceed to devise policies of defence against them, the *Kenkyūkai* must take the lead in bringing all the factions together, we must list all the Government's political failures and present a petition to the Throne.[23]

Thus it was that 'arrangements for a grand concerted attack',[24] centring on Hirata, Kiyoura, and those Diet members appointed by the Emperor who were Yamagata faction bureaucrats, as well as on the *Kenkyūkai*, made steady progress, so that by the beginning of October 'the opposition had obtained a majority'.[25]

It is not, however, the case that the *Kenseitō* Cabinet completely lacked supporters in the House of Peers. Prince Konoe Atsumaro, leader of the *Sanyōkai* in the House of Peers, although he feared for the future path of the Cabinet, noted in his diary that 'the formation of the present party Cabinet is a matter for hearty congratulations as a step forward in the political world'.[26] Moreover, there were those Peers in the *Sanyōkai* and *Konwakai* who hoped that Konoe would become a member of the *Kenseitō* Cabinet, and contended that this would constitute a blow against the forces of the *Kenkyūkai* and benefit their own factions. For instance:

We humbly pray that your Excellency seize this opportunity to become the scourge of the *hanbatsu*, to direct a concerted attack against the *Shōyūkai* [electoral body for the *Kenkyūkai*] which corrupts the atmosphere of the House of Peers and is harming the progress of our nation, and to do sterling service by spreading the good word on behalf of our stalwart group. If you were able to persuade the Cabinet to stop appointing prefectural governors and others, as previously, from the *Shōyūkai* and select them instead from the *Sanyōkai* and *Konwakai*, this would give our groups a boost at the expense of the *Kenkyūkai*, and would surely be of great benefit for the future of the House of Peers. This is only one example. If there is any other position which our men ought to obtain, it will be possible to obtain it through your Excellency's good offices.[27]

Thus it can be seen that the 'office seeking' which the bureaucrats were wont to criticize was not confined to members of political parties. Within the *Sanyōkai* and the *Konwakai* there were some who, in order to arrest the decline in their fortunes which followed the elections of July 1897, wished to enter into a coalition with the party Cabinet. Moreover the *Kenseitō* Cabinet itself entered into negotiations with Konoe, with a view to appointing him Director-General of the Judicial Office, in order to obtain the support of the *Sanyōkai* and the *Konwakai*.[28] As we have already seen, however, the balance of forces in the House of Peers underwent a sudden change at the time of the reselection of the three classes of peerage in July of the previous year. The *Sanyōkai* and the *Konwakai* had now become very minor groupings. The House of Peers as a whole was coming round to the view, centred on the *Kenkyūkai*, that the party Cabinet ought to be overthrown.

This movement among the bureaucrats and forces in the House of Peers to overthrow the Cabinet resulted – because of the disintegration of the *Kenseitō* from internal splits – in a situation were 'there was no opportunity for real bullets to be fired',[29] and the trend within the House of Peers, which were being reported as they happened by the Inspector-General of Police, Nishiyama Shichō, restrained the Government authorities, and this in turn increased the dissatisfaction of *Kenseitō* party members in general.

The *Kenseitō* Cabinet marked a big step forward in the emergence of party power, but the fact that the House of Peers joined with the bureaucrats to block it sentenced the Cabinet to an abbreviated life span. The party forces, which possessed a majority in the House of Representatives, were strong enough to keep the *hanbatsu* bottled up so far as the questions of post-war reconstruction and land tax increase were concerned, and to deprive them temporarily of their power. So long, however, as the parties were unable to exert a similar degree of influence in relation to the House of Peers, a party Cabinet was plainly unable even to prorogue a session of Parliament. Just how weak a party Cabinet was when compared to a Cabinet of *hanbatsu* is evident from the fact that whereas the latter had the power to dissolve the House of Representatives, the former had no such power over the House of Peers. In practice, the *Kenseitō* Cabinet fell apart before the House of Peers was required to demonstrate its strength, but as we shall see later on, its falling apart was indirectly accelerated by the movement aimed at its overthrow involving the Army and Navy Ministers, the bureaucrats and the House of Peers. Moreover, had the Cabinet managed to reach the thirteenth session of the Diet without splitting, it is highly doubtful whether it would have been able to come through the whole session unscathed.

INTERNAL FACTORS: THE INTERNAL CONTRADICTIONS OF THE *KENSEITŌ*

Those most intimately acquainted with the seriousness of the internal situation within the Cabinet were the *Kenseitō* leadership group, including especially Ōkuma and Itagaki. When Itō Hirobumi urged Ōkuma and Itagaki to form a Cabinet, Ōkuma expressed his fears about reaction from the bureaucrats in the following words: 'Since the situation has greatly changed, shall I, if I enter the Cabinet, be able to sustain my prestige as before?'[30] Itagaki, too, was worried about the strength of the bureaucratic forces: 'Even when I was Minister for Home Affairs, I had to act at all times with caution, and there were many things which were impossible to attain. The forces of Satsuma and Chōshū were more than a match for the political party forces.'[31] Itō in reply advised that provided the existing position of bureaucrats were preserved when meeting the demands of party members for official positions, it should be possible to soften bureaucratic antipathy. As he put it: 'It will be sufficient if you give the bureaucrats reassurance and consideration for the security of their positions ... It is impossible to force them to give up the whole castle.'[32] Fukuzawa Yukichi gave similar advice:

> The party itself contains respected leaders rich in experience, and so when your party takes over the reins of government, you should not think that everything should be precipitately overturned. Unless you are prepared to deal with this, many party members may become so overenthusiastic and overbearing as a result of their victory that unpredictable consequences may ensue.[33]

Caught between the *genrō* and the bureaucrats, who were opposed to bureaucrats being replaced, and party members, who strongly desired bureaucratic positions, Ōkuma as Prime Minister sought a solution in an idea which he had long held, namely that a distinction[34] should be made between 'political party officials and permanent officials'. Shortly after the Cabinet was formed, he called a meeting of local officials and addressed them in the following terms:

> With a party Cabinet clear distinction should be made between political officers – ourselves and our party friends – and administrative officers, who are different, and have different responsibilities from their political counterparts. This will avoid unnecessary replacement of staff and slowing down of work, and so long as the administrative officers do not refuse to obey the orders of their superiors or obstruct the work of political officers, it should not be necessary to make replacements.[35]

The distinction here being made by Ōkuma between political and administrative officers was between *sōnin* [government officials of second rank] and below, whose qualifications were determined by the Civil Service Appointments Ordinance, and those Imperial appointees whom Cabinet could freely designate. This being the case, it was in fact impossible to satisfy both those who looked for a further tightening up of the Civil Service Appointments Ordinance, and those party members who, on the contrary, wanted free appointment of all officials through abolition of the Civil Service Appointments Ordinance itself. Ōkuma's compromise proposal could not 'satisfy all the demands of party members',[36] and as we have seen, the idea that all positions should be occupied by party members except for the vice-ministers, councillors and some bureau directors of each ministry, private secretaries, governors and so on who were excluded from the regulations of the Appointments Ordinance, certainly did not seem to the bureaucrats like a compromise proposal at all. We have already investigated the bureaucrats, so now we shall turn to the demands on the party side for admission to official positions.

Soon after it was formed, the Cabinet established an Extraordinary Administrative Affairs Investigation Bureau, with Itagaki, the Minister of Home Affairs, as its chairman, and officials who originated from the *Kenseitō* as members. The task the bureau was given by the Cabinet was to prepare for administrative reform, but conflict between the *Jiyūtō* and *Shinpotō* factions within the party ensured that virtually no conclusions were reached.[37] As a result, many local groups and prefectural branches of the *Kenseitō* were angered by the Cabinet's indecisiveness, and pressed their respective resolutions upon it. One of the earliest was a petition delivered to the Prime Minister just after the Cabinet was formed, on 10 July, by several representatives from Kumamoto Prefecture, demanding 'the dismissal of all officials with illegal and unfair prejudices, from the Kumamoto Prefectural Governor to district mayors'.[38] On 13 July former *Jiyūtō* members in Ibaragi Prefecture got together, resolved that 'besides overthrowing the *hanbatsu*, there must be a widespread weeding out of officials, the *hanbatsu* gang must be thoroughly purged and the party Cabinet must stand up for itself',[39] and decided to send a representative to the party headquarters and to Ministers. This shows the kind of things that were expected by local party members of the first party Cabinet.

These demands from local party members became local bloc resolutions and were gradually brought together at the centre. First of all, on 29 August, the *Dōshi* Club held a general meeting, which passed two resolutions: '1: Weed out all *hanbatsu* elements among officials at central and local level; 2: Extirpate the evils of factionalism and promote genuine talent'.[40] Shortly afterwards, on 6 September, the *Kantō* Club also held a general meeting and resolved, among other things: abolition of the Civil Service Appointments Ordinance; weeding out of *hanbatsu* elements from the ranks of officialdom at central and local level, and fundamental administrative reform; and convening of an extraordinary party congress. In order to promote its resolutions, the *Kantō* Club general meeting appointed an executive committee, and resolved to lobby the party's Executive Committee, and also to lobby other local blocs, urging them to join in the same movement.[41] Since, as we have already seen, Ōkuma, from the time the Cabinet was established had advanced a policy of appointing party members, so far as possible, as 'political officers'; it was the implementation of this policy that was the meaning of the slogan 'weed out *hanbatsu* elements'. On the other hand, it was the demand to appoint party members as 'administrative officers' also (whereas Ōkuma had said that he would replace administrative officers) that was signified by the slogan 'abolition of the official appointments ordinance'. The following statement by Haseba Sumitaka, of the *Dōshi* Club, shows how strong was the demand for party members to be appointed to 'administrative positions' within the party:

> The present Cabinet scrupulously pays attention to many other things, but seems unwilling to take seriously the plan of reform that we have presented. Indeed we are disgusted by its total lack of initiative. The Cabinet itself talks of being a party Cabinet, of conducting a second Restoration, and hopes to conduct reform with spectacular boldness, taking measures which will command the astonished attention of the world. When, however, Itō handed over the reins of government to Ōkuma and Itagaki, they spoke of hoping to give attention to the replacement of lower-level officials, but they seem to have shelved these questions and hesitate to undertake reform. The base of political parties essentially lies in the aspirations of ordinary people, and if this, with the sanction of the Emperor, becomes national law and politics, it is devoutly to be hoped that the wishes of ordinary party members will not be cast aside, and that the Cabinet will stop shilly-shallying and act as quickly as it possibly can.[42]

These resolutions and appeals by the *Dōshi* Club and the *Kantō* Club rapidly spread to other groups as well. The 'Political Intelligence Report' sent by the Inspector-General of Police, Nishiyama Shichō, to the Prime Minister, Ōkuma, on 4 October, reported the current situation as follows:

> The proposal to abolish the Civil Service Appointments Ordinance is unanimously supported by ten *Kenseitō* groups (but not by Kōchi and Ōsaka). On the 5th a committee of a ten-group alliance extending throughout the nation will be inaugurated at the *Kenseitō* headquarters, the present question will be presented to the *Kenseitō* Congress, and if a favourable resolution is passed, then there will be discussion of using the party rules to bind party members who are in the Cabinet to implement the resolution.[43]

Moreover, after the *Kinki Club* had discussed what attitude it should take at the ten-group alliance committee, it resolved that 'Cabinet Ministers who do not implement party rules should incur some penalty from the Party'.[44] The view that the Civil Service Appointments Ordinance ought to be abolished, and that *Kenseitō* members should be appointed even to lower-ranking official positions, had become the general trend of the *Kenseitō* as a whole, and the gap between the party and the Cabinet, which hesitated to take such action, gradually opened wider.

A considerable difference was seen in the ways in which the *Kenseitō* headquarters and the Cabinet respectively handled demands from various *Kenseitō* groups. The *Kenseitō* headquarters established an investigation committee separate from the Extraordinary Administrative Affairs Research Bureau which had been set up by the Cabinet, and drew up an administrative revision proposal which was fairly close to the demands of the party members. The proposal was as follows: 1 Revise the Civil Service Appointments Ordinance and widen the scope for non-examined appointments; 2 Replace all imperial appointees and officials of *sōnin* rank; 3 Abolish the Police Department.[45] But the Extraordinary Administrative Affairs Research Bureau set up by Cabinet rejected this, arguing that the 'Cabinet is responsible for its own independent policy, and does not have to accept advice from the *Kenseitō*'.[46] On 22 October the bureau announced its own public service reform. This involved two main points: 1 Establish counsellors (*sanyokan*) below the vice-ministers (*jikan*) in each ministry, in order to increase the number of imperial appointees; and 2 Make all bureau heads (*kyokuchō*) imperial appointees.[47] The *Kenseitō* Cabinet thus continued as before to make a distinction between 'political officials' (*seimukan*) and 'administrative officials (*jimukan*), and sought to expand the number of party members appointed, within the limits of the distinction. Since, however, even under the existing system for each ministry, there were sixteen bureau heads who were imperial appointees and seven bureau heads of *sōnin* rank,[48] even under a reform which would also bring counsellors into the picture, this could not increase the number of posts available for party members by more than fourteen. Certainly compared to previous reforms this was quite bold, but party members held inflated expectations of the first party Cabinet, and it was impossible to satisfy their demands with this degree of reform. In the 'Outline of the Reforms', issued at the same time as the public service reforms themselves, it was written: 'Every time there is a change of minister, many officials are needlessly shifted, and this is likely to cause problems similar to those caused by the dismissal of a colleague who is skilled at his work. This amounts to an unnecessary disorganization of work and frustration of government commands. Henceforth the promotion and retirement of administrative officials must be treated with care, and by giving them long security of tenure in their positions it should be possible to make them work diligently'.[49] The statement thus rejected the abolition of the Civil Service Appointments Ordinance, and again refused to contemplate the replacement of 'administrative officials', thus diametrically opposing the view of all groups in the *Kenseitō*.

As we have seen, within the party there was a great ferment of demands for government positions at all levels – central and local, high ranking and low – and dissatisfaction with a government that was unable to satisfy such demands was increasing. This constituted a major background cause of the internal disintegration of the *Kenseitō* Cabinet.

THE FINANCIAL POLICY OF THE *KENSEITŌ* CABINET

We have already discussed how an increase in the land tax, the indispensable condition for post-war reconstruction, became impossible with the formation of the *Kenseitō*, and how this was the most important reason why the *hanbatsu* Government handed over power to a political party. In what way, then, did the *Kenseitō* Cabinet attempt to handle this problem? After the collapse of the Cabinet, Itagaki wrote:

> I, along with Count Ōkuma, obeyed the Imperial Command and formed the Cabinet, but already after the inauguration of the thirteenth Diet, the whole Cabinet suddenly tendered its resignation. Consequently, only its budget expenditure bill went through Cabinet and was put into effect, whereas the revenue bill had yet to be presented to Cabinet. At the time, however, it was unanimously admitted among Cabinet members that it was quite impossible to bring down the revenue bill without introducing some tax increases.[50]

The expenditure budget bill, which was passed by a meeting of the *Kenseitō* Cabinet, was taken over without alteration by the second Yamagata Cabinet, which succeeded it. Matsukata Masayoshi, Minister of Finance in the Yamagata Cabinet, in explaining the budget at the thirteenth Diet session, said on this point:

> The fact that the budget for 1899 could not help but be expan-

sionist, given the progress of national development, should be well known to you all. In fact the 1899 budget was already drawn up during the previous Cabinet, and before I became Minister, so that this Government, judging that it was acceptable, presented it in its existing form.[51]

In other words, so far as the expenditure budget was concerned, the draft prepared by the *Kenseitō* party Cabinet was taken over intact by a *hanbatsu* Cabinet, the second Cabinet of Yamagata. This is the most striking demonstration of the fact that there was absolutely no conflict between the *hanbatsu* and the parties over the post-war reconstruction plan, which centred on the expansion of the Army and the Navy.

We can learn about this in detail from the 'Financial and Economic Policy in the 1899 Budget'[52] published immediately after the fall of the Cabinet by Soeda Juichi, who as Vice-Minister of the Ministry of Finance had been at the centre of budget making in the *Kenseitō* Cabinet. Soeda, in this document, confessed that the inflated expenditure was something that could not be prevented even under a party Cabinet:

> Even in the budget for 1899 drawn up by the *Kenseitō* Cabinet, despite the earnest efforts that were employed, it was regrettably impossible to find any means of reducing the huge level of expenditure. The amount, however, rose to ¥230 million.[53]

Next he admitted that the main reason was increased Army and Navy spending, and wrote that military expenditure even under a party Cabinet 'could not be reduced below ¥100 million'.[54] This is just about the same expenditure as for the previous year. Soeda,[55] who had reached the position of Vice-Minister in the party Cabinet, was of course not averse to criticizing armaments expansion. As he put it:

> From an economic point of view, expenditure on armaments militates against increased production, and if such expenditure is needlessly increased, then not only will this itself harm production, but it will encroach on other areas of expenditure which are required for the purposes of production. General economic damage will surely result. When, therefore, the budget for 1899 was drawn up, we adopted a policy of reducing unproductive expenditure and, so far as possible, making expenditure that was productive.[56]

Even at the time when there was a general upsurge of support for armaments expansion, immediately after the Sino-Japanese War, Soeda criticized 'increasing military preparations without regard to the nation's capacity', on the grounds that

> Today victory or defeat depends less on military strength than on financial strength. The most important factor is general industrial development. However much of our national interest in the future may depend upon our aggressiveness, if we are at least to maintain the development and defence of Japan, as well as helping and guiding nations poorer and weaker than ourselves, we must cultivate our strength to the utmost, make sure that our sources of revenue are large enough to deal with emergency needs, and aim at victory in peacetime trade as though it were a wartime campaign.[57]

It cannot be denied that this was why the efforts of Soeda and others in the *Kenseitō* Cabinet were frustrated by the strong opposition of the Army and Navy ministers. This was probably what underlay the statement of the Army Minister, Katsura, that:

> According to the policy of the Ministry of Finance survey of the budget for 1899, all new works are to be stopped, apart from expenditure on anti-cavalry batteries all new projects in the army budget have been deleted, and revisions will not be accepted. The Prime Minister has already accepted it, and I think that if the slightest departure from the Finance Ministry survey is introduced at the Cabinet conference, there is bound to be a great argument.[58]

It appears to be the case that Soeda and the Ministry of Finance strove to cut back the armaments expansion plan. The fact, however, that in the end the party Cabinet, like the *hanbatsu* Cabinet before it, accepted the demands of the Army and Navy subsequently placed the parties in a great quandary. If they were to disintegrate to the extent experienced by the *Jiyūtō* and *Shinpotō* with their internal strife, it was merely necessary for them to reject the budget demands of the Army and Navy and thus be overthrown. In the case of the second Saionji Cabinet [1911–12], which rejected an increase of the two divisions, the result was to place its life in jeopardy. To make its position in power secure, a party had to restrict its policy choices.

If a party Cabinet could not cut back the armaments expansion plan, and thus was unable to reduce its expenditure, the only thing it could do was to increase taxation. This was particularly the case in view of the fact that Soeda had served for many years as an official of the Ministry of Finance, and that in believing that 'the deficit must not be made up by increasing the national debt or even by redemption of bonds',[59] he was echoing the thoughts of the Ministers of Finance in the previous two Cabinets. Earlier he had said that

> If you want to establish the national finances on a sound foundation, it is necessary to find a way of creating a sound long-term source of revenue by increasing taxation'.[60]

For the *Kenseitō* Cabinet, however, which opposed increases in taxation but held the reins of power, it was desirable to avoid simply implementing an increase in land tax. As Soeda himself put it:

> Now that increases in taxation are inevitable, we have adopted a policy of preventing a greater burden from falling on producers. We wish to raise the following taxes on non-productive consumption: increase the tax on *sake*, and raise the official sale price of leaf tobacco; impose a new tax on sugar, and introduce an equalization tax on those imported goods which would adversely affect those and other consumer items. We expect to raise in 1899 more than ¥26 million from the increase in *sake* tax, the rise in the official price of leaf tobacco and the tax on sugar.[61]

In order to cover the rest of the deficit, the policy was to increase income tax and registration tax. As we have seen, the Cabinet fell without having come to a decision on a proposal to make up the required revenue, but quite possibly the proposal of the Ministry of Finance would have prevailed in Cabinet.

Thus the *Kenseitō*, which had beaten the *hanbatsu* Government and come to power itself through its opposition to any increase in the land tax, was deciding to present a new tax increase bill to the House of Representatives. If it intended to hold on to power without cutting the armaments expansion plan and without increasing the land tax, it had no other choice than to do so. If, however, we remember that one of the main motivating forces behind political changes between the Russo-Japanese War and the early part of the Taishō period [1912–25] was going to be the demand for reduction in the indirect consumer taxes which the *Kenseitō* Cabinet had decided to impose, then we may readily draw the conclusion that its financial policies bring out in sharp relief the nature of the parties of that time. They would have found it difficult to refute the attack of Taguchi Ukichi, who, as ideologist for commercial and industrial interests, advocated increasing the land tax, when he said: 'It is easy to speak admiringly of the beginning of the party Cabinet, but in fact it spelled progressive reduction of welfare for poor people. What contributed to this above all was the increases in consumer taxes.'[62]

The consistent contradiction of the political parties after the Sino-Japanese War was that they gave wholehearted support to the post-war reconstruction plan, and particularly to armaments expansion, and yet in their desire to represent the interests of the landlords who were their base of support they wished to avoid increasing the land tax. This was revealed most graphically when they themselves took over the reins of office. The parties at this point were faced with a certain number of choices. One of these was to tread the path mapped out by the *Kenseitō* Cabinet. This clearly meant abandoning all interests apart from the landlords and peasants, and going ahead with post-war reconstruction by sacrificing commerce and industry and the poor of the cities. It was, in fact, possible to remain in power in these circumstances. The second way was to accept the idea of increasing the land tax, as a means of carrying out post-war reconstruction. This was the quickest shortcut to participating in office, but it carried the risk of reducing party support. It was important, therefore, since the landlords were the party base, to keep to a minimum any increase in the burdens they had to bear, and at the same time to augment their strength by attracting industrialists. The third way, naturally enough, was to give up for the time being the idea of taking office, and as a party of opposition to proclaim the necessity of relief from taxes. The difference between choice number three and choice number one was that embarking on the third did not entail compensating for opposition to higher land taxes by proposing to increase other taxes. Once power was relinquished it would be possible to criticize basic expansion of military expenditure, requiring tax increases, and therefore to oppose land tax increases without talking about increasing any other kind of taxation. After the fall of the *Kenseitō* Cabinet the mainstream of the *Kenseihontō* made the first choice; the *Kenseitō*, led by Hoshi Tōru, made the second; while the anti-mainstream of the *Kenseihontō* made the third; and the outlines of these differences could be seen even in the period of the *Kenseitō* Cabinet. The following statement is obviously a mixture of choice one and choice two:

> If it is possible to cover the deficit with other sources of taxation this will lead to a happier result, but if we are to obtain a positive outcome we must propose immediately an increase in land tax and so avoid trouble.[63]

On the other hand the next statement is clearly choice three:

The present Cabinet has not reduced the budget below that of its predecessor, and the only difference is that it does not make demands on the land tax; but even so, how can we really tell it from the previous Cabinet?[64]

Hoshi Tōru, Shimada Saburō and others seem to have hit on choice two when they argued that 'land tax should be increased, the economy should be stabilized and the revival of the industrial world should be targeted.'[65]

THE *KENSEITŌ* SPLIT

As we have seen, it was Hoshi Tōru, of the former *Jiyūtō*, who brought the coalition Government – already facing all kinds of difficulties – to the point of a split. The report from Nishiyama, Inspector-General of Police, to the Prime Minister, Ōkuma, dated 13 September 1898, noted that

It was previously reported that Kaneko Kentarō, Sone Arasuke and others recently, in the Nippon Club, discussed a plan to organize a new party, to the detriment of the *Kenseitō*, centred on the *Kokumin Kyōkai*. We have heard that an announcement was made immediately afterwards, and that this unfortunately led to the *Kenseitō*'s closing ranks. The opportunity was thus lost of splitting that party – indeed an unprofitable situation. We now secretly plan, postponing any announcement, on the one hand to divide the Kenseitō, and on the other hand to negotiate with the faction of Hoshi Tōru and the faction of Shimada Saburō and Taguchi Ukichi on certain conditions (with Hoshi the question of the chairmanship; with Shimada, Taguchi and others, no doubt, the tax increase problem); we shall seek to absorb one or other of these factions, and in anticipation of a favourable outcome of the above we shall dissolve the *Kokumin Kyōkai* and at the same time organize a new party to be called the *Aiminto* [literally: Party of Those Loving the People].[66]

It seems that Hoshi did not in fact make a positive response to this invitation, but it can well be imagined that having been excluded from the coalition Government he would have regarded that Government with dissatisfaction. Also, considering his consistent opposition to a coalition of popular parties, he would doubtless have been hostile to a coalition Government of the *Jiyūtō* and the *Shinpotō*. In fact his activities during the two and a half months following his enforced return from his position as consul in the United States were focused on attempts to split the coalition Government, relying on the Kantō Club for help.[67] Concerning the activities of Hoshi and the Kantō Club, Nishiyama reported to Ōkuma:

> Only the former *Jiyūtō* faction within the Kantō faction feels a great sense of inequality, and is secretly plotting a split. Even though the Central Executive Committee members work for a compromise, the activities behind the scenes of Hoshi's forces are causing great disquiet. At the meeting, of the Kantō Club the other day at the *Kōyōkan*, however, Hoshi brought together his sympathisers from neighbouring prefectures, and hinted that he was planning a show of his own strength, but subsequently he became dissatisfied with the conditions for achieving his aim, and gathering his supporters together he presented all kinds of difficult questions, showing that his ambition was to disrupt that day's meeting.[68]

The meeting of the Kantō Club which Nishiyama refers to is possibly the previously mentioned general meeting of the Kantō Club held on 6 September. If this is the case, the activities of the Kantō Club in pressing party headquarters and Cabinet for abolition of the Civil Service Appointments Ordinance, and for exclusion of *hanbatsu* elements, and in calling upon other local blocs to act in the same manner, were already directed towards the splitting of the *Jiyūtō–Shinpotō* coalition, and were led by Hoshi Tōru. Hoshi's plan of provoking a split in the *Kenseitō* (an amalgam of the *Jiyūtō* and the *Shinpotō*) and then building a party under his own leadership with a clear majority becomes obvious from the following story which Hoshi is said to have related:

> Since the formation of the present Cabinet the political and administrative situation has been hopeless; the present ministers have fulfilled none of the promises they made when in opposition and have simply procrastinated. We do not propose in the future to spend our time praising the *Kenseitō*. We must build up our own faction, double its strength and then double it again, and create a single mighty force in the Diet. We recognize the necessity for the Kantō faction to build up the unity of its will, and both to prepare for the period following the split and to determine its policy towards the Diet.[69]

From about the time of the fourth Diet session, or even further back, from the time of the Movement to Destroy False Parties [a movement in 1883 which aimed to destroy the *Kaishintō*], Hoshi Tōru had consistently and strongly opposed the idea of a coalition of popular parties. Because of the strength of antipathy towards the *Kenseitō* Cabinet felt by the *genrō*, the bureaucrats and the House of Peers, the inability of the coalition Cabinet to present a coherent policy on matters of finance, and the fact that he himself was not able to take the leadership of a coalition Government formed in his absence, Hoshi went out of his way to foster the dissatisfaction felt within the party over the Civil Service Appointments Ordinance question, and worked towards a split between the old membership of the *Jiyūtō* and *Shinpotō*.

Incidentally, there were some interesting aspects of the activities of Shimada Saburō and others, who were dissatisfied elements within the former *Shinpotō*. Shimada was upset that the Education Ministry portfolio had gone to Ozaki Yukio, and planned to have the House of Peers take up the question of Ozaki's 'republican' speech [in August 1898 Ozaki alluded to the possibility of Japan's becoming a republic in a speech directed against big business – the Meiji Emperor became angry at this and demanded his removal from office], in order to have him removed from his position of Education Minister.[70] He is also said to have worked enthusiastically to have himself sworn in as the successor to the Education portfolio once Ozaki was removed.[71] Thus the Shimada faction, with its discontents, conducted a fierce attack upon the Cabinet, much like Hoshi and the Kantō Club, over administrative reform,[72] and at the same time reacted with great sensitivity to the direction in which Hoshi and the Kantō Club were moving.[73] The Hoshi faction and the Shimada faction had a great deal in common concerning their treatment in the Kenseitō Cabinet and also concerning the land tax increase question. Therefore the fact that the one was rapidly increasing its influence within the *Jiyūtō* faction, while the other was gradually becoming heretical within the *Shinpotō* faction, may well have had a good deal to do with the differences in direction subsequently taken by the *Kenseitō* and the *Kenseihontō*.

The immediate cause of the split, however, was not anything to do with Hoshi Tōru, but was the result of a pre-emptive attack by the *Shinpotō* people. The *Jiyūtō* and *Shinpotō* factions were locked in conflict over who should replace Ozaki, who had relinquished his Education portfolio following his 'republican' speech, but when the matter was unresolved at the Cabinet meeting of 26 October, Ōkuma announced that he would recommend Inukai Tsuyoshi to the Emperor and went to the Palace. At the Palace, before recommending Inukai, Ōkuma announced his own resignation on the grounds of Cabinet disunity. On being dissuaded from this, he then recommended Inukai as the next Minister of Education.[74] It was a fairly high-handed way of forcibly breaking the impasse. For the *Jiyūtō* faction, which thought that 'if this Cabinet is really a coalition Cabinet it should not take any action when one side disagrees', there was a sense of complete betrayal. The *Jiyūtō* faction is said to have 'experienced great consternation upon hearing the Imperial proclamation of Inukai's appointment'.[75] The *Jiyūtō* faction thereupon began to counterattack, and on 28 October informed the *Shinpotō* faction: 'Since our alliance has been irrevocably broken we must withdraw our three Ministers, so please replace your Ministers from the *Shinpotō*; but in that case the *Kenseitō*, will have to be dissolved, and if that is not accepted it will unfortunately have to be put to a party congress'.[76] On the 29th the *Jiyūtō* faction independently convened a congress of the *Kenseitō*, and resolved to disband that party and to form a new *Kenseitō*, while Itagaki, (Minister of Home Affairs), Matsuda (Minister of Finance), and Hayashi (Minister of Communications) simultaneously tendered their resignations. At this point Ōkuma and the others in his Cabinet were forced once again to tender their resignations, only this time the resignations were accepted, and so on 30 October the *Kenseitō* Cabinet fell. Thus Japan's first party Cabinet disintegrated without completing even a single Diet session. It lasted a mere four months.

The end of this Cabinet however, was not brought about by direct action to overthrow it by the *genrō*, bureaucracy or the House of Peers. Nor was the immediate cause of its fall to be found in conflict between it and the Army Minister over matters of military expenditure. If the first party Cabinet did have to fall within four months, the situation would no doubt have looked much better had it been overthrown by outside pressure, such as an impeachment petition by the House of Peers or the resignation of the Minister of the Army. Its disintegration as a direct result of squabbling between Cabinet ministers of the *Jiyūtō* and *Shinpotō* factions was a too ignoble ending. Indeed, it would probably have been better if the Cabinet had been able to last a little longer before handing over power, and in the thirteenth Diet had chosen to fall rather than itself present a bill to increase land tax.

7   Concluding the land tax increase bill

A bill to increase the land tax – the most controversial of all issues since the end of the Sino-Japanese War – passed through both houses during the thirteenth Diet; and thus the conflict between policies of 'enriching the Nation and strengthening the armed forces' versus 'lightening the people's burdens', which had been raging ever since the first Diet between the *hanbatsu* Governments and the political parties, was for the time being extinguished. Of the calls for 'retrenchment of Government spending' and 'reduction of taxation', which had been the main policies of the popular parties during the early sessions of the Diet, the first had completely disappeared since the ninth Diet. The fact that the expenditure budget of the first Ōkuma Cabinet (the *Kenseitō* Cabinet) was accepted as it stood by its successor, the second Yamagata (*hanbatsu*) Cabinet, shows most clearly that the parties had entirely lost interest in 'retrenchment of government spending'. Even the *Kenseihontō*, which opposed the land tax increase bill in the thirteenth Diet and continued to call for tax reductions, could not oppose the expenditure budget which it itself had drawn up. The circumstances of the time seem clearly indicated by the criticism of the *Kenseihontō* made by the *Mainichi Shinbun*:

> The responsibility for inflating government expenditure and rapidly increasing the burdens falling on the people does not rest entirely with the *Jiyūtō*. The *Shinpotō*, given that this expenditure bill had been drawn up during the period of the Ōkuma Cabinet, could not demand its reduction, and there was not even anybody strong-minded enough to support our argument that military administration should be streamlined.[1]

Moreover, as we have already seen in the last chapter, because the party Cabinet itself drew up an expenditure budget which almost entirely accepted the post-war reconstruction plan, if on the revenue side an increase in the land tax were to be avoided, other tax increases would have to be envisaged. We have already seen that what the Ministry of Finance was planning was principally an increase in indirect consumer taxes. The parties were now supporting armaments expansion, and were backing increases in taxation to pay for it, and the only thing they were opposed to was that the tax increase should fall on the land tax. Moreover, the parties, which since the Sino-Japanese War had been gradually advancing to political power, wished to avoid, so far as possible, those policies which would result in their being completely excluded from power. Putting all these things together, it becomes not all that surprising that during the thirteenth Diet the *Kenseitō* should have arrived at a position of support for increasing the land tax.

Even so, it cannot be denied that for the parties, which a few years before had been demanding a reduction in the land tax, to support an increase in that same tax was a risky adventure. Apart from providing the general background leading to such a fundamental change of direction by the parties, we must explain why the *Kenseitō* underwent such a change of direction, whereas the *Kenseihontō* did not. In order to investigate the subsequent changes in direction of the two parties, we must explicate the political process of the land tax increase question, and this means going over some matters already discussed in the previous chapter.

THE POLITICAL EMERGENCE OF COMMERCIAL AND INDUSTRIAL INTERESTS, AND THE LAND TAX QUESTION

We saw in Chapter 3 how shocked were the commercial and industrial interests when, in the period of reconstruction following the Sino-Japanese War, they were for the first time ordered to share the burden of the *hanbatsu* Government's policies of enriching the nation and strengthening the armed forces'. This was an opportunity for businessmen to join political movements, where previously they had been 'the type of people who are not interested in politics and whose opinions lean towards those of the Government parties'.[2] Unlike the landlords and farmers who, continuously since the Restoration, had had to bear the burden of expansionist policies, businessmen and industrialists had hitherto felt no reason to have a movement independent of the Government. After the Sino-Japanese War, when the national business tax was first instituted, businessmen criticized the Government's expansionist policies for a brief period. As we have seen, the criticisms of armaments expansion made by the Tokyo Chamber of Commerce and by Taguchi Ukichi and others were of this kind. Even with Taguchi, however, opposition to armaments expansion and support for raising land tax went together from the start; and as this shows, the opposition of the Chamber of Commerce to business tax was more likely to develop into a movement opposing taxation of commercial and industrial interests and supporting increased land tax than into a movement criticizing postwar reconstruction. This constitutes the exact antithesis of the failure of the parties to push through their opposition to 'enriching the nation and strengthening the armed forces', together with the ultimate limitation of their opposition to increases in the burdens falling on the landlords. The progress of the post-war depression beginning in 1897 accentuated this trend. Certainly at the outset of the depression there were quite a few 'people who proposed as a method of treatment the reduction of armaments'.[3] As the depression deepened, however, and as relief for commerce and industry became increasingly urgent, then naturally the view that 'rearmament should be given first priority, and measures for the relief of industry should be treated with urgency'[4] became stronger. The argument that the economic situation could be eased by reducing spending on armaments, and the argument that it could be improved by raising more money from an increase in land tax differed in the sense that the latter was far more realistic. Ishikawa Yasujirō, of the *Mainichi Shinbun*, wrote on the recent situation at the beginning of 1899:

> When the Government presented its plan for armaments expansion at the ninth Diet, representatives of the chambers of commerce met in Nagoya, resolved that excessive armaments expansion risked leading to a decline in national strength, and petitioned the Government to this effect. The rearmament which they opposed, however, was decided upon, but the result has been problematic for financial management and has had a great effect in economic circles. It has meant that tax increases are being actively discussed, and yet chamber of commerce members lack the guts to come out with the straightforward argument that military spending ought to be cut back, instead they go along with reckless ideas such as nationalizing the railways, and thus cause a great fuss. Their indecisiveness is nothing short of astonishing.[5]

The view that the economy could be salvaged by cutting back the plans for armaments expansion held that by making use of preparations, it would be possible to speed up the repayment of Government war loans and Government industrial loans, and to overcome financial stringency. Against this was ranged the argument that rearmament was rearmament and help for the economy was help for the economy, that the national finances could be strengthened by increasing the land tax and that the economy could be revived by attracting foreign capital. The central proponents of the latter argument were the *Keizai Kenkyū Dōshikai* (Economic Research Association), which consisted principally of the railway executives Amemiya Keijirō, Nezu Kaichirō, Inoue Kakugorō, Tanaka Heihachi and Takeuchi Tsuna. The *Keizai Kenkyū Dōshikai*, on 12 May 1898, sent a statement of their opinion concerning relief for the economy to the members of the House of Peers and the House of Representatives. This statement consisted of three points: 1 relief for the economy through Sino-Japanese War reparations; 2 nationalization of the railways and repayment of Government loans by means of foreign borrowing; 3 reduction in the Bank of Japan interest rate.[6]

It is particularly interesting that the *Jiyūtō* from the beginning was connected with the *Keizai Kenkyū Dōshikai* movement. On 27 April 1898, at the meeting of the *Gaishi Yunyū Dōmeikai* (League for the Import of Foreign Capital), in which the *Keizai Kenkyū Dōshikai* played a central role, the *Jiyūtō* President, Itagaki Taisuke, made a speech in which he said:

> The economic policy of the present Cabinet is thought to be forward-looking, but recently it is being rumoured that it has become negative ... The present policy for [stimulating] the economy lies in importing capital and with it nationalizing the railways. This should be done by buying up the four lines which constitute the principal railways of the whole country, namely the Kyūshū, the Sanyō, Nippon, and Kōbu lines.[7]

When the bulk of commercial and industrial interests shifted from advocating economic recovery by cutting back the armaments expansion plan to economic recovery through positive financial management, the *Jiyūtō* quickly began to align itself with this trend. As we have already seen, the *Jiyūtō*, shortly after this, opposed the third Itō Cabinet's bill to increase land tax, and amalgamated with the *Shinpotō* to form the *Kenseitō*, but if their advocacy of railway nationalization through importation of foreign capital were not to be accompanied by a strengthening of the financial base by an increase in land tax, then there would be no prospect of future payment of loans. This may indicate that the leadership of the *Jiyūtō* at this point basically supported the idea of increasing the land tax.[8] In the eyes of

Inoue Kakugorō, a driving force behind the *Keizai Kenkyū Dōshikai,* the *Jiyūtō* of that time did appear in such a light. When the *Jiyūtō* and *Shinpotō* amalgamated and formed the *Kenseitō* Cabinet, Inoue predicted that the two parties would split over financial policy:

> The present Cabinet can be said to be without policy and without doctrine. This is because the doctrines of the *Jiyūtō* and the *Shinpotō* are mutually opposed ... The one wants to nationalize the railways and the other does not. The one wants to import foreign capital and the other does not. The one calls for expansion of armaments and the other does not. In other words it is positive versus negative ... How can such an entity possibly hold together?[9]

As to why after the fall of the *Kenseitō* Cabinet the former *Jiyūtō* section of the [new] *Kenseitō* should have moved in favour of increasing the land tax, one reason that may be considered is the kind of connection that existed between the party on the one hand and commercial and industrial interests on the other. An editorial in the *Tōyō Keizai Shinpō* at the beginning of 1899 reports as follows on this point:

> Previously for a while the argument that the railways should be nationalized was heard, and greatly engaged the attention of politicians, but in reality it was only a temporary fad, and failing to emerge into the real world of economics it appeared to have faded from sight. Recently, however, voices have been raised once again concerning this question. The *Kenseitō* intends soon to present a motion for railway nationalization, and the Government is interviewing the presidents of private railway companies, conducting surveys of shareholders' opinions and so on, so that concerning this question there is a tendency for activity gradually to increase both in government and outside.[10]

As we shall be describing later, after it supported an increase in land tax during the thirteenth Diet, the *Kenseitō* (formerly *Jiyūtō*) gradually began to advocate 'positive' [i.e. expansionist] policies, and recommended restoration of local profitability through such measures as railway nationalization, acceleration of railway building, payment for prisons out of the National Treasury and repair of harbours. What is interesting to note, though, is that the links between railway capitalists and the *Kenseitō* were an important reason why the *Kenseitō* should have come to support increasing the land tax. The restoration of local profits by expansionist policies was something that was frequently advocated by the parties, but in any case this was a means of preventing a decline in party strength caused by the increase in land tax. The parties did not support an increase in the land tax in order to achieve a growth in party strength through expansionist policies, but rather, because they supported an increase in land tax, it gradually became necessary that they support such policies. In contrast to this, the connection between the industrialists' railway nationalization argument and the *Kenseitō* was more concrete, and may well have been one of the reasons why the *Kenseitō* came to support an increase in land tax. In fact when the alliance was formed between the second Yamagata Cabinet and the *Kenseitō*, the above-mentioned *Keizai Kenkyū Dōshikai* and the *Tōkyō Shōkō Sōdankai* (Tokyo Council of Commerce and Industry), whose principal officers included Ōkura Kihachirō, Ōe Taku, Watanabe Kōki, Masuda Takashi and Kondō Renpei, used their good offices to bring about the alliance. The day before the alliance between the Yamagata Cabinet and the *Kenseitō* was finalized, an Itō faction bureaucrat named Kuki Ryūichi reported to Itō:

> From yesterday morning through last night and into today the *Tōkyō Shōkō Sōdankai* and the *Keizai Kenkyūkai* members – about eighty of them – have been stating their opinions, and have frequently been pressing the Government to compromise.[11]

At about the same time both groups were also working on the *Kenseihontō*. A statement of opinion addressed to Ōkuma from the *Keizai Kenkyū Dōshikai* and dated 27 November 1898 desired support for an increase in the land tax:

> The Cabinet has just been formed and the Diet will soon be inaugurated. When one secretly inspects the situation of the Cabinet and the Diet, it is immediately clear that both are pitted against each other and an early clash between them is unavoidable. If that is so, then important affairs of state will be held up, financial management will be unable to cope with post-war reconstruction and an enfeebled commerce and industry will sink into the distress of stagnation and decline ... May I respectfully ask you to act as conciliator between Honourable Members of the Cabinet and your political friends in the Diet ... you should strengthen the financial base and thus lighten the [tax] burdens of the people.[12]

A statement of opinion by the *Tōkyō Shōkō Sōdankai* dated 28 November expressed practically the same sentiment.[13] Considered in the light of these statements, the approaches made to the *Kenseitō* by the two businessmen's organizations, as mentioned in Kuki's letter, may well have contained much the same content. In other words, the *Keizai Kenkyū Dōshikai* and the *Tōkyō Shōkō Sōdankai* were presumably urging the *Kenseitō* to support the Yamagata Cabinet's land tax increase, and were also working on the *Kenseihontō* for the same purpose.

As has become evident, therefore, by the beginning of 1898 business interests were strongly urging that the financial situation be stabilized by raising the land tax, and that on that basis the tight money policy be eased by raising foreign loans. Moreover, the *Jiyūtō* (*Kenseitō*) was quickly coming to accept this argument, as can be seen from the following:

> The new Japan, which we have opened up to the world, must multiply its national wealth with agriculture, industry and commerce all pulling together. When it is a question of supporting them we must deliberately weigh the pros and cons, and we must consider the speed of development of already developed and yet-to-be developed sectors with the national interest as our primary concern. The notion that agriculture is the basis of the State is an economic argument reminiscent of the days when Japan was still sealed off from the outside world.[14]

This assertion by Itagaki shows that the *Kenseitō* headquarters was vigorously looking for support from the industrial and commercial classes.

THE INCREASE IN THE LAND TAX AND LAND ASSESSMENT REVISION

However much the leadership of the *Kenseitō* may have desired the support of commerce and industry, so long as that support could be obtained only at the cost of totally losing the backing of the landlords and peasants, the *Kenseitō* could never move in favour of increasing the land tax. How was it, therefore, that in the thirteenth Diet, the *Kenseitō* did back an increase in the land tax and yet broadly speaking retained the support of the landlords? This has already been studied from many different angles, and the following arguments have been put forward:

1 that there was a fall in real terms in the land tax burden because of an incrase in the rice price;
2 that a bourgeoisification of interests had occurred with the acquisition of stocks by landlords who had become parasitical;

3 that there were regional discrepancies in the real rate of increase of the land tax because of land assessment revision;
4 that a compromise between the Governnent and the *Kenseitō* led to a reduction in the rate of increase and a restriction in the tax increase period (3.3 per cent of assessed value, over five years).[15]

These four points practically exhaust the question, but each posits causality in a different dimension, so that unless we clarify the mutual relationships between them, it will be difficult to produce a readily comprehensible explanation.

First of all, taking the rice price increase question, it is essential to consider separately the increase in the rice price as a direct cause of the passage through the thirteenth Diet of the land tax rise, and the long-term aspect involved in the fact that the land tax question had been declining in importance since the early sessions of the Diet. As a direct cause, the rice price increase was quite unimportant. From the landlords' point of view, it was a natural economic trend, and did not directly result from the expansionist policies of the Government. The argument that the rice price rise brought about the land tax increase was appealing to bureaucrats, as well as to commercial and industrial interests. It had no rationale for landlords. For a landlord, the view that the land tax was increased because the price of rice rose was incomprehensible unless if the rice price were to fall, the land tax would be reduced.

Table 7.1 Average rice price in Tokyo (per *koku*)

Year	Price in yen (¥)
1873	4.80
1887	5.00
1890	8.95
1891	7.04
1892	7.24
1893	7.38
1894	8.83
1895	8.88
1896	9.65
1897	11.98
1898	14.80
1899	10.03

Source: Ishihara Yasuhide, *Beika Hendō Shi*. Yaraidō Shuppanbu, 1914

If, however, we think of this in a long-term perspective, then the question has an important meaning. The fact that the price of rice was about three times as high in 1898 as it was in 1887 meant that in real terms the burden on landlords of the land tax had declined to one-third of what it had originally been. Of course there was also the question of price inflation and the lowering in the value of the currency which this entailed. Seen, however, in terms of the real burden of the land tax, currency devaluation itself serves to demonstrate the point, and the increase in the cost of production resulting from price inflation had no immediate impact on landlords, who were not producers in a direct sense.

Thus the land tax issue gradually came to have less and less significance for landlords. Although the tax had increased from 2.5 per cent to 3.5 per cent (i.e. an increase of 32 per cent), nevertheless, the burden on landlords had clearly decreased in comparison with 1887. What, then, is the meaning of the fact that under expansionist policies incomparably more thoroughgoing following the Sino-Japanese War than anything experienced in the pre-war period, landlords found themselves carrying burdens at any rate no heavier than they had borne ten years earlier?

At this point we should consider the increase in a whole series of consumer taxes following the war. Revenue from the tax on *sake* alone rose approximately threefold between 1894 and 1899, the amount of the increase being ¥32,000,000, about four times the ¥8 million increase in revenue from land tax. The burden of post-war reconstruction was thus not borne only by the landlords; the greater part of it took the form of increased taxation on the people at large – both city and country dwellers – through consumption taxes, and on direct producers. The argument of the political parties, that the burden of expansionist policies fell on the landlords and that retrenchment was therefore in order, was already losing credibility. As we have seen, however, this cannot explain the immediate reaction of landlords to the land tax increase question, since however much of the tax burden was being reduced in real terms, there were no landlords actually wishing for a tax increase. To find the immediate cause we must seek elsewhere. Even so, we should not forget that if the landlords were now no longer sole carriers of the burden of expansionist policies, this derived significantly from changes in the structure of politics since the Sino-Japanese War.

The same sort of distinction should also be made in respect of the second argument, that the landlords had developed bourgeois characteristics. It is probably erroneous to argue as a direct cause that the landlords were becoming bourgeois through the ownership of stocks. It is true that industrialists and businessmen were advocating the redemption of Government loans by increasing the land tax, in order to overcome the economic recession. This was wholly a call to take economic remedies by placing the burdens onto another class, and if they, like the landlords, had had to bear increased taxation, they could not have put forward such a solution. According to research which specifically pursued the relationship between landlords and enterprises in Niigata prefecture, the stock holdings of landlords of the landlord areas [i.e. the rice-producing areas of the prefectures of Tōhoku and Niigata Prefecture], although involving an element of risk, were mostly in property, while their interest in participating in local enterprises was extremely slight.[16] If this was the case, then even if they were to pay more taxes this would hardly pull enterprises out of recession. Assuming that they bought largely property shares, then a short-term recovery of share prices could not be expected in exchange for an actual increase in the tax burden through an increase in the land tax. Just like the rise in rice prices, the question of the bourgeoisification of parasitical landlords indicates that the landlords were becoming no longer simply the victims of expansionist policies, and the political structure was changing, gradually, from the first Diet sessions and rapidly, since the end of the Sino-Japanese War. It is impossible, however, to regard this as the immediate reason for the passage of the land tax increase bill.

In contrast, the third and fourth questions relate more directly to the land tax increase question. The Yamagata Cabinet, as a concession to the *Kenseitō*, modified the original proposal for the land tax rate of 2.5 per cent, to be raised to 4 per cent. From this initial proposal it was reduced to 3.3 per cent, and the period of the increase was restricted to five years. Moreover, a land assessment revision bill was proposed at the same time, and most regions, excepting the prefectures of the Tōhoku and Hokuriku regions – saw their land assessment reduced. Since land tax was determined on the basis of land assessment, for these regions a reduction in land tax went along with a land tax increase. If, after land reassessment, the new land values were assessed at 85 per cent of the old land value, then an increase in tax by 0.8 per cent would mean, for that region, an actual tax increase of only 0.3 per cent. Moreover, since after five years the land tax rate was to revert to 2.5 per cent, at that time there would be a tax reduction of about 0.4 per cent. Table 7.2 illustrates these relationships prefecture by prefecture.

In Ōsaka Prefecture an 0.8 per cent increase in land tax because of

Table 7.2 Actual land tax increases as a result of land revaluation (rice paddy)

	New land valuation / Old land % valuation	Actual increase in tax rate (%)	Actual tax rate after return to old valuation (%)	Number of Kenseitō Diet Members	Number of Kenseihontō Diet Members	Total number of Diet Members	Non-tax increase faction in Kenseitō
Ōsaka	80.3	0.15	2.01	3	0	10	
Tokyo	80.5	0.16	2.01	4	8	14	
Mie	81.7	0.20	2.04	1	6	7	
Kanagawa	81.9	0.20	2.05	3	2	5	
Gunma	82.1	0.21	2.05	4	1	5	
Wakayama	82.2	0.21	2.06	2	3	5	2
Shizuoka	82.6	0.23	2.07	2	6	8	
Okayama	82.8	0.23	2.07	2	6	8	
Hiroshima	82.8	0.23	2.07	6	0	10	1
Saitama	82.9	0.24	2.07	5	3	8	2
Hyōgo	83.6	0.26	2.09	6	6	12	
Kōchi	83.7	0.26	2.09	4	0	4	
Aichi	84.1	0.28	2.10	6	1	11	1
Tochigi	85.0	0.31	2.13	3	2	5	
Gifu	85.0	0.31	2.13	2	2	7	
Shiga	86.5	0.35	2.16	2	3	5	1
Chiba	87.0	0.37	2.18	5	3	9	
Ehime	87.0	0.37	2.18	4	3	7	4
Kagoshima	87.1	0.37	2.18	0	0	7	
Ōita	87.2	0.38	2.18	0	3	6	
Tokushima	87.2	0.38	2.18	0	4	5	
Kagawa	88.1	0.41	2.20	2	2	5	2

				total	total	total	total
Yamanashi	89.4	0.45	2.24	2	1	3	
Tottori	89.4	0.45	2.24	3	0	3	
Fukui	89.5	0.45	2.24	3	1	4	3
Ishikawa	90.0	0.47	2.25	4	2	6	
Kumamoto	90.0	0.47	2.25	1	0	8	
Ibaragi	90.3	0.48	2.26	5	3	8	
Kyōto	90.7	0.49	2.27	1	4	7	
Nagasaki	90.9	0.50	2.27	4	1	7	1
Nara	91.4	0.52	2.29	2	2	4	2
Shimane	91.7	0.52	2.29	2	0	6	2
Miyazaki	93.3	0.58	2.33	3	0	3	
Fukuoka	93.8	0.60	2.35	5	4	9	3
Nagano	94.4	0.62	2.36	5	2	8	
Fukushima	95.2	0.64	2.38	0	7	7	
Saga	95.7	0.66	2.39	1	3	4	
Toyama	97.7	0.72	2.44	1	4	5	
Niigata	100.0	0.80	2.50	4	9	13	4
Miyagi	100.0	0.80	2.50	2	3	5	2
Iwate	100.0	0.80	2.50	1	4	5	
Aomori	100.0	0.80	2.50	0	4	4	
Yamagata	100.0	0.80	2.50	4	1	6	2
Akita	100.0	0.80	2.50	0	4	5	
Yamaguchi	100.0	0.80	2.50	0	0	7	
	86.7	0.36	2.17	119	123	300	32
	average	average	average	total	total	total	total

Sources: Compiled from Meiji Zaisei Shi, vol. 1, and Gikai Seido Nanajūnen Shi – Seitō Kaiha Hen, pp.320–3

land reassessment meant a tax increase of only 0.15 per cent, whereas in Tōhoku, where no land reassessment took place, it meant the full increase of 0.8 per cent. It was natural therefore, that with such regional discrepancies the attitudes of landlords to the land tax increase should have been so divided. Of course as we saw in Chapter 4 the inequalities of land valuation before the reassessment were quite severe, and the reassessment was a rational thing to undertake.

Despite this, however, even though the tax increase of 0.15 per cent for landlords in Ōsaka was almost negligible, the increase affecting landlords in Tōhoku seemed excessive. Ōsaka prefecture, however, was an extreme example, and the average increase was in fact 0.36 per cent, while no region enjoyed an actual reduction in taxation. Also it was scarcely possible to be completely confident that the tax increase was for five years only. Thus even though land reassessment had taken place, this did not mean that there was a positive case *for* the land tax increase. This may only be understood, however, if it is considered in relation to the question whether the land tax increase could continue to be rejected right to the last. We have already seen in Chapter 2 that it was extremely difficult for the *hanbatsu* Government to increase the land tax by means of an emergency ordinance as laid down in article eight of the Meiji Constitution. But depending on circumstances, it was not absolutely impossible. If circumstances had arisen such that the House of Representatives continued to reject a land tax increase bill three or four times, and this were having an important effect on post-war plans for armaments expansion, it would not have been impossible to effect a tax increase by means of article 8. Moreover, before this happened successive dissolutions would naturally have been considered. If total opposition to the land tax increase were to persist but to end in defeat, then since some degree of tax relief was possible through land reassessment, and there might be some tax reduction in five years' time if the former tax rate were then resumed, the attitude of local landlords would most likely be that a land tax increase was inevitable, and that some profit could be gained from land reassessment. Since, in contrast to general questions such as rice price inflation and the bourgeoisification of the landlords, land reassessment emerged concretely as having the opposite effect to a land tax increase, it was this that was most specifically likely to bring about a change of attitude on the part of landlords. Indeed, to repeat, land reassessment was not a positive cause of land tax increase. It was not the case that those Diet Members from regions where there was no profit at all from land reassessment or only a very little profit, strongly opposed the land tax increase bill, whereas Diet Members from regions where the land reassessment produced a large profit, reacted positively to the land tax increase. This is clear if we look at the relationship to land reassessment of Diet Members belonging to the *Kenseitō*, which supported the land tax increase, and those belonging to the *Kenseihontō*, which opposed it. In regions where some profit was to be gained from land reassessment, there was no difference at all in the distribution of Diet Members from the *Kenseitō* and from the *Kenseihontō*, even though those from the latter were the more numerous. But if one looks at the prefectures of Hokuriku and Tōhoku, *Kenseihontō* Members predominated, and most of the few *Kenseitō* Members in those prefectures belonged to the anti-tax increase faction within the *Kenseitō*, which held out against the land tax increase and demanded a free vote. Thus Diet Members from regions where land reassessment brought no advantage at all were strong opponents of increasing land tax, whether they belonged to the *Kenseitō* or to the *Kenseihontō*, while Members from regions where it did bring some advantage did not necessarily support the land tax increase. For this reason, if there were differences in attitude to the land tax increase bill between the *Kenseitō* and the *Kenseihontō*, this was only because the *Kenseihontō* happened to contain a relative majority of those Members who came from regions where there was absolutely no advantage to be obtained from land reassessment. This, however, has a significance which ought not to be ignored in relation to the deciding of attitudes by both parties. If we compare Diet Members belonging to both parties for those regions with an actual tax increase rate of more than 0.6 per cent, we see that the *Kenseihontō* had 45, while the *Kenseitō* had 23. As we shall see, whereas the *Kenseitō* was able to suppress the non-tax-increase faction, through the use of party regulations, this was not possible in the case of the *Kenseihontō*.

THE *KENSEITŌ*

In the thirteenth Diet the *Kensietō* rallied all its Members except a mere seven who defied party rules, and almost unanimously assented to the land tax increase.[17] Resolution of the party regulations, however, was anything but smooth. At the general meeting of Diet Members held on 8 December 1898, the Executive Committee expressed the view that a land tax increase was inevitable, but it proved impossible to obtain a decision from the Diet Members' general meeting.[18] Before this, several groups, including the Kinki group, the *Hokushin hasshūkai* [Association of the Eight Regions of

Hokuriku and Shinshū] and the *Dōshi Club*, resolved to oppose a land tax increase, and in particular the *Hokushin hasshūkai* expressed the hard line attitude that 'if support for a tax increase is resolved at the general meeting of Diet Members, the *Hokushin* Members will independently strive to achieve their goal.'[19] The general meeting of Diet Members reconvened on 12 December and resolved by 51 to 33 to make support for the tax increase binding on its Members.[20] Thirty-two of those who had opposed the resolution, however, demanded *en bloc* to be released from the binding nature of the resolution, and to be allowed a free vote.[21] The Executive Committee refused a free vote, but instead pressed the Yamagata Cabinet and obtained a compromise whereby the rate of land tax increase was to be cut back to 3.3 per cent and the period of increase was to be restricted to five years. In this way it was able with difficulty to overcome the non-tax-increase faction.[22] The leadership of the *Kenseitō* decided to support the land tax increase, and in a fairly tough way led the whole party in the desired direction. This was based upon the power strategy of the *Kenseitō* leadership, which took into account the attitudes towards the land tax increase of the commercial and industrial classes as well as the landlord class.

After entering into a coalition with the second Yamagata Cabinet and co-operating with its land tax increase bill, the *Kenseitō* leader Hoshi Tōru treated the coalition as a preparatory process to bring into being a party Cabinet and put forward the following four points as the task of the *Kenseitō*:

1 It is essential to aim high. An old man once said: 'If you do not flinch from ambitious goals, neither will you neglect matters of detail.' It is important not to pursue great goals with impatience. More haste, less speed. Trying to do everything at once may rob us of victory.
2 We should be prepared to open the door wide. We must invite a broad range of talent and allow great men into the party. Even if they come of their own accord, they should not be rejected even if they are *genrō*.
3 Party rules must be strictly enforced. The party should always be completely united. If it is moderate and ordered, keeps the law and stays united, it will go from strength to strength.
4 We must consolidate our local bases of power. The foundation of the party's strength is in the regions. Victories and defeats in politics depend on the parties victories and defeats, while those of the party depend on those in the local areas. Speaking crudely, poli-

tical changes may spring immediately from meetings held at Ōiso, Waseda and the Imperial Hotel, whereas the more long-term causes are to be found in victories or failures at the local level. What happens locally is the most important.[23]

The first and third points were a development of Hoshi's consistent criticism of popular party coalition. Hoshi also wrote:

> The era of minor party splits has passed. If any party fails to secure a majority in the Diet by its own independent efforts, it will not achieve the success it ought to achieve in politics.[24]

In other words for Hoshi the first task was to turn the *Kenseitō* into a party having an independent majority in its own right.

The second point, about 'opening the door', was aimed at bringing over Itō and Itō faction bureaucratics, as well as businessmen. The idea, not simply of a coalition between the *genrō* Itō and the *Kenseitō*, but the kind of amalgamation that later took place with the founding of the *Rikken Seiyūkai*, apparently began to be discussed for the first time from the period when a coalition was set up between the second Yamagata Cabinet and the *Kenseitō*. Hara Kei wrote in his diary on 27 November – the day when the coalition was established:

> When Itō recommended to Hoshi at Kōbe that he should gain the confidence of high and low by assisting the government, Hoshi replied that in his opinion there ought to be an unconditional alliance. But the *Jiyūtō* seemed to regard Itō as a future prime minister.[25]

The very next day, Kuki Ryūichi reported to Itō:

> The *Kenseitō*, because of your efforts, has entirely withdrawn the first and second of their demands, asks for a political platform to be announced, wants a unification of opinions and has decided to work for an alliance.[26]

Also Itō Miyoji, in March 1899, wrote to Itō:

> Concerning the change in the movement of the political parties up to this summer, as I have told you before, I have tried to discover the opinion of Hoshi, and I have the impression that he is relying upon you yourself.[27]

The fact that the *Kenseitō*, departing from its previous strategy of *hanbatsu* – party coalition Cabinets, was not providing a single

Cabinet minister, and was supporting the Yamagata Cabinet merely on one agreed item of policy – the great question of increasing the land tax – was no doubt premised on a matter of considerable weight, namely that the party had achieved some degree of understanding with Itō on the future course that it should take. This was why, according to Hara Kei, it was 'essential to aim high'. The fact that the alignment of Itō faction bureaucrats with the *Kenseitō* was becoming conspicuous at this period also underlay these developments. Itō's son-in-law, Suematsu Kenchō, just after the fall of the *Kenseitō* Cabinet, officially joined the *Kenseitō* (formerly *Jiyūtō*) while Kaneko Kentarō was invited to join and gave it serious consideration. Kaneko reported the circumstances to Itō in the following words:

> For some time past my friends in the *Jiyūtō* have been visiting me and have been urging me to join the *Jiyūtō*. I have been replying that since this was an important decision affecting my future, I definitely wanted to have the benefit of your advice on the matter before committing myself. Since at present there are three possible roads to take – join an existing party, form a new party as you were planning this spring, or else maintain a strictly transcendentalist position and await future changes in political fortune – at present I am being cautious, and concerning when to make a decision, I should like to resolve on a policy after you have returned to Tokyo and you have been kind enough to give me your respected opinion.[28]

We can see that although they had some worries about it, the Itō faction bureaucrats were beginning to think seriously about turning to the political parties. 'Opening the door' was aimed not only at the *genrō* and the bureaucrats but also at businessmen. Since the time of its predecessor, the *Jiyūtō*, the *Kenseitō* had exerted itself to make contact with groups of businessmen such as the *Keizai Kenkyū Dōshikai*, and the party's decision to support the land tax increase bill in the thirteenth Diet gradually improved its chances of absorbing members of the business class. Moreover, because the Itō Cabinet had presented to the twelfth Diet a House of Representatives election law revision bill, and was planning a bill for independent city constituencies which was advantageous for business and commercial interests, the possibility was emerging that the party's absorption of businessmen might be linked directly to an expansion of party strength premised on an increase in the number of Diet Members.

The election law revision bill presented by the third Itō Cabinet to the twelfth Diet session consisted of these four main provisions:

1 abolition of minimum tax payment limits for candidates, and maintenance only of the lower age limit of 30 years and restriction to males;
2 lowering the tax qualifications for electors to those paying land tax of at least ¥5, or income tax or business tax of ¥3;
3 division of electoral constituencies into city and rural district constituencies with the rural districts having a single large (multi-member) constituency per prefecture, and the cities having independent constituencies;
4 adopting a single entry secret ballot system.[29]

There is no space here to go into details about the election law revision topic as a whole,[30] but we must touch briefly on the question of independent city constituencies, which is relevant to our argument. At the time of the twelfth Diet, both the *Jiyūtō* and the *Shinpotō* were opposing the land tax increase bill, and therefore also opposed independent urban constituencies, which they regarded as a means which the Government was using to achieve an increase in land tax.[31] The revised bill in the House of Representatives changed the provision that cities should have one representative for every 50,000 people to one per 80,000, and eliminated the provision in the original bill that concentrations of population of less than 50,000, provided that they were cities, should each have one representative.[32] Evidently the parties rejected the Government notion of supremacy of the commercial and industrial classes. In the thirteenth Diet, however, the situation was changing. The leadership of the *Kenseitō*, which now supported the land tax increase bill, decided, upon the question of electoral revision, to support the bill for independent city constituencies.

On 1 February 1899 the *Kenseitō* leaders held a conference, to which they invited representatives of chambers of commerce and industry from all parts of the nation, as well as members of election law revision committees from every city, who had come up to Tokyo because of the electoral issue. One of the participants, Takagi Bunpei from Kyōto, representing the National League of Chambers of Commerce and Industry, spoke as follows:

As business colleagues from the National Chamber of Commerce and Industry, we feel that if it proves possible to create a united movement with the *Kenseitō* over the land tax issue, we should also like to work together with the party on electoral reform and other issues in the future.

Hoshi Tōru, representing the *Kenseitō*, replied:

> We too should organize a movement taking full consideration of your sentiments.[33]

The leaders of the *Kenseitō* were now intending to respect the views of commercial and industrial interests not only concerning the land tax increase question, but also on the issue of revising the electoral law, while businessmen and industrialists expected a great deal from the *Kenseitō*. The *Kenseitō* leaders, including Hoshi Tōru, worked extremely hard within the party (as their views, expressed at the conference, indicate) to bring about independent city constituencies. Within the party there was a serious controversy between supporters of large multi-member constituencies in rural districts combined with the single entry ballot, and those who wanted the large constituencies but with a plural entry ballot. This was intertwined with the issue of separate city electorates, and it was not easy to reach a conclusion. On 18 February 1899 at a meeting of party Diet Members Hoshi Tōru argued that the question of separate city constituencies should be given prior consideration and that it should be treated separately from the issue of single or plural entry ballot in rural constituencies. He succeeded by the narrowest of margins (43 votes to 41) in having separate city constituencies made official *Kenseitō* policy.[34] Hoshi subsequently went on to make the proposal that any city, whatever the size of its population, should be entitled to at least one Diet representative. This too was accepted.[35] Hoshi Tōrū, like the Itō Cabinet, in the twelfth Diet, was working hard for the realization of separate city constituencies. Incidentally also on 18 February the *Kenseihontō* held a general meting of its Diet Members which established as party policy that only cities with populations of more than 50,000 should be treated separately.[36] This, in effect, emasculated the separate city electorate system as in the previous Diet. In the *Kenseihontō*, too, however, the proposal of its political affairs research committee, like that of Hoshi, was that each city should have at least one Diet Member, irrespective of its population, but this did not pass the general meeting of party Diet Members.[37] There was not so much difference in attitude between the leaders of the two parties, and when we consider that the Hoshi proposal passed the *Kenseitō* Diet Members' general meeting only by a mere two votes, it is clear that there was not much difference in attitude there either. The end result, however, was that the two general meetings of Diet Members revealed a difference in direction between the *Kenseitō*, which was positive towards separate city constituencies, and the *Kenseihontō*, which was negative towards them. The difference between the *Kenseitō* and the *Kenseihontō* positions on electoral reform, just like their differences over the land tax increase issue, became clear during the thirteenth Diet. In the thirteenth Diet, however, the electoral law revision bill failed to pass, because the discussions between the House of Representatives and the House of Peers did not reach an agreed conclusion on the matter of rural districts. Nevertheless, the process of discussion concerning the electoral law revision indicates just how enthusiastic the *Kenseitō* had become about absorbing the commercial and industrial classes.

The fourth point put forward by Hoshi Tōru, namely the expansion and consolidation of the party's rural base, had as its immediate target the re-election of prefectural assembly members in September 1899. The policy proclaimed by the *Kenseitō* for these elections included nationalization of railways, the rapid completion of railway lines, assumption by the State of the cost of prisons, reconstruction of harbours and expansion of educational establishments.[38] This was a more clearly expressed version of the expansionist policies put forward by the *Jiyūtō* after the Sino-Japanese War, given the fact that the land tax issue was at an end. Hoshi himself made speech after speech preaching expansionist policies throughout the six prefectures of Tōhoku, which were the strongest electoral base of the *Kenseihontō* and were most insistent in their demands for tax reductions. In April 1899 the party held a conference at Sendai which resolved on harbour construction for Tōhoku, completion of railways in Tōhoku and establishment of universities in Tōhoku.[39] Participating at the conference, Hoshi linked the concrete interests of Tōhoku with the *Kenseitō* expansionist policies:

> Tōhoku, when compared with the southwest, is most backward in the state of its agriculture. In the economic sphere industry and commerce are similar, while financial institutions are also behind. Communications facilities in Tōhoku are also underdeveloped when compared with Kansai and must be improved. It is very backward too in basic and higher education ... If Tōhoku is to be placed on as good a footing as Kansai, then there is no alternative to expansionist policies.[40]

Thus 'the practice of the *Jiyūtō* was to play on local issues and help the party increase its support'.[41]

At this time, however, it is a little doubtful how specific were the local interests capable of being controlled by the *Kenseitō*. Still, it is true that if the *Kenseitō* adopted such a policy then the supreme issue for it was how to place itself in the position of a long-term party in power. In other words:

> A government party in the *hanbatsu* era meant a friend of the *hanbatsu*, but a government party in the party era means the executor of policy. But if the aim of parties is to put their policies into effect, then today a government party needs to become popular.[42]

The policy of putting forward expansionist policies and seeking to expand local party support pointed the way towards the *Rikken Seiyūkai*.

As we have been arguing, the direction taken by the *Kenseitō* after it moved to support the land tax increase bill was in all respects towards the *Rikken Seiyūkai*. Considering the *Kenseitō* policies of aiming for a Diet majority in its own right, propounding expansionist policies and seeking to expand its local support, and attempting to absorb Itō faction bureaucrats and also members of the business class, there was no other path that it could take. Moreover, the direction taken by the party after land tax was increased may also explain the attitude which it took to the land tax increase question itself. By helping the forces of the *hanbatsu*, which wanted to increase land tax in order to accomplish postwar reconstruction, the *Kenseitō* would force the *hanbatsu* to recognize it as an element in its own power structure. It would also help commercial and industrial interests which wanted to assist economic circles by means of increasing land tax in order to lift the economy out of recession, and thus it would gain their support. It would, so far as possible, ease the increased burdens on farmers caused by the land tax rise, by such measures as land reassessment, reduction in the rate of tax increase and limiting the period of increase. Finally it would put forward expansionist policies, advocate such counter-attractions as railways, harbours and schools, and reverse the loss of support from landlords occasioned by the land tax increase. Thus the *Kenseitō* would try, so far as possible, to expand its party strength.

THE *KENSEIHONTŌ*

Unlike the *Kenseitō*, the *Kenseihontō* opposed the land tax increase bill in the thirteenth Diet, and after the bill was passed organized a movement to return the tax to its old rate in anticipation of the prefectural assembly elections in September 1899 and the fourteenth Diet. In April 1899 the party held tax reduction conferences in

Shikoku and Tōhoku,[43] and on 27 May held a tax reduction
conference in Kansai.[44] Ōkuma himself participated and spoke at the
Tōhoku and Kyōto conferences. As we showed, however, when we
were investigating the financial policy of the *Kenseitō* Cabinet, the
arguments of the *Kenseihontō* in generally supporting armaments
expansion and tax increases and yet opposing any increase in the land
tax, rather lacked persuasive power. Why then did the *Kenseihontō*
persist in opposing a land tax increase? It is of course possible to say
that since opposition to an increase in land tax had been a consistent
policy of the *Jiyūtō* and the *Shinpotō* even after the Sino-Japanese
War, it is the change from opposition to support by the *Jiyūtō*
(*Kenseitō*) that particularly needs explaining, whereas there is no real
requirement to explain the attitude of the *Kenseihontō*, which did not
change. The factors, however, which induced a reversal of policy in
the *Kenseitō* were also operative in relation to the *Kenseihontō*, and
so to explain the *Kenseitō* change of direction without explaining the
absence of such a change in the *Kenseihontō* goes no further than to
report a fact as a fact.

First, we need to repeat the point that the *Kenseihontō* had more
Diet Members than did the *Kenseitō* representing regions which
received no advantage at all from land reassessment and which were
saddled with the land tax increase at its face value. Compared to the
Kenseitō, therefore, its freedom of action was restricted.

Second, concerning the party's relations with the business world,
the *Kenseihontō* (leaving aside railway nationalization) had from an
early stage been advocating the necessity of economic rehabilitation
through the purchase and redemption of government securities,
which would involve increased taxation. Right from the middle of the
twelfth Diet the *Shinpotō* [predecessor of the *Kenseihontō*] had been
putting forward an economic recovery policy whereby the Government should buy government securities using reparations from the
Sino-Japanese War, keep the reparations money in the form of
negotiable stocks, and redeem these later either through increased
taxation or through imports of foreign capital.[45] It was supremely
important for the *Kenseihontō* to avoid the proposed land tax
increase, and the party was by no means indifferent to the demands
of business interests for economic assistance. As we have already
seen, the leadership of the *Kenseihontō* in the thirteenth Diet session
expressed support for the proposal for separate city electorates as an
aspect of electoral law reform, which businessmen were demanding;
but since this was immediately after the passage of the land tax
increase bill, the proposal was not accepted by the general meeting of

Diet Members. This is corroborated by the fact that in the fourteenth Diet the *Kenseihontō* did not express dissent from the proposal for separate city electorates.

Third, there was a miscalculation about which way the voting would go on the land tax increase bill in the thirteenth Diet. This point is quite important when considering elections. Since, as we have seen, there was within the *Kenseitō* a fairly strong current of opposition to increasing the land tax, it was not beyond the bounds of possibility that the bill might again be defeated. If this had happened it would have meant Diet dissolution and general elections, and the *Kenseihontō*, which had opposed the bill, would presumably have performed much better than the *Kenseitō*, which had supported it. On the other hand, the *Kenseitō*, which gave the bill its support, may well have been significantly motivated by the fact that once the bill had passed there would be no issues necessarily leading to a confrontation with the *hanbatsu*, and thus no elections would have to be held until 1902. Since if the elections took place in 1902, the land tax rate would probably be about to return one year later to its original level, the land tax question was unlikely to have much influence on the election result. This is pure speculation concerning the attitude of the *Kenseitō*, but there is some evidence about the attitude of the *Kenseihontō*.

First, there is the overestimation of the strength of the anti-land tax increase faction in the *Kenseitō*. Hiraoka Kōtarō, a member of the *Kenseihontō* General Executive Committee, thought that 'from observation thirty or forty people are opposed',[46] while Tsunoda Shinpei put the 'faction in the *Jiyūtō* which opposes land tax increase at about twenty people'.[47] On about the 4th or 5th of December these figures were fairly accurate, but the problem was that they regarded the twenty or thirty members of the opposition faction as being unchangeably opposed.

Second, and linked with this, is the paucity of information concerning the compromise proposal that was being worked out between the Yamagata Cabinet and the *Kenseitō*. In the *Kenseihontō* there were some who thought that 'the 0.25 per cent rate will inevitably have to rise to 0.3 or 0.33',[48] but in the end that party concluded that 'the 0.25 rate will rise to 0.4 and this will yield ¥3,600,000, or ¥3,700,000, as the revisionists wish'.[49] This was why, when the compromise plan of 0.33 per cent and a five-year period, was devised by the Yamagata Cabinet and the *Kenseitō*, the *Kenseihontō* was rather dismayed. A letter from Tsunoda Shipei to Ōkuma dated 20 December, expressed something of this:

According to what I hear, the land tax rate will not be 0.4 per cent, but 0.33 per cent. Also there will be land reassessment. Also there will be a limited special tax increase on residential land. Also while some, clad in warm clothing and with enough to eat, make speeches in favour of increasing the land tax, others have nothing to eat and neither wine nor tea to drink. Many gentlemen including the previous Prime Minister, who ought to be handing out free lunches in their comings and goings, have been using illegal methods and oppressing those who are against increasing the land tax. Also they are violating the human rights that are the glory of the Constitution.[50]

It can be deduced from this that the *Kenseihontō* had not imagined that the Yamagata Cabinet would reduce the 0.4 per cent rate to a rate of 0.33 per cent, and place a time limit on the tax increase. Thus the party's failure to anticipate a concession by the Yamagata Cabinet was connected with its overestimation of the strength of the anti-tax increase faction within the *Kenseitō*. In fact, as we have seen, if this concession had not been made, that faction might well have forced a free vote.

Fourth, it should not be overlooked that the land tax increase question was the only point at issue at the time between the *hanbatsu* Government and the political parties, and the *Kaishintō–Shinpotō–Kenseihontō* had since the fourth Diet session come to replace the *Jiyūtō* in playing the central role in the popular parties, while there were far more 'popular party' men among its supporters than in the case of the *Jiyūtō*.

It is true that in some quarters it was argued that the land tax increase was of concern only to the landlords, whereas small cultivators were, on the contrary, oppressed by the burdens of indirect consumer taxes advocated by political parties. A typical example of this was the statement of Taguchi Ukichi to Tani Tateki that 'the reason why "General Tani" was opposed to increasing land tax and insisted instead on consumer tax was that he was concerned about small farmers and tenants. But the small farmers would be disadvantaged more as a result of consumption tax than of land tax.'[51] Whatever the merits of the economic argument, there was a fear that 'the big landlords would make good the losses they suffered from the tax increase by raising the amount of rice deliveries required of the small farmer'.[52] On the other hand, however that may be, 'in Japan there are large numbers of small owner-cultivators', and there was a strong feeling that by increasing the land tax, 'confiscation of the lands of small farmers would be accelerated'. The opposition to a land tax increase, whatever its motivation, was now able to present itself as representing the interests of the small farmers who were suffering under the expansionist policies of the *hanbatsu* Government. Therefore the movement opposed to increasing the land tax, whatever its ultimate goals may have been, was capable of absorbing some people who expected radical reform. An example of this is a remark in the diary of Kōtoku Shūsui, who was a member of the Socialism Association along with Abe Isoo and Katayama Sen: 'Frankly I do not think that it is possible to return to the *status quo* concerning the land tax either in this Diet or for several years. But this is not the place to look back on past successes and failures. Even if the land tax is not returned to the *status quo*, we may expect to destroy a part of the *Jiyūtō* in Tosa in the future with this as our banner. Also it may be a step for us to enter the political world.'[55] Kōtoku was clearly participating in this movement as a socialist,[56] and as is seen in Tani Tateki's remark to Kōtoku that 'German socialism envisages the equal division of land between small farmers',[57] the movement in opposition to the land tax included early socialists. This means that it could attract people from popular parties including socialists, and therefore it was difficult for the *Kenseihontō*, which insisted that it was the only popular party in order to oppose the *Jiyūtō*, to change its attitude quickly.

As we have seen, the *Shinpotō*, like the *Jiyūtō*, supported post-war reconstruction centring on expansion of armaments and aimed to achieve power on this basis. So during the Kenseitō Cabinet, when it had itself achieved power, it did not alter this attitude. Thus, although in the circumstances described above, the *Kenseihontō* opposed any increase in land tax, nevertheless, the situation inside its headquarters was fairly complicated. The problem lay in the conflict between those who advocated both expansion of armaments and increasing the land tax and, on the other hand, the opposing intra-party faction which wanted to reduce arms spending but also opposed any land tax increase.[58] The matter did not emerge during the thirteenth Diet session, but in the Diet discussions on the land tax bill, the party was defeated in its opposition to the bill, and the division within the party did not come to the surface. But when the Diet began discussing the budget after the passage of the land tax bill, the conflict within the party finally emerged. As we have already noted several times, the expenditure budget for 1899, which was brought before the thirteenth Diet by the second Yamagata Cabinet, had been drawn up and had received Cabinet assent in the days of the *Kenseitō* Cabinet. Therefore it was difficult for the leaders of the *Kenseihontō*, who as members of the previous Cabinet had participated in the budget decision making, to oppose it. This, however, affected only the Cabinet, and the budget for 1899 had not been written with all the members of the *Kenseitō* participating. Thus, within the *Kenseihontō*, which had been especially opposed to a land tax increase during the thirteenth Diet, the view gradually became dominant that 'it is contradictory to support the Goverment's ten-year plan while opposing the land tax increase. The party should therefore boldly oppose rearmament.'[59]

This conflict continued even after consideration of the expenditure budget had been completed. The Government, in order to make good a deficit in the revenue budget, could no longer cover it with a land tax increase, so it proposed a new house tax, as well as increases in postal charges and in the soya sauce tax. Increasing the land tax, which ever since the second Matsukata Cabinet had been seen as a last-ditch means of meeting a budget deficit, nevertheless did not come up to expectations. Since, in its attempt to secure its passage through the House of Representatives, the Yamagata Cabinet had made broad concessions (by revising land assessment and cutting it to 0.33 per cent), the revenue from it fell far below the level of ¥17,600,000 envisaged in the first plan, and did not exceed ¥8,470,000. Therefore, as has been noted, the Government aimed to raise an additional ¥6,000,000 through a house tax, soya sauce tax and increases in postal charges. At this point the arms-cutting faction within the *Kenseihontō*, having lost at the time of discussions on the expenditure budget, once again made an issue of it. On 31 January 1899 there was a meeting of the anti-military faction arranged by Ishihara Hanemon and Satō Muneya. After discussing the matter, they reached an agreement, signed by 48 members, that

> Since we believe that there is an alternative either to cut back military spending or to increase taxation, we have therefore resolved to reject a supplementary revenue budget, have decided on a method of achieving reduced expenditure, and shall work towards this aim.[61]

For the leadership of the *Kenseihontō*, however, there was an obvious contradiction between opposing arms expansion and even opposing taxation increases designed to achieve it (except for land tax increase), on the one hand, and their previous policies, on the other. Since they might thereby forfeit the chance of attaining power, they could not readily agree to this demand. Even so, it was also impossible to ignore the demands of 48 party Diet Members. As a conciliatory step the party leadership therefore set up an investigation committee in order to study party policy on reduction of arms spending and administrative retrenchment.[62] At the committee meeting of 20 February, the following three points were resolved:

1 to adopt a policy of cutting back total government expenditure as far as possible;
2 to return land tax, postal charges and soya sauce tax to their previous levels;
3 to oppose all and any tax increases.[63]

Since, however, the budget had been sent to the House of Peers, and both the postal charge and soya sauce tax increases had passed the House of Representatives, the whole issue had to be held over to the following year. By achieving a postponement through the device of setting up an investigating committee, the *Kenseihontō* leadership had successfully survived the thirteenth Diet. In name, however, it was a victory for the anti-military faction. If it was a question of opposing 'all and any tax increases', then naturally if they did not propose cutting back the plan for increased military spending, it would not be possible for the *Kenseihontō* as a party to put forward a consistent financial policy. The party leadership was thus placed in quite a difficult position.

Taketomi Tokitoshi, known as the 'financial expert' of the *Kenseihontō*, drew up the 'Taketomi proposal', which was designed to show that the land tax could be returned to its former rate without reducing the expenditure envisaged in the armaments expansion plan. The fact that the party was trying to use this plan as the basis of its financial policy reflects the difficult situation in which the party leaders found themselves. Taketomi was a thoroughgoing opponent of reductions in military spending. He wrote, of Tani Tateki, who from the time of the Matsukata Cabinet had been an opponent of armaments expansion, and had enthusiastically participated in the tax reduction movement:

For a long time he has repeatedly attacked armaments expansion. When members of our party follow his example, it leads to the most unfortunate spectacle of our party members also inveighing against increased military spending.[64]

Since in April 1899, when this letter was written by Taketomi to Ōkuma, the financial retrenchment advocated by the supporters of reduced military spending had more or less become party policy, it is obvious that the party leadership was almost completely ignoring the decisions of the party's administrative retrenchment committee. Taketomi seems not to have been particularly enthusiastic about the land tax reduction movement as such. He wrote to Ōkuma, opposing the fact that Ōkuma, who was the supreme leader of the *Kenseihontō*, should have supported in his local speeches the land tax reduction movement, and addressed him in the following terms:

> It is reported in the press that you have been asked to participate in congresses of the Anti-Land-Tax League to be held in Kyōto and Ōsaka. I am rather worried about this, and I feel that your journey to the Sendai region may also have been imprudent. I believe it would also be imprudent for you to go to the Kansai. If the critical time should come for you, I do not disagree that you should venture forth openly, but for the time being please leave this to the party rank and file.[65]

Why should the fact that Ōkuma, apparently the key figure in the *Kenseihontō*, was at this precise moment leading the movement to return the land tax to its original level, be regarded as 'imprudent'? This can only be understood if we take into account that Taketomi did not regard the land tax reduction movement at all seriously.

This was the point of view from which Taketomi put forward the 'Taketomi proposal' as one of the proposals for financial retrenchment, and he had already shown it to Ōkuma in April 1899. At that time he explained to Ōkuma the intention of his draft in the following terms:

> Even though the tax reduction argument is, of course, attractive to the people as a whole, many reasonable people even among its supporters realize that at a time when government expenditure is rapidly increasing year by year, the argument for a tax reduction is merely a means of arousing the baser elements in the population. I should like to show people the relevant figures in order to persuade them.[66]

The proposal which Taketomi showed to Ōkuma for this purpose was the following:

1 Revise the law relating to the Taiwan militia and instead send a regiment or a battalion intact from the twelve divisions on the mainland. This will result in about a two-thirds cost saving from the ¥6,000,000 militia budget.
2 Abolish the Taiwan military police and use ordinary police instead,

so that the present cost of ¥2,000,000 will be approximately halved.

3 If revenue from Taiwan can be increased, and supplementary civilian expenditure can be abolished, it should be possible to save ¥3 million.

If we take these three measures, we should be able to achieve a reduction in expenditure of about ¥8,000,000, so that even if the land tax is reduced from 0.33 per cent to its former rate of 0.25 per cent, there is no danger of running a deficit.[67]

Since the total income from the land tax increase was ¥8,470,000, if the reductions proposed for expenditure in Taiwan amounted to ¥8,000,000 it should have been possible to achieve a return to the old rate of land tax. Taketomi, at the Executive Committee of the *Kenseihontō* in August 1899, made the following proposal:

We should save ¥4,000,000 by amending the Taiwan militia ordinance, save a further ¥1,000,000 by abolishing the military and increasing the ordinary police, abolish the ¥3,000,000 subsidy from the Japanese mainland and reduce other administrative expenses. Moreover, if we add increases in indirect taxes, we should be able to return land tax, soya sauce tax and postal charges to their former rates.[68]

Against this, Kōmuchi Tomotsune, Ishihara Hanemon and others, who belonged to the faction supporting reduced arms spending, opposed the Taketomi proposal, arguing:

We should cut down the period of reserve service to two years, and so reduce military spending, save ¥1,500,000 by reducing general administrative expenses by 5 per cent, save ¥500,000 by returning the salaries of Diet members to their previous level and by these means return to the earlier rates of the three taxes.[69]

Thus, Taketomi's financial policy proposal attempted to fuse an acceptance of arms expansion with the cutting of the land tax to its former rate. In Taketomi's own words: 'It should be easily possible to reduce taxation without going through the trials of a fundamental financial reorganization.'[70] According to the newspaper of the rival *Kenseitō*:

The reason why the members of the Taketomi faction do not speak directly of military retrenchment but merely of making savings in Taiwan is that if they call for military retrenchment they may one day find themselves in charge of the Cabinet and then face great difficulties.[71]

Their way of saying it was different, but in fact both were speaking the same message. Taketomi's financial policy was an expression of the dilemma of the *Kenseihontō* leadership in expecting to have to form the next Government and yet needing to project the image of a party of opposition.

It was nevertheless impossible in a party out of power to ignore men concerned with principles. Those putting forward a compromise proposal had nothing to bargain with. The fact that in the budget debates in the fourteenth Diet Taketomi himself had to represent the opinions of the arms reduction faction is an extreme example of this. He spoke as follows:

> What must be reduced is first of all expenditure on Taiwan, given the fact that the militia has become far too big and is essentially unnecessary. As a result, Taiwan receives a large subsidy every year, and it becomes impossible to establish its finances on an independent basis. It is essential to reduce the expenses of the Taiwan Government General. Secondly, there is room for large-scale reduction in what are now excessively inflated general administrative expenditures. Thirdly, we must cut back army expenditures. Although nobody would deny the necessity of expanding the armed forces, there is a great problem of inflated expenditure. We must make savings in all areas of military spending.[72]

The fact that, while trying to make a point of avoiding criticism of military expansion, Taketomi was nevertheless forced to criticize it, shows the nature of the *Kenseihontō*, which, while hoping to come to power, was becoming a permanent opposition party. After enduring many years of confrontation between a revisionist and an anti-revisionist faction within the party, it was only with the formation of Katsura's *Rikken Dōshikai* Party in 1913 that we can say that Taketomi and his friends finally reached their goal.

Conclusion

The conflict which unfolded from the first Diet session, between the oligarchs who wanted to 'enrich the nation and strengthen the armed forces' and the political parties, who were demanding reduction of the tax burdens on landlords and farmers, took the form of a struggle between the idea of a 'transcendental Cabinet' and a 'party Cabinet', but between 1898 and 1900 this conflict had more or less spent itself. This is demonstrated by the passage of the land tax increase bill at the end of 1898 and by the formation of the *Seiyūkai* Party in September 1900, which brought party politicians and bureaucrats together in the same party. Of course, the land tax issue did not completely disappear from the political stage when the land tax increase bill was passed, and the struggle for power between the *hanbatsu* and the parties was not ended by the formation of the *Seiyūkai*. The land tax question was a contentious issue up to the outbreak of the Russo-Japanese War [1904–5] and with the struggle for power both publicly and behind the scenes, between Yamagata faction Cabinets and the *Seiyūkai*, it can even be said to have become more intense. The issue however was not now focused on opposition to the expansionist policies of the Meiji State. Moreover, the choice between Katsura Cabinets and *Seiyūkai* Cabinets did not encompass a choice between expansionist and retrenchment policies. The Meiji State was successful in assimilating to itself the change of system involved in the proclamation of a constitution and the establishment of a parliament. In the true sense the Meiji constitutional system may be said to have been consolidated between 1898 and 1900.

As we have repeatedly maintained throughout the book, however, this change did not come about suddenly, but took place gradually right from the first Diet session. If we divide this process broadly into a number of stages we can find four turning-points, in the fourth, ninth, twelfth and thirteenth Diets. While the fourth Diet was a turning-point in the sense that however much the popular parties dressed up their policies, they were forced to realize the incompatibility between 'enriching the nation and strengthening the armed forces' and 'reducing the tax burdens of the people', it was also a turning-point in the sense that the *Jiyūtō* was forced to choose, and was very quickly exploring the possibilities of changing direction. The support for tax reduction, which had come from demands originating with the *Minken* [popular rights] movement, was essentially dropped by the parties from this point onwards.

The ninth Diet was a turning-point in that the parties clearly came out in support of expansionist policies. If, ever since the fourth Diet, the tax reduction position had effectively been abandoned, it was from the ninth Diet that the demand to retrench administrative expenditure also came to be dropped. Coalition Cabinets between the *hanbatsu* and the parties, which were no longer in conflict with each other on policy matters, emerged for a while at this period.

The twelfth Diet was an even more dramatic turning-point, in that it showed the impossibility of continuing with the coalition Cabinets as a result of the proposal to increase the land tax. The parties, which now supported arms expansion and had abandoned their support for land tax reduction, could not easily accept an actual increase in land tax. This was why the *hanbatsu* and the parties from the third Itō Cabinet and the first Ōkuma Cabinet to external appearances were waging a more intense struggle against each other than they had been during the early Diet sessions. In fact, however, the political differences between them were far smaller than during the early sessions of the Diet. There was almost no difference on the expenditure side of the budget. The only conflict was on the revenue side. The fact that the first Ōkuma Cabinet planned to continue policies of arms expansion by increasing taxes other than land tax is a tragic indication of this.

The particular importance of the thirteenth Diet does not need to be reiterated. The passage through the House of Representatives of the land tax increase bill is evidence enough.

Policies of military expansion pursued by the Meiji State, however, were to continue without interruption, but the supporters of tax reduction who opposed it never completely disappeared. As is widely known, various tax reduction demands were behind 'people's movements' such as the anti-peace treaty campaign and the movement to 'overthrow the *hanbatsu* and support the constitution' from the Russo-Japanese War until the early years of Taishō. An important reason for this was obviously that an increase in indirect taxation meant an increase in the tax burdens falling upon the people. But instead of the landlords bearing the main financial burdens of the Meiji State, the burdens were now felt by the middle and lower orders, irrespective of class. The proportion of total national taxation accounted for by land tax went steadily down from 60.6 per cent in 1890 to 32.5 per cent in 1898, and to 17.8 per cent in 1911. In contrast, indirect taxation on *sake* and other items (including revenue from government sales) went up from 23.7 per cent in 1890 to 35.5 per cent in 1899, to 43.5 per cent in 1911. The change from the tax reduction demands of landlords to the tax reduction demands of 'the people' (it is impossible to define how the burden was distributed in class terms among the people) should be thought of as a point of divergence between the period from the end of the Russo-Japanese War and the period dealt with in this book.

Appendices

Appendix 1: Sessions of the Imperial Diet in the 1890s

First session	29 November 1890–8 March 1891
Second session	26 November 1891–25 December 1891
Third session	6 May 1892–15 June 1892
Fourth session	29 November 1892–1 March 1893
Fifth session	28 November 1893–30 December 1893
Sixth session	15 May 1894–2 June 1894
Seventh session	18 October 1894–22 October 1894
Eighth session	24 December 1894–27 March 1895
Ninth session	28 December 1895–29 March 1896
Tenth session	25 December 1896–25 March 1897
Eleventh session	24 December 1897–25 December 1897
Twelfth session	19 May 1898–10 June 1898
Thirteenth session	13 December 1898–10 March 1899
Fourteenth session	12 November 1899–24 February 1900

Source: *Nihon kindaishi jiten*. Tōyō keizai shinpōsha, 1958, p. 756

Appendix 2: Prime Ministers and their Cabinets in the 1890s

First Yamagata Cabinet	24 December 1889–6 May 1891
First Matsukata Cabinet	6 May 1891–8 August 1892
Second Itō Cabinet	8 August 1892–18 September 1896
Second Matsukata Cabinet	18 September 1896–12 January 1898
Third Itō Cabinet	12 January 1898–30 June 1898
First Ōkuma [party] Cabinet	30 June 1898–8 November 1898
Second Yamagata Cabinet	8 November 1898–19 October 1900

Source: *Nihon kindaishi jiten*, pp. 682–4

Appendix 3: General election results for the House of Representatives in the 1890s

First election, 1 July 1890	seats
Jiyūtō	127
Shinpotō	44
Taiseikai	80
Independents	49
Total	300

Second election, 15 February 1892	
Jiyūtō	94
Shinpotō	37
Chūō Kōshōbu	83
Independent Club	32
Others	15
Independents	39
Total	300

Third election, 1 March 1894	
Jiyūtō	121
Kaishintō	51
Kokumin Kyōkai	28
Rikken Kakushintō	37
Others	10
Independents	54
Total	300

Fourth election, 1 September 1894	
Jiyūtō	104
Kaishintō	45
Kokumin Kyōkai	30
Rikken Kakushintō	41
Others	31
Independents	49
Total	300

Fifth election, 15 March 1898	
Jiyūtō	105
Kaishintō	104
Kokumin Kyōkai	29
Rikken Kakushintō	26
Others	14
Independents	22
Total	300

Sixth election, 10 August 1898

Kenseitō	120
Kenseihontō	124
Kokumin Kyōkai	21
Hiyoshi Club	9
Independents	26
Total	300

Source: *Nihon kindaishi jiten*, p. 767

Appendix 4: Political divisions in the House of Peers in the 1890s

	Group affiliations in various years			
	1892	*1894*	*1898*	*1900*
Sanyōkai	29	26	16	22 (Asahi Club)
Kenkyūkai	70	68	70	66
Konwakai	50	59	59	40
Sawakai	–	15	18	34
Mokuyōkai	–	–	19	29
Mushozoku-ha	–	–	32	38
Others	125	124	112	98
Total	274	292	326	327

(See also Table 4.1).

Appendix 5: Notes on various groups

Sanyōkai

Founded by Duke Konoe Atsumaro in 1891. Took a position of neutrality between the Government and the political parties. Reorganized as the *Asahi Kurabu* (Asahi Club) in 1898.

Kenkyūkai

Established in 1891. The largest group in the House of Peers and the one most loyal to *hanbatsu* (but not party) Cabinets.

Konwakai

The precise date of its establishment is unknown, but its name began to appear from the fourth Diet session (November 1892 to February 1893). Its most famous leader was Viscount Tani Tateki. Like the Sanyōkai, it took an attitude of neutrality between the *hanbatsu* Governments and the political parties. It was amalgamated into the Doyōkai in 1901.

Sawakai

Established at the end of 1893. It was composed of Imperial nominees to the House, with some exceptions. It maintained loyalty to the *hanbatsu* Governments and hostility to Cabinets based on political parties.

Mokuyōkai

Founded by Baron Senge Takatomi in 1898. Composed of barons, with a few exceptions.

Mushozoku-ha

There were two such groups of 'Independents' in the House of Peers. One comprised Independent members of the House. The other was composed of anti-party members among Imperial nominees. The latter group was organized in 1898, and the reason why a group so similar to the Sawakai was formed at that time is unknown.

Appendix 6: Notes on personalities

name	dates	place of origin	comments
Abe Isoo	1865–1949	Fukuoka Prefecture	a leading Christian Socialist
Abei Iwane	1852–1916	Iwashiro Nihonmatsu domain (Fukushima Prefecture)	nationalist; later a leader of *Kokumin Jiyūtō*
Adachi Kenzō	1864–1948	Kumamoto Prefecture	leader of *Kokumin Kyōkai*; later Minister of Home Affairs
Amemiya Keijirō		Yamanashi Prefecture	businessman
Aoki Shuzō	1844–1914	Chōshū domain (Yamaguchi Prefecture)	Vice-Minister of Foreign Affairs; later Foreign Minister
Asano Nagakoto	1842–1937	Hiroshima domain (Aki)	former Lord of Hiroshima domain; marquis

name	dates	place of origin	comments
Egi Kazuyuki	1853–1932	Iwakuni domain	official of Home Ministry; local governor
Fujita Denzaburō	1841–1912	Yamaguchi Prefecture	founder of Fujita-gumi; one of the most influential business leaders in Osaka
Fukumoto Makoto (Nichinan)	1857–1921		a pan-Asianist who supported Sun Yat-Sen
Fukuzawa Yukichi	1835–1901	Nakatsu domain (Ōita)	one of the most prominent thinkers and journalists in Meiji Japan; owner of *Jiji Shinpō* newspaper. His autobiography and *Outline of Civilization* available in English
Furusawa Urō (Shigeru)	1847–1911	Tosa domain (Kōchi)	learned parliamentary democracy in England and drafted Petition for a Popularly elected Parliament in 1874; Chief editor of *Jiyū Shinbun*; member of *Jiyūtō*, but left it at end of 1880s, becoming official of several ministries
Furushō Kamon	1840–1915	Ehime Prefecture	nationalist and pan-Asianist; member of *Kumamoto Kokkentō*; Member of House of Representatives
Gotō Shōjirō	1838–97	Tosa domain (Kōchi)	one of the most influential leaders in Tosa at time of Meiji Restoration; *de facto* President of *Daidō Danketsu* movement; served as Minister of Agriculture and Commerce, and of Transport

name	dates	place of origin	comments
Hara Rokurō	1842–1933	Hyōgo Prefecture	businessman in Yokohama; president of various banks, including Yokohama Specie Bank
Hara Takashi (Kei)	1856–1921	Iwate Prefecture	chief editor of Ōsaka Mainichi Shinbun; later President of *Rikken Seiyūkai* and Prime Minister
Haseba Sumitaka	1854–1914	Kagoshima Prefecture	leader of *Kyūshū Kaishintō, Jiyūtō* and later *Seiyūkai* parties
Hatoyama Kazuo	1856–1911	Okayama (Mimasaki Katsuyama)	a leader of *Shinpotō* and *Kenseihontō* parties; graduate and later professor at Tokyo Imperial University
Hayashi Yūzō	1842–1921	Tosa domain (Kōchi)	a leader of *Shinpotō* within *Jiyūtō*
Hiraoka Kōtarō	1851–1906	Fukuoka domain	one of founders of the *Genyōsha*; owner of mining companies
Hirata Tōsuke	1849–1925	Yonezawa domain (Yamagata Prefecture)	one of the most influential of Yamagata faction bureaucrats; Minister of Home Affairs
Horiuchi Kenrō		Nagano Prefecture	
Hoshi Tōru	1850–1901	Edo	a powerful and pragmatic leader of *Jiyūtō* and *Kenseitō* parties
Hotta Masayoshi			a leader of the *Kenkyūkai* faction in the House of Peers; Count
Ichijima Kenkichi		Niigata Prefecture	journalist on *Yomiuri Shinbun*; *Kaishintō*
Ikeda Eiryō		Chiba Prefecture	Member of *Jichitō*; later, Diet Member of *Taiseikai*

name	dates	place of origin	comments
Inoue Kakugorō	1860–1938	Hiroshima	Member of House of Representatives for *Taiseikai,* later *Kokumin Kyōkai, Kenseitō,* and later Member of *Seiyūkai;* owner of railway and mining companies
Inoue Kaoru	1836–1915	Chōshū domain (Yamaguchi Prefecture)	Genrō, Foreign Minister, Minister of Agriculture and Commerce, Minister of Finance
Inoue Kowashi	1844–95	Kumamoto (Higo) domain	one of the most important contributors to the Meiji Constitution
Inukai Tsuyoshi	1855–1932	Okayama Prefecture	Diet Member; leader of the *Kaishintō, Shinpotō* and *Kenseihontō* parties
Ishihara Hanemon			Diet member, *Kenseihontō*
Ishikawa Yasujirō	1872–1925	Okayama Prefecture	journalist
Itagaki Taisuke	1837–1919	Tosa domain (Kōchi Prefecture)	President of *Jiyūtō, Kenseikai*
Itō Daihachi			*Kenseitō;* later, Secretary of *Seiyūkai*
Itō Hirobumi	1841–1909	Chōshū domain	Genrō; Prime Minister; Chairman of Privy Council; the first Speaker of the House of Peers; President of *Seiyūkai*
Itō Miyoji	1858–1934	Nagasaki Prefecture	Chief Secretary of Cabinet; Minister of Agriculture and Commerce
Iwasaki Yanosuke	1851–1908	Tosa domain	head of Mitsubishi group; president of Bank of Japan
Kabayama Sukenori	1837–1922	Satsuma domain (Kagoshima Prefecture)	Navy Minister; one of the most militaristic leaders of the Meiji Government

name	dates	place of origin	comments
Kanai Noburu	1865–1933	Hamamatsu Prefecture	one of the founding members of the Japanese Association for Social Policies; Professor at University of Tokyo
Kaneko Kentarō	1853–1942	Fukuoka domain	a bureaucrat who contributed to drafting of Meiji Constitution; later Minister of Agriculture and Commerce; member of *Seiyūkai*
Kashiwada Morifumi			member of *Kokumin Kyōkai*
Katayama Sen	1859–1933	Okayama Prefecture	a prominent and moderate socialist in Meiji and Taishō Japan
Katō Heishirō			a member of *Kenseitō*
Katsura Tarō	1843–1914	Chōshū domain (Yamaguchi Prefecture)	War Minister; one of the most influential among the Yamagata faction bureaucrats
Kawakami Sōroku	1848–99	Satsuma domain (Kagoshima Prefecture)	Chief of Army General Staff
Kiyoura Keigo	1850–1942	Kumamoto domain	Minister of Justice; one of the leaders of the Yamagata faction bureaucrats
Koizuka Tatsu			a leader of *Kaishintō*, *Shinpotō* and *Kenseihontō* parties; Diet Member and journalist
Kōmuchi Tomotsune	1848–1905	Tango Yosa gun	a retired bureaucrat who became a liberal but nationalistic party politician; Diet Member and member of *Kenseihontō*
Kondō Renpei	1848–1921	Tokushima (Awa) domain	businessman; Managing Director of *Nippon Yusen KK*

name	dates	place of origin	comments
Konō Hironaka	1849–1923	Fukushima Prefecture	one of the best known leaders of the *Minken* (Popular Rights) movement in the 1880s; a leader of *Jiyūtō*; later changed sides and became leader of *Shinpotō* and *Kenseihontō* parties
Konoe Atsumaro	1863–1904		highest ranking of Court aristocracy; father of Prime Minister, Konoe Fumimaro; Chairman of House of Peers
Kōtoku Shusui	1871–1911	Kōchi Prefecture	one of the most radical socialists in Meiji Japan; executed for allegedly plotting assassination of Meiji Emperor
Kuga Minoru (Katsunan)	1857–1907	Tsugaru domain	editor of *Nippon* newspaper; one of the most prominent Meiji nationalist leaders
Kuki Ryūichi			a bureaucrat-politician of the Itō group
Kunitomo Shigeaki	1862–1909	Kumamoto (Higo) domain	journalist on *Nippon* newspaper; leader of pan-Asianist movement
Kurihara Ryōichi	?–1911	Toba domain	a leader of *Jiyūtō* and *Kenseitō* parties
Kuroda Kiyotaka	1840–1900	Satsuma domain (Kagoshima Prefecture)	Prime Minister; top leader of Satsuma faction within Meiji Government, after deaths of Saigō Takamori and Ōkubo Toshimichi
Madenokoji Michifusa			member of *Kenkyūkai* faction in House of Peers; Count
Masuda Takashi	1848–1938	Sado	an important member of Mitsui group business élite; managing director of Mitsui Bussan

name	dates	place of origin	comments
Matsuda Masahisa	1845–1914	Saga (Hizen) domain	Member of House of Representatives from first Diet session; leader of *Jiyūtō, Kenseitō* parties; later one of three most important leaders of *Seiyūkai*, along with Saionji and Hara
Matsudaira Masanao			Government official who served mainly in Ministry of Home Affairs; Governor of Kumamoto Prefecture; one of the most active Yamagata faction bureaucrats
Matsukata Masayoshi	1835–1924	Satsuma domain (Kagoshima Prefecture)	Minister of Finance; Prime Minister; one of the very few financial experts in Meiji Japan; *genrō*
Matsumoto Gōkichi			rather famous as a political broker between the bureaucratic faction and the political parties
Minoura Katsundo	1855–1929	Ōita Prefecture	Leader of *Rikken Kaishintō, Shinpotō,* and *Kenseihontō* parties
Miura Gorō	1847–1926	Chōshū domain (Yamaguchi Pref.)	member of *Konwakai* faction in House of Peers; Army general
Miyake Setsurei (Yūjirō)	1860–1945	Ichikawa Prefecture	Founder of the journal *Nihonjin*; centre-left nationalist; his book *Dōjidaishi* (History of the Age in which I Lived) still read even today
Motoda Hajime	1858–1938	Ōita Prefecture	Leader of *Kokumin Kyōkai*; later entered *Seiyūkai*
Motoda Nagazane (Eifu)	1818–91	Kumamoto domain	Personal consultant (*Jikō*) to Emperor Meiji; Confucianist

name	dates	place of origin	comments
Mutsu Munemitsu	1844–97	Kishū domain	one of the best known foreign ministers of prewar Japan, who accomplished revision of the unequal treaties with Western powers and who signed Peace Treaty with China in 1895. Also famous as government leader with strongest ties with *Jiyūtō*
Nakai Hiroshi		Chōshū domain	Governor of Shiga Prefecture
Nakayama Takamaro			Leader of *Kenkyūkai* faction in House of Peers; Marquis
Narushima Giichirō		Chiba Prefecture	
Nezu Kaichirō	1860–1940	Yamanashi Prefecture	head of a local *zaibatsu* in Yamanashi Prefecture
Nijō Motohiro			Leader of *Sanyōkai* faction in House of Peers; Duke
Nishimura Ryōkichi			member of *Konwakai* in House of Peers
Nishimura Shigeki	1828–1902	Sakura domain (Chiba)	a founder of the *Meirokusha*, which sought to introduce Western civilization into Japan; contributed to drafting of Imperial Ordinance on Education
Nishiyama Shichō		Tosa domain (Kōchi)	Inspector-General of Police; leader of Tosa group liberals from 1880s
Nomura Fumio		Hiroshima Prefecture	
Nomura Yasushi		Chōshū domain (Yamaguchi Pref.)	Minister of Home Affairs; a leader of Yamagata faction bureaucrats
Ōe Taku	1847–1921	Tosa domain (Kōchi)	party man and businessman of Tosa origin

name	dates	place of origin	comments
Ōgimachi Michimasa			Member of House of Peers; count
Oishi Kumakichi			Secretary of Prime Minister's Office
Ōishi Masami	1855–1935	Kōchi Prefecture	Leader of *Daidō Danketsu* movement; leader of *Shinpotō*, *Kenseihontō*; Diet Member
Okabe Nagamoto	1855–1925	Kishiwada domain	Member of House of Peers; one of the top leaders of *Kenkyūkai* in that House; viscount
Ōkōchi Masachika			Member of House of Peers; count
Ōkuma Shigenobu	1838–1922	Hizen domain (Saga)	the founder of the *Kaishintō*; one of the founding fathers of the Meiji Government, top leader of *Shinpotō* and *Kenseihontō* parties
Ōkura Kihachirō	1837–1928	Niigata Prefecture	the founder of the *Ōkura zaibatsu*
Ōoka Ikuzō	1856–1928	Chōshū domain (Yamaguchi Pref.)	Diet Member of *Kokumin Kyōkai*
Ōura Kanetake	1850–1918	Satsuma domain (Kagoshima Pref.)	Governor of several Prefectures; Superintendent of Tokyo Metropolitan Police
Ozaki Yukio	1859–1954	Mie Prefecture	one of the best known liberals in pre-war Japan; leader of *Kaishintō*, *Shinpotō* and *Kenseihontō*
Saigō Tsugumichi	1843–1902	Satsuma domain (Kagoshima Pref.)	Navy Minister; one of the most influential Satsuma leaders; brother of Saigō Takamori; President of *Kokumin Kyōkai*

name	dates	place of origin	comments
Saionji Kinmochi	1849–1940	Kyōto	one of the most liberal of the Court lords; second President of *Seiyūkai*; the last *genrō* from latter half of 1920s to his death
Saitō Shūichirō			a government official in Ministry of Agriculture and Commerce
Sasa Tomofusa	1854–1906	Kumamoto Prefecture	Leader of *Kumamoto Kokkentō*; one of the founders of *Kokumin Kyōkai*
Seki Naohiko	1857–1934	Wakayama Prefecture	managing director of *Tōkyō Nichinichi Shinbun*
Senge Takanori			Member of House of Peers; Baron
Shiba Shirō	1852–1922	Aizu domain	Secretary to Minister of Agriculture and Commerce; well known novelist writing under name of 'Tōkai san shi'; a leader of the Japanist movement
Shibusawa Eiichi	1841–1931	Musashi no kuni	Earlier an official of Ministry of Finance, who founded the First National Bank (*Daiichi Kokuritsu Ginkō*); one of the most influential members of the business élite in prewar Japan
Shiga Shigetaka	1863–1927	Aichi Prefecture	Editor of journal *Nihonjin*; a leader of Meiji period nationalists; member of *Shinpotō, Kenseihontō*; geologist
Shimada Saburō	1852–1923	Shizuoka Prefecture	A founder of the *Rikken Kaishintō*; also belonged to *Shinpotō* and *Kenseihontō*; chief editor of Tokyo (Yokohama) *Mainichi Shinbun*

name	dates	place of origin	comments
Shinagawa Yajirō	1843–1900	Chōshū domain (Yamaguchi Prefecture)	Minister of Home Affairs; Vice-President of *Kokumin Kyōkai*; Viscount
Shirane Senichi	1850–98	Chōshū domain (Yamaguchi Prefecture)	Vice-Minister of Home Affairs; Minister of Communications
Soeda Juichi	1864–1929	Chikuzen domain (Fukuoka Prefecture)	Liberal bureaucrat of Ministry of Finance; Vice-Minister of Finance
Soga Sukenori			A leader of *Konwakai* in House of Peers
Sone Arasuke	1849–1910	Chōshū domain	Minister of Justice, Minister of Agriculture and Commerce
Suehiro Shigetaka	1849–96	Uyo Iwajima domain	editor of *Chōya Shinbun*; a leader of *Daidō Danketsu* movement; well known novelist writing under the name of 'Tetchō'
Suematsu Kenchō	1855–1920	Fukuoka Prefecture	a bureaucrat of the Itō group; member of *Taiseikai* and *Kenseitō*; graduated from Cambridge University
Sugita Teiichi	1851–1929	Fukui Prefecture	a leader of the *Minken* (Popular Rights) movement, and of the *Jiyutō, Kenseitō*
Sugiura Jūgō	1855–1924	Ōmi domain	Ministry of Education official who was sent by the Ministry to study in England; leader of Japanist movement after retirement
Taguchi Ukichi			one of the most prominent economists outside the Meiji Government; believer in *laissez-faire*; editor of *Tōkyō Keizai Zasshi*; author of *Nihon Kaika Shōshi* (Short History of the Japanese Enlightenment)

name	dates	place of origin	comments
Takada Sanae	1860–98	Edo (Tokyo)	a leader of *Kaishintō*, *Shinpotō* and *Kenseihontō*; editor of *Yomiuri Shinbun*; later, President of Waseda University
Takagi Bunpei			businessman in Kyōto; a leader of the National Assembly of Chambers of Commerce and Industry
Takahashi Tomonosuke	1844–1916	Satsuma domain (Kagoshima Prefecture)	Army Minister
Takegoshi Yosaburō	1865–1950	Tokyo	journalist, historian; member of *Rikken Seiyūkai*
Taketomi Tokitoshi			a leader of *Shinpotō*, *Kenseihontō*
Takeuchi Masashi	1854–1920	Okayama Prefecture	graduated from Keiō Gijuku; Leader of the *Chūgoku Shinpotō*; member of *Kenseihontō*
Takeuchi Koretada			Member of House of Peers
Takeuchi Tsuna	1840–1922	Tosa domain (Kōchi)	a leader of *Jiyūtō*; managing director of Seoul-Pusan Railway; father of Yoshida Shigeru (Prime Minister after Second World War)
Tani Tateki	1837–1911	Tosa domain (Kōchi)	Army general, famous for his defence of Kumamoto Castle against the attack of Saigō Takamori; Minister of Agriculture and Commerce; Member of House of Peers; well known leader of Japanist movement
Terajima Munenori	1832–93	Satsuma domain (Kagoshima Prefecture)	Minister of Foreign Affairs; Chairman of Privy Council; Count

name	dates	place of origin	comments
Tokudaiji Sanenori	1840–1919	Kyōto	Grand Chamberlain; elder brother of Saionji Kinmochi
Tokugawa Iesato	1863–1940		son of the last Shogun (Yoshinobu); Chairman of House of Peers; Duke
Tokutomi Iichirō (*Sohō*)	1863–1957	Kumamoto Prefecture	founder of *Kokumin no Tomo* (People's Friend) and *Kokumin Shinbun* (People's News)
Torii Tadafumi			Leader of *Kenkyūkai* faction in House of Peers; Count
Tsunoda Shinpei			a leader of the *Kenseihontō*
Tsuzuki Keiroku	1861–1923		official of Ministry of Home Affairs; Vice-Minister of Foreign Affairs; Member of House of Peers
Ueki Emori	1857–92	Tosa domain (Kōchi)	Leader and theorist of *Minken* movement; Diet Member of *Jiyūtō*
Utsumi Tadakatsu	1843–1905	Chōshū domain	local governor; official of Home Ministry
Watanabe Kōki	1848–1901	Fukui Prefecture	career bureaucrat in Ministry of Foreign Affairs; the first President of Tokyo Imperial University a founder of the *Kokumin Kyōkai*
Watanabe Kunitake	1846–1919		career bureaucrat in Ministry of Finance; Minister of Finance; later entered *Rikken Seiyūkai*
Yamada Nobumichi		Kumamoto Prefecture	one of the local governors who were loyal to Yamagata's transcendentalism

name	dates	place of origin	comments
Yamagata Aritomo	1838–1922	Chōshū domain (Yamaguchi Prefecture)	second only to Itō Hirobumi, the most influential leader of the Meiji Government after deaths of Saigō Takamori, Ōkubo Toshimichi and Kido Takayoshi; his influence over the military and Home Ministry was even greater than that of Itō
Yasuba Yasukazu	1835–99	Kumamoto domain	governor of Fukushima, Aichi and Fukuoka prefectures; during his period in office in Fukuoka he became close to *Genyōsha*
Yoshii Tomozane	1828–91	Satsuma domain (Kagoshima Prefecture)	Vice-Minister of Imperial Household
Yoshikawa Akimasa	1842–1920	Awa domain (Tokushima Prefecture)	Minister of Education; Minister of Home Affairs

Guide to sources

The following is a guide to the principal sources used in this book.

UNPUBLISHED SOURCES

A Private papers

1 *Hirata Tōsuke kankei monjo* (Hirata Tōsuke Papers), in *Kenseishi hensankai shūshū monjo*
2 *Inoue Kaoru kankei monjo* (Inoue Kaoru Papers)
3 *Katsura Tarō kankei monjo* (Katsura Tarō Papers)
4 *Kobayashi Motoo kankei monjo* (Kobayashi Motoo Papers)
5 *Kojima Kazuo monjo* (Kojima Kazuo Papers)
6 *Mutsu Munemitsu kankei monjo* (Mutsu Munemitsu Papers)
7 *Okuma monjo* (Okuma Papers)
8 *Sakatani Yoshio kankei monjo* (Sakatani Yoshio Papers)
9 *Sasa Tomofusa kankei monjo* (Sasa Tomofusa Papers)
10 *Tsuzuki Keiroku kankei monjo* (Tsuzuki Keiroku Papers)
11 *Itō ke monjo* (Itō Family Papers)

Note All the above papers except no. 7 belong to the *kensei shiryōshitsu* (Parliamentary History Section) of the *kokuritsu kokkai toshokan* (National Diet Library) in Tokyo. No. 7 belongs to Waseda University. No. 11 (*Itō ke monjo*), which has been used very extensively in this book, also belongs to the *kensei shiryōshitsu*, but has subsequently been published as: Itō Hirobumi kankei monjo kenkyūkai (ed.), *Itō Hirobumi kankei monjo*, Hanawa Shobō, 1973–1980.

B Newspapers

Chōya shinbun
Chūō shinbun
Hōchi shinbun
Jiji shinpō
Jinmin
Kokkai
Kokumin
Mainichi shinbun
Nippon
Osaka mainichi shinbun
Tōkai shinbun
Tōkyō nichinichi shinbun
Tōkyō shinbun

C Party organs (periodical)

(Jiyūtō) tōhō
Kenseihontō tōhō
Kenseitō tōhō
Rikken kaishintō tōhō
Seiron
Shinpotō tōhō

D Journals

Kokumin no tomo
Nihonjin
Shakai zasshi
Taiyō
Tōyō keizai shinpō
Tōkyō keizai zasshi

Notes

Titles have not been translated in these notes, but the following brief vocabulary may be useful:

den	biography
nikki	diary
zenshū	complete works
jiden or *jijoden*	autobiography
kankei monjo	papers

Place of publication is Tokyo unless otherwise stated.

Some notes have been simplified from the original, and a few minor corrections and additions have been made. In addition, a few have been omitted entirely. Where there is a discrepancy, reference to notes in the original is provided in brackets after the numbers used here.

Introduction

1 An oligarchy derived from the south-western domains of Satsuma, Chōshū, Tosa and Hizen, which were victorious over the shogunate at the time of the Meiji restoration.

1 Some problems of transcendentalism

1 Shihara Yasuzō, 'Meiji seishi', in Meiji bunka kenkyūkai (ed.), *Meiji bunka zenshū – seishi hen*, part 2. Nihon hyōronsha, 1929, p. 37.

2 Tsuzuki Keiroku, 'Chōzenshugi', drafted 24 July 1892. Kokuritsu kokkai toshokan kensei shiryōshitsu.

3 Letter from Yamada Buho to Yano Fumio, 1887 (precise date unknown), in Hiratsuka Atsushi (ed.), *Itō Hirobumi hiroku*, 1929, p. 389.

4 On the *Jichitō*, see pp. 12–22.

5 Tani Tateki nikki, 27 February 1889, in Shimanouchi Toshie (ed.), *Tani Tateki ikō*, vol. 2, p. 711. Seikonsha, 1912.

6 Shihara, *Meiji seishi*, p. 50.

7 (8) Watanabe Ikujirō, *Meiji tennō to hohitsu no hitobito*. Chikura Shobō, 1936, pp. 329–38.

224   *Notes*

8   (9) Tani Tateki nikki, 14 March 1889, in op. cit., pp. 720–1.
9   (10) Letter from Nomura Yasushi to Yamagata Aritomo, 1889 (precise date unknown), in Tokutomi Iichirō, *Kōshaku Yamagata Aritomo den*, 1933 vol. 2, p. 1057.
10   (11) Letter from Inoue Kaoru to Itō Hirobumi, 2 September 1887, in *Itō ke monjo*. Kokuritsu kokkai toshokan kensei shiryōshitsu, vol. 16, p. 329. This may now be read in Itō Hirobumi kankei monjo kenkyūkai (ed.), *Itō Hirobumi kankei monjo*, Hanawa Shobō, 1973, vol. 1.
11   (12) op. cit.
12   (13) Inada Masatsugu, *Meiji kenpō seiritsu shi*. Yūhikaku, 1962, vol. 2, pp. 522–34.
13   (14) Letter from Inoue to Itō, 16 December 1888, in *Itō ke monjo*, vol. 16.
14   (15) Letter from Furusawa Shigeru to Mutsu Munemitsu, 20 October 1888, in *Mutsu Munemitsu kankei monjo*. Kokuritsu kokkai toshokan kensei shiryōshitsu.
15   (16) Letter from Mutsu to Inoue, 16 May 1888, in *Inoue Kaoru kankei monjo*, Kokuritsu kokkai toshokan kensei shiryōshitsu.
16   (17) Inoue Kaoru kō denki hensankai (ed.), *Segai Inoue kō den*, vol. 4. Naigai shoseki, p. 11.
17   (18) Miyake Setsurei, *Dōjidai shi*, vol. 2. Iwanami shoten, 1950, p. 341.
18   (19) Letter from Inoue to Itō, 23 July 1888, in *Itō ke monjo*, vol. 15, p. 273.
19   (20) Letter from Inoue to Itō, 24 July 1888, in *Itō ke monjo*, vol. 16, p. 339.
20   (22) *Segai Inoue kō den*, vol. 4, p. 11.
21   (23) See note 10 (11).
22   (24) Ōkubo Toshiaki, 'Meiji jūyonen no seihen', in Meiji shiryō renrakukai (ed.), *Meiji seiken no kakuritsu katei*. Ochanomizu Shobō, 1957, pp. 52–3.
23   (25) Op. cit., p. 110.
24   (26) See note 14 (15).
25   (27) Letter from Mutsu to Inoue, 3 May 1889, in *Inoue Kaoru kankei monjo*.
26   (28) *Segai Inoue kō den*, vol. 4, p. 55.
27   (29) Letter from Inoue Kaoru to Tsuzuki Keiroku, 2 January 1889, in Keikōkai (ed.), *Tsuzuki Keiroku den*. Keikōkai, 1926, p. 65.
28   (30) See note 25 (27).
29   (31) See note 14 (15).
30   (32) Oyama Azusa (ed.), *Yamagata Aritomo ikensho*. Hara Shobō, 1966, p. 191.
31   (33) Letter from Nomura Yasushi to Yamagata Aritomo, 1888 (date unknown), in *Segai Inoue kō den*, vol. 4, pp. 19–23.
32   (34) *Segai Inoue kō den*, vol. 4, pp. 19–23.
33   (35) op. cit.
34   (36) *Seiron* (organ of the Daidō Danketsu movement), no. 8, pp. 10–12.
35   (37) Tokutomi Iichirō, *Waga kōyūroku*. Chūō kōronsha, 1938, pp. 24–5.
36   (38) *Segai Inoue kō den*, vol. 4, pp. 54–7. Concerning the relationship of Saionji Kinmochi with the Jichitō, see Tokutomi Iichirō, *Sohō jiden*. Minyūsha, 1935, p. 273.

37 (39) Seki Naohiko, *Nanajūnana nen no kaiko.* Sanseidō, 1933, p. 121.
38 (40) Ibid.
39 (41) See note 14 (15).
40 (42) See note 25 (27).
41 (43) See note 25 (27).
42 (44) Letter from Nakai Hiroshi to Inoue Kaoru, end of 1889 (precise date unknown), in *Inoue Kaoru kankei monjo.*
43 (45) The Ōsaka Dōyūkai and its organ, the *Ōsaka Mainichi Shinbun,* seem to have belonged to the Jichitō. See Ōsaka mainichi shimbunsha (ed.), *Ōsaka mainichi shinbun gojūnen shi.* Ōsaka mainichi shinbunsha, 1932, p. 44. Concerning the relationship of the Kyōto kōminkai with it, see *Meiji bunka zenshū – seishi hen,* op. cit., vol. 1, p. 594.
44 (46) The plan to found a party called the Jichitō seems to have been given up by the time when this letter was written at the end of 1889. The label itself, however, appeared in newspaper reports of the first general election of July 1890. This fact suggests that local activities of the Jichitō had continued even after the plan to form such a party had been abandoned at the central level.
45 (47) See note 42 (44).
46 (48) Letter from Takasaki Chikaaki to Shinagawa Yajirō (enclosed in Inoue's letter to Itō of 1 January 1889).
47 (50) *Tōkai shinbun,* 1 May 1889.
48 (51) *Meiji seishi,* p. 199.
49 (52) Tani, 'Yōkō nikki', 13 November 1886, in *Tani Tateki ikō,* op. cit., vol. 1, pp. 587–8.
50 (53) Ibid., p. 577.
51 (54) Ibid., p. 584.
52 (55) Ibid., p. 576.
53 (56) Letter from Tani to Hirota Masao 1892 (precise date unknown), in *Tani Tateki ikō,* vol. 2, p. 570.
54 (57) Letter from Tani to Soga Sukenori, 23 January 1887, ibid., p. 520.
55 (58) Ibid., p. 95.
56 (59) Ibid., pp. 95–6.
57 (61) Letter from Terajima to Itō, 9 September 1887, in *Itō ke monjo,* vol. 55, Terajima Munenori, pp. 4–5. See also Hiratsuka Atsushi, *Zoku Itō Hirobumi hiroku.* 1930, pp. 61–3.
58 (62) Nishimura Shigeki, *Ōjiroku,* privately published, 1905, p. 194.
59 (63) Nishimura Shigeki, 'Jōyaku kaisei ni tsuki kengi', in Itō Hirobumi (ed.), *Hisho ruisan gaikō hen.* Hisho ruisan kankōkai, 1934, vol. 1, p. 588.
60 (64) Ibid., p. 589.
61 (65) *Tani Tateki ikō,* vol. 1, pp. 681–2.
62 (66) Ibid., p. 683.
63 (67) Nishida Nagatoshi and Uete Michiari, Introduction to *Kuga Katsunan zenshū,* op. cit., pp. 797–9.
64 (68) Nikki, 1 April 1889, in *Tani Tateki ikō,* vol. 1, p. 740.
65 (69) Nikki, 18 and 19 March 1889, in ibid., p. 724.
66 (70) Nikki, 15 March 1989, in ibid., p. 722.
67 (71) Nikki, 11 April 1889, in ibid., p. 740; and Nikki, 19 April 1889, p. 748.

68   (72) Shōji Kichinosuke, 'Daidō danketsu undō to seitō seiritsu', in Horie Eiichi and Tōyama Shigeki (eds), *Jiyū minkenki no kenkyū*. Yūhikaku, 1960, vol. 3, pp. 119–30.

69   (73) Nikki, 5 May 1889, in *Tani Tateki ikō*, vol. 1, p. 754.

70   (74) Ibid., p. 762.

71   (75) Letter from Sasa Tomofusa to the comrades in Kumamoto, 11 July 1889, in Sasa kokudō sensei ikō kankōkai (ed.), *Kokudō Sasa sensei ikō*. Kaizōsha, 1936, p. 432.

72   (76) Ibid., pp. 429–37.

73   (77) Inoue Kiyoshi, *Jōyaku kaisei*. Iwanami shinsho, 1955.

74   (78) *Tani Tateki ikō*, vol. 1, p. 788.

75   (79) Seikyōsha (ed.), *Kanju shōgun kaikoroku*. Seikyōsha, 1925, pp. 270–1.

76   (80) Tsuzuki Keiroku graduated from the Faculty of Letters of the University of Tokyo in July 1881. From January 1882 he spent four years studying in Germany, and soon after he returned to Japan in May 1886, he was appointed a junior official in the Ministry of Foreign Affairs. In 1890 he moved to the Ministry of Home Affairs, and in 1894 was promoted to the senior position in its Bureau of Public Works. Expecting much of his future, the *genrō* Inoue Kaoru persuaded him to marry his adopted daughter, Mitsuko. Yamagata Aritomo also had the very highest opinion of his legal erudition and knowledge of foreign languages. During his period at the Home Ministry he appears to have exercised considerable influence, and was leader of a faction within the Ministry.

77   (81) Uzaki Rojō, *Hitsu dan*. Isobe kōyōdō, 1915, pp. 46–7.

78   (82) Tsuzuki, 'Chōzenshugi', pp. 1–2.

79   (83) Ibid., p. 4.

80   (84) Ibid., pp. 18–19.

81   (85) Satō Seizaburō, 'Ōkubo Toshimichi', in Kamishima Jirō (ed.), *Kenryoku no shisō*. Chikuma Shobō, 1965, p. 38 and pp. 52–3.

82   (86) Maruyama Masao, 'Meiji kokka no shisō', in Rekishigaku kenkyūkai (ed.), *Nihon shakai no shiteki kyūmei*. Iwanami shoten, 1949, p. 184.

83   (87) Tsuzuki, 'Chōzenshugi', pp. 9–10.

84   (88) Tsuzuki, 'Kitei saishutsu no hōri', in *Hisho ruisan teikoku gikai shiryō*, op. cit., vol. 3, p. 323.

85   (89) Ibid., pp. 332–3.

86   (90) Itō Hirobumi's interpretation of 'those already fixed expenditures' was as follows:

'"Already fixed expenditures based by the Constitution upon the powers appertaining to the Emperor" include all the expenditures which are based upon the sovereign powers of the Emperor, as set forth in Chapter I of the Constitution, to wit: ordinary expenditures required by the organization of the different branches of the administration, and by that of the Army and Navy, the salaries of all civil and military officers and expenditures that may be required in consequence of treaties concluded with foreign countries. Such expenditures, whether their origin be prior to the coming into force of the present Constitution or subsequent to it, shall be regarded as permanent expenditures already fixed at the time of the bringing of the budget into the Diet.'

Hirobumi Itō, *Commentaries on the Constitution of the Empire of Japan.* Second edition, 1906. Greenwood Press reprint, 1978, pp. 140–1.

It may be noted that 'ordinary expenditures ... already fixed at the time of the bringing of the budget into the Diet' were not in practice much different from the previous year's budget defined by article 71.

87 (91) *Hisho ruisan teikoku gikai shiryō,* vol. 3, p. 267.
88 (92) Ibid., pp. 268–70.
89 (93) Ibid., p. 267.
90 (94) Tsuzuki, 'Minseiron', April 1892, pp. 9–10.
91 (95) Ibid., p. 18.
92 (96) Ibid., pp. 22–3.
93 (97) Tani Tateki, 'Tsuzuki Keiroku shi no kitei saishutsu no hōri o yomu', in *Tani Tateki ikō,* vol. 2, p. 131.
94 (98) Ibid., p. 125.
95 (99) Opinion paper of Inoue Kowashi addressed to the Prime Minister, Minister of Justice and Minister of Home Affairs, dated 29 August 1892, in *Inoue Kowashi den – shiryō hen,* vol. 2, p. 528.
96 (100) Ibid., p. 526.
97 (101) Tsuzuki, 'Chōzenshugi', p. 31.
98 (102) Letter from Mutsu Munemitsu to Inoue Kaoru, 3 May 1899.
99 (103) Letter from Mutsu to Inoue, 2 March 1889, in *Inoue Kaoru kankei monjo.*
100 (104) *Inoue Kowashi den – shiryō hen,* vol. 2, p. 527.

2 'Enrich the nation and strengthen the armed forces' and 'lighten the people's burdens' as issues in the early Diet sessions

1 Yamagata Aritomo, 'Teikoku no kokuze ni tsuite no enzetsu', Ōyama Azusa (ed.), *Yamagata Aritomo ikensho.* Hara Shobō, 1966, pp. 205–7.
2 Ibid., p. 207.
3 Meiji zaiseishi hensankai, *Meiji zaiseishi.* Meiji zaiseishi hensankai, 1926, vol. 3, pp. 460–1.
4 Hirobumi Itō, *Commentaries,* p. 141.
5 Inoue Kowashi, 'Gikai taisaku iken', 5 February 1891, in *Inoue Kowashi den – shiryō hen,* vol. 2, p. 326.
6 Itō, *Commentaries,* p. 141.
7 'The Hall of the Baying Stag' – an establishment which flourished between 1885 and 1887, where members of the post-Restoration élite, together with their wives, affected Western dress, manners and activities (such as ballroom dancing).
8 (7) Inoue Kowashi, 'Dai ni gikai taisaku iken', in *Inoue Kowashi den – shiryō hen,* vol. 2, p. 383.
9 (8) Ibid., p. 385.
10 (9) Ibid., p. 390.
11 (10) Ibid.
12 (11) Ibid., p. 388.
13 (12) Shūgiin, Sangiin (ed.), *Gikai seido nanajū nenshi – seitō kaiha hen.* Shūgiin, Sangiin, 1961, p. 261.
14 (13) Ibid., p. 255.
15 (14) Ibid., p. 260.
16 (15) Ibid., p. 266.

17   (16) Inoue Kowashi to Itō Hirobumi, 25 October 1891, in *Itō ke monjo*, vol. 39, p. 23.
18   (17) Itō Miyoji to Itō Hirobumi, 20 December 1891, in *Itō ke monjo*, vol. 34, p. 1093.
19   (18) *Meiji zaiseishi*, vol. 3, pp. 569–71.
20   (19) Ibid., p. 571.
21   (20) *Kokkai*, 27 December 1891.
22   (21) *Jiji shinpō*, 15 December 1891.
23   (22) *Meiji zaiseishi*, vol. 3, p. 583.
24   (23) Ibid., pp. 583–4.
25   (24) The only exemption from this was expenditure for nationalization of railways.
26   (25) *Meiji zaiseishi*, vol. 3, p. 575 and p. 577.
27   (26) Ibid., p. 586.
28   (27) *Inoue Kowashi den – shiryō hen*, vol. 2, p. 524.
29   (28) Ōtsu Junichirō, *Dai Nihon kenseishi*, vol. 3, 1927, p. 638.
30   (29) Itō Miyoji to Itō Hirobumi, 20 December 1891, in *Itō ke monjo*, vol. 34, pp. 1090–1.
31   (30) *Rikken kaishintō tōhō*, 7 August 1893, no. 14, p. 3.
32   (31) Ozaki Yukio, 'Keihi setsugen an', in *Ozaki gakudō zenshū*, Kōronsha, 1955, vol. 4, p. 170.
33   (32) Ibid., p. 175.
34   (33) Ibid., p. 182.
35   (34) Ibid., p. 183.
36   (35) Tsuzuki, 'Chōzenshugi', p. 9.
37   (36) Shūgiin, Sangiin (ed.), *Gikai seido nanajū nenshi – teikoku gikai gian kenmei roku*. Shūgiin, Sangiin, 1961, pp. 482–502.
38   (37) *Chūō shinbun*, 11 December 1891.
39   (38) This did not mean that the *hanbatsu* Government had no difficulty in passing legislation. When the government wanted to enact new laws or to revise existing laws, the consent of the House of Representatives was a necessary condition. In other words, while both the *hanbatsu* Government and the House of Representatives could rely on the Constitution as long as they were satisfied with the *status quo*, they lacked constitutional advantage when they wished to bring about change.
40   (39) Kajiwara Otoki (ed.), *Seihi setsugen saku*. Gakuyūkan, 1891, p. 14.
41   (40) *Ozaki Yukio zenshū*, vol. 4, p. 199.
42   (41) Kajiwara, op. cit., pp. 14–15.
43   (42) Ōtsu, op. cit., vol. 3, p. 644.
44   (43) *Kokkai*, 18 December 1891.
45   (44) op. cit.
46   (45) *Chōya shinbun*, 15 December 1891.
47   (46) Toriumi Yasushi, 'Tetsudō fusetsu seitei katei ni okeru tetsudō kisei dōmeikai no atsuryoku katsudō', in *Tōkyō daigaku kyōyō gakubu jinbun kagaku kiyo*, no. 43.
48   (47) Shibusawa Eiichi denki hensankai, *Shibusawa Eiichi denki shiryō*. Kyūmonsha, 1956, vol. 10, pp. 101–6. See also *Kokkai*, 16 December 1891.
49   (48) Minoura Katsundo, 'Zōzei oyobi shinzei o ronzu', in *Rikken kaishintō tōhō*, no. 1, 20 December 1892, p. 17.

50 (49) op. cit.
51 This tendency was strong during the first session of the Diet among Diet Members who were large landowners. See Araki Moriaki, 'Daiichi gikai ni okeru jinushi giin no dōkō', in *Shakai kagaku kenkyū*, vol. 16, no. 1, p. 21.
52 Yoshitsu Dairoku, *Daini gikai shimatsuki*. 1982, p. 9. This leaflet was published in order to explain the stance of the Taiseikai at the time of the second general election in 1892.
53 'Kokumin kyōkai shi', no. 5, in *Chūō shinbun*, 29 June 1893.
54 *Hattori Shisō chosakushū*. Kironsha, 1956, vol. 7, p. 98.
55 *Tōkyō keizai zasshi*, no. 561, 28 February 1891, pp. 268–9.
56 Inoue Kowashi to Watanabe Kunitake, 28 July 1892, in *Shakai kagaku kenkyū*, vol. 18, no. 5.
57 Toriumi Yasushi, 'Shoki gikai ni okeru jiyūtō no kōzō to kinō', in *Rekishigaku Kenkyū*, no. 255, pp. 23–4.
58 *Chūō shinbun*, 28 May 1892.
59 *(Jiyūtō) tōhō*, no. 17, 25 July 1892, p. 3.
60 Ibid., no. 29, appendix, 25 January 1892, p. 1.
61 Inoue Kaoru to Itō Hirobumi, 26 November 1892, in *Itō ke monjo*, vol. 17, pp. 489–90.
62 *(Jiyūtō) tōhō*, no. 28, 10 January 1893, p. 5.
63 *Kokkai*, 3 October 1893.
64 See note 60 (61).
65 *(Jiyūtō) tōhō*, no. 28, p. 4.
66 Ibid., p. 31.
67 *(Jiyūtō) tōhō*, no. 33, 25 March 1893, p. 19.
68 (69) Ibid., no. 28, pp. 27–8.
69 (70) Ibid., no. 29, appendix, p. 1.
70 (71) 'Takeuchi Tsuna jijoden', in *Meiji bunka zenshū – zasshi hen*, Nihon hyōronsha, 1956, pp. 445–6.
71 (72) Hattori Kazumi to Inoue Kaoru, 31 August 1892, in *Itō ke monjo*, vol. 17, p. 401.
72 (73) Suematsu Kenchō to Itō Hirobumi, 1892 (precise date unknown), in *Itō ke monjo*, vol. 47, p. 77.
73 (74) *(Jiyūtō) tōhō*, no. 1, 25 October 1891, p. 9.
74 (75) Ibid., no. 33, 25 March 1893, p. 21.
75 (76) Letter from Inoue Kaoru to Itō Hirobumi, 7 January 1893, in Shunpo kō tsuishōkai (ed.), *Itō Hirobumi den*. Tōgensha, 1943, vol. 2, p. 872.
76 (77) *Tōkyō nichinichi shinbun*, 27 July 1892.
77 (78) *(Jiyūtō) tōhō*, no. 35, 25 April 1893, pp. 4–5.
78 (79) Ibid., no. 51, 25 December 1893, p. 1.
79 (80) Letter from Itō Miyoji to Itō Hirobumi, 11 August 1893, in *Itō ke monjo*, vol. 25, p. 27.
80 (81) Yoshitsu, op. cit., p. 56.
81 (82) *Chūō shinbun*, 27 June 1893.
82 (83) Ibid., 12 July 1893.
83 (84) Ibid., 29 June, 30 June, 6 July, 11 July, 1893.
84 (85) Public announcement in the *Chūō shinbun* throughout June and July 1893.

85   (86) *Chūō shinbun*, 12 July 1893.
86   (87) *Kyūshū nichinichi shinbun*, 15 August 1893.
87   (88) Miyake Setsurei, *Dōjidai shi*. Iwanami shoten, 1950, vol. 2, p. 473.
88   (89) *Chūō shinbun*, 18 August 1891.
89   (90) *Kokudō Sasa sensei ikō*, op. cit., pp. 59–60.
90   (91) Ibid., p. 61.
91   (92) Itō Miyoji to Itō Hirobumi, 22 June 1889, in *Itō ke monjo*, vol. 34, p. 1026.
92   (93) Letter from Sasa Tomofusa to Kobayashi Motoo, 31 October 1892, in *Kobayashi Motoo kankei monjo*.
93   (94) Opinion paper of Sasa Tomofusa, dated 6 November 1892, in *Kokudō Sasa sensei ikō*, p. 77.
94   (95) Letter from Itō Miyoji to Itō Hirobumi, 11 August 1893, in *Itō ke monjo*, vol. 25, pp. 26–7.
95   (96) *Kokudō Sasa sensei ikō*, pp. 95–6.
96   (97) Ibid., p. 96.
97   (98) Shiga Fujio (ed.) *Shiga Jūkō zenshū*. Shiga Jūkō kankōkai, 1928, vol. 1, p. 60.
98   (99) *Kokumin no tomo*, vol. 13, no. 197, 23 July 1893, p. 17.
99   (100) Inoue Tetsujirō, 'Naichi zakkyo ron', September 1889.
100 (101) *Kokumin no tomo*, vol. 12, no. 188, p. 43.
101 (102) See note 85 (87).
102 (103) *Rikken kaishintō tōhō*, no. 6, p. 1, 5 March 1893.
103 (104) Ibid., p. 5.
104 (105) Ibid., p. 1.
105 (106) *Nihonjin* (reissued), no. 1, p. 12.
106 (107) *Nippon*, 30 July 1893.
107 (108) *Rikken kaishintō tōhō*, no. 21, 5 December 1893, p. 3.
108 (109) Ibid., p. 2.
109 (110) Ibid., no. 23, 3 January 1894, pp. 1–2.
110 (111) op. cit.
111 (112) (*Jiyutō) tōhō*, no. 54. 10 February 1894, p. 1.
112 (113) Ibid., p. 4.
113 (114) *Rikken kaishintō tōhō*, no. 21, 5 December 1894, p. 16.
114 (115) Ibid., p. 17.
115 (116) Ibid., no. 8, 18 May 1893, p. 46.
116 (117) Ibid., no. 23, 3 January 1894, pp. 10–11.
117 (118) *Nippon*, 7 July 1893.
118 (119) *Rikken kaishintō tōhō*, no. 1, 20 December 1892, p. 16.
119 (120) Ibid., no. 16, 9 September 1893, p. 1.
120 (121) Ibid., no. 1, 20 December 1892, p. 17.
121 (122) Ibid., no. 15, p. 2.
122 (123) *Kokumin no tomo*, vol. 13, 23 July 1893, pp. 17–18.
123 (124) *Kokkai*, 4 October 1893.
124 (125) *Hattori Shisō chosakushū*, vol. 7, pp. 105–6.
125 (126) Letter from Itō Miyoji to Itō Hirobumi, 5 June 1894, in *Itō ke monjo*, vol. 31, p. 688.
126 (127) *Kokumin no tomo*, vol. 14, no. 222, 3 April 1894, pp. 554–5.
127 (128) *Chūō shinbun*, 16 June 1894.
128 (129) op. cit.

129 (130) Tokutomi Iichirō, *Sohō jiden.* Chūō kōronsha, 1935, pp. 289–90.
130 (132) *Kokumin no tomo,* vol. 14, no. 222, p. 555.
131 (133) *(Jiyutō) tōhō,* no. 57, 25 March 1894, p. 15.

3 Post-war reconstruction and the reactions of various political forces

1 Itō Hirobumi (ed.), *Hisho ruisan zaisei shiryō* (Hisho ruisan kankōkai, 1935), vol. 2, p. 56. Opinion paper dated 15 August 1895.
2 Opinion paper dated September 1895, in ibid., pp. 81–2.
3 Ibid., p. 56.
4 Ibid., pp. 108–10.
5 Ibid., p. 59.
6 Opinion paper dated November 1895, in ibid., p. 99.
7 Ibid., p. 103.
8 Ibid., p. 104.
9 Ibid., p. 59.
10 Ibid., p. 104.
11 *(Jiyutō) tōhō,* no. 106, 11 April 1896, p. 1.
12 *Tōkyō keizai zasshi,* no. 810, 1 February 1896, p. 136.
13 *Itō Hirobumi monjo.* Kokuritsu kokkai toshokan kensei shiryōshitsu. This demand seems to have been presented to the Prime Minister in March 1896. No card index was available when this book was originally published.
14 Tani Tateki to Kuga Minoru [Katsunan], 26 September 1896, in *Tani Tateki ikō,* vol. 2, p. 608.
15 *Tōkyō keizai zasshi,* no. 888, p. 297, 7 August 1897.
16 Shibusawa Eiichi denki kankōkai (ed.), *Shibusawa Eiichi denki shiryō,* vol. 22, pp. 5–6.
17 *Tokyo keizai zasshi,* no. 811, 8 February 1896, pp. 206–7.
18 Ibid., no. 812, 15 February 1896, pp. 206–7.
19 *Shibusawa Eiichi denki shiryō,* vol. 22, p. 77.
20 See note 17.
21 *Shibusawa Eiichi denki shiryō,* vol. 22, pp. 79–80.
22 Ibid., vol. 22, pp. 227–8.
23 *Tōkyō keizai zasshi,* no. 815, 7 March 1896, pp. 380–1.
24 *Shibusawa Eiichi denki shiryō,* vol. 22, p. 309.
25 Ibid.
26 *Tōkyō keizai zasshi,* vol. 36, no. 904, 27 November 1897, p. 1232.
27 Taguchi Fumiyo (ed.), *Teiken Taguchi Ukichi zenshū,* Teiken Taguchi Ukichi zenshū kankōkai, 1929, vol. 6, p. 31.
28 Ibid., p. 451.
29 Kawai Eijirō, *Meiji shisō no ichi danmen – Kanai Yutaka o chūshin toshite.* Nihon hyōronsha, 1941, pp. 171–4.
30 Shimada Saburō, 'Rōdō mondai shokan', *Shakai zasshi,* vol. 7, p. 6, November 1897.
31 *Teiken Taguchi Ukichi zenshū,* vol. 6, p. 38.
32 Shioda Shōbei, *Zōho – Kōtoku Shūsui no nikki to shokan,* diary entry for 28 November 1899. Miraisha, 1965, p. 111.
33 *Nippon,* 12 January 1897.
34 Ibid., 8 January 1897.

35   *Shinpotō tōhō*, no. 5, 1 July 1897, pp. 13–15.
36   *Nippon*, 5 March 1897.
37   *Teiken Taguchi Ukichi zenshū*, vol. 6, p. 28.
38   On Taguchi's respect for and criticism of Tani Tateki, see ibid., pp. 40–1.

4 The formation of the Yamagata faction

 1   Hirobumi Itō, *Commentaries*, p. 133.
 2   For examples, see Toriumi Yasushi, 'Shoki gikai ni okeru [rikken] jiyūtō no kōzō to kinō, *Rekishigaku kenkyū*, no. 255; Uno Shunichi, 'Rikken seiyukai kessei no zentei jōken', *Nihon rekishi*, no. 209; Yasui Tatsuya, 'Hanbatsu shihai no henyō – Itō Hirobumi no baai', in Shinohara Hajime and Mitani Taichirō (eds), *Kindai nihon no seiji shidō*; and George Akita, *Foundations of Constitutional Government in Modern Japan*. Cambridge, Mass., Harvard University Press, 1967.
 3   The most important exception in this regard is Oka Yoshitake, *Yamagata Aritomo*, Iwanami shoten, 1958.
 4   See Ōkubo Toshiaki, *Nihon zenshi – kindai III*. Tōkyō daigaku shuppankai, 1964.
 5   See Masumi Junnosuke, *Nihon seitōshi ron*. Tōkyō daigaku shuppankai, 1968, vol. 4.
 6   Hayashida Kametarō, *Nihon seitōshi*, Dai nihon yūbenkai, 1927, vol. 1, p. 442.
 7   *Itō ke monjo*, vol. 28, p. 411.
 8   Yamada Nobumichi to Sasa Tomofusa, 7 February 1896, in *Sasa Tomofusa kankei monjo*.
 9   Egi Kazuyuki ō keireki dan kankōkai (ed.), *Egi Kazayuki ō keireki dan*. Kankōkai, 1933, vol. 1, pp. 196–8.
10   Ibid., p. 197.
11   Ibid.
12   Dai nihon teikoku gikai kankōkai (ed.), *Dai nihon teikoku gikaishi*. 1927, vol. 3, p. 1410.
13   Kuki Ryūichi to Itō Hirobumi, 8 February 1895.
14   Uzaki Rojō, *Chōya no godaibatsu*. Tōa shobō, 1912.
15   Yamada Nobumichi to Sasa Tomofusa, 14 April 1896, in *Sasa Tomofusa kankei monjo*.
16   Kiyoura Keigo to Yamagata Aritomo, 31 April 1896, in Inoue Masaaki (ed.), *Hakushaku Kiyoura Keigo den*, vol. 1, pp. 407–8. See also Oka Yoshitake, *Yamagata Aritomo*. Iwanami Shoten, 1968, pp. 65–6.
17   (18) It is difficult to date precisely the emergence of the 'Yamagata faction bureaucrat'. According to Oka, the faction was formed during Yamagata's stay in the Ministry of Home Affairs between 1873 and 1890 (See Oka, op. cit., p. 47). I do not disagree with Oka about this. The Yamagata faction, however, as a political group potentially capable of challenging Itō Hirobumi's Rikken Seiyūkai, seems to have been formed about the time of Itagaki Taisuke's appointment as Minister of Home Affairs in April 1896.
18   (20) Itō Miyoji to Itō Hirobumi, 8 June 1894, in *Itō ke monjo*, vol. 31, p. 687.
19   (21) Shinagawa Yajirō to Sasa Tomofusa, 5 August 1896, in *Sasa Tomofusa kankei monjo*.

20 (22) Ōoka Ikuzo to Sasa Tomofusa, 27 August 1896, in *Sasa Tomofusa kankei monjo.*
21 (23) Motoda Hajime to Sasa, 19 August 1896, in *Sasa Tomofusa kankei monjo.*
22 (24) Ōura Kanetake to Inoue Kaoru, 1 May 1896, in *Inoue Kaoru kankei monjo.* Kokuritsu kokkai toshokan kensei shiryōshitsu.
23 (25) Shinagawa Yajirō to Sasa Tomofusa, 26 August 1896, in *Sasa Tomofusa kankei monjo.*
24 (26) *Nippon,* 21 February 1894.
25 (27) Itō Miyoji to Itō Hirobumi, 8 February 1894, in *Itō ke monjo,* vol. 27, p. 310.
26 (28) Kaneko Kentarō to Itō Hirobumi, 20 December 1891, in Itō Hirobumi (ed.), *Hisho ruisan teikoku gikai shiryō,* vol. 1, pp. 434–5.
27 (30) Itō Miyoji to Itō Hirobumi, 25 March 1896, in Shinteikai (ed.), *Hakushaku Itō Miyoji.* Shinteikai, 1938, vol. 1, pp. 194–5.
28 (31) See note 16.
29 (32) Kizokuin jimukyoku (ed.), *Dai kyū kai teikoku gikai kizokuin iinkai kaigiroku,* 1896, p. 1001 and p. 693. Concerning Senge Takatoshi and Ōgimachi Michimasa, see Sakamoto Tatsunosuke, *Nihon teikoku seiji nenpyō.* Shōbundō, 1930, p. 20 and p. 24.
30 (33) See note 27 (30).
31 (34) Yamada Nobumichi to Sasa Tomofusa, 3 September 1896, in *Sasa Tomofusa kankei monjo.*
32 (35) Yamada to Sasa, 22 September 1896, in *Sasa Tomofusa kankei monjo.*
33 (36) Ibid.
34 (37) Yamada to Sasa, 26 September 1896.
35 (38) Yamada to Sasa, 14 October 1896.
36 (39) Ōura Kanetaka to Sasa, 28 December 1896, in *Sasa Tomofusa kankei monjo.*
37 (40) Shinagawa Yajirō to Sasa Tomofusa, 6 November 1896, in ibid.
38 (41) Ibid.
39 (42) Shinagawa to Sasa, 9 December 1896.
40 (43) Adachi Kenzō, *Adachi Kenzō jijoden.* Shinjusha, 1960, p. 97.
41 (44) Shinagawa Yajirō to Adachi Kenzō, 23 September 1897, in *Adachi Kenzō kankei monjo.*
42 (45) Adachi Kenzō, op. cit., pp. 95–6.
43 (46) Shinagawa to Sasa, 29 December 1897.
44 (47) See note 36 (39).
45 (48) Shinagawa to Sasa, 29 December 1897.
46 (49) Konoe Atsumaro nikki kankōkai (ed.), *Konoe Atsumaro nikki.* Kajima kenkyūjo shuppankai, 1968, vol. 1, p. 55.
47 (50) Ibid., p. 57.
48 (51) Ibid., pp. 57–8.
49 (52) Ibid., p. 69.
50 (53) Tani Tateki to Kuga Minoru [Katsunan], 26 September 1896, in *Tani Tateki ikō,* vol. 2, p. 606.
51 (54) Ibid., p. 608.
52 (55) Tani Tateki nikki, 15 September 1896, in ibid., vol. 1, p. 909.
53 (56) *Tōkyō keizai zasshi,* vol. 36, no. 904, 27 November 1897, p. 1232.

54   (57) See note 50 (53).
55   (58) *Shinpotō tōhō*, no. 9, 1 September 1897, p. 2.
56   (59) Meiji zaiseishi hensankai, *Meiji zaiseishi*, Kankōkai, 1926, vol. 3, p. 903.
57   (60) Ibid.
58   (61) Satō Tatsuo, *Kizokuin taisei seibi no kenkyū*. Jinbun kaku, 1943, p. 17; and Noma Gozō, *Rippō ichigen ron*. Hakuyōsha, 1927, vol. 2, p. 152.
59   (62) Diary entry for 24 February 1897, in *Konoe Atsumaro nikki*, vol. 1, p. 177.
60   (63) Ibid.
61   (64) Diary entry for 28 February 1897, in ibid., p. 179.
62   (65) Ibid.
63   (66) Ibid.
64   (67) Diary entry for 8 March 1897, in ibid., p. 186.
65   (68) *Kizokuin giji sokkiroku furoku* (tenth session), p. 264.
66   (69) The table is based on *Kizokuin tōha ichiranhyō* (Makino monjo); *Nippon*, 7 June 1897; and *Kizokuin giji sokkiroku furoku*. More accurate figures are now available in Saketa Masatoshi, *Kizokuin kaiha ichiranhyō*. Kindai nihon shiryō kenkyūkai, 1974.
67   (70) Hanabusa Sakitarō, *Kizokuin kaku kaiha no enkaku*. Private publication, 1942, pp. 10–11.

5 The question of increasing the land tax

1   Matsukata haku danwa hikki, 4 December 1897, in *Sakatani Yoshio kankei monjo*. Kokuritsu kokkai toshokan kensei shiryōshitsu.
2   Ibid.
3   Ibid.
4   Ibid.
5   Ibid.
6   Ibid.
7   Matsukata haku jimu dan (Kokumin shinbunsha, 1897), in *Sakatani Yoshio kankei monjo*.
8   Matsukata haku no danwa (January 1898), in ibid.
9   *Meiji zaiseishi*, vol. 1, pp. 50–1.
10   See note 8.
11   *Tōkyō keizai zasshi*, vol. 36, no. 888, 7 August 1897, p. 1.
12   Oshima Kiyoshi, *Nihon Kyōkō shiron*. Tōkyō daigaku shuppan, 1952, vol. 1, pp. 190–1.
13   See note 8.
14   *Tani Tateki ikō*, vol. 2, p. 317. The publication of this argument has been wrongly dated by the editor. Judging from internal evidence, the article was published in June 1902, not in 1898.
15   See note 8.
16   Kō Sakatani shishaku kinen jigyōkai (ed.), *Sakatani Yoshio den*. Kō Sakatani Yoshio shishaku kinen jigyōkai, 1951, p. 202.
17   Ozaki Yukio, 'Waga tō ga gen naikaku to tatsu no riyū', *Shinpotō tōhō*, no. 14, 15 November 1897, pp. 1–4.
18   Ōtsu Junichirō, *Dai nihon kensei shi*. Hara shobō, 1970 (originally

published 1927), vol. 4, p. 732.
19 *Segai Inoue kō den*, vol. 4, p. 732.
20 Yasui Tetsuya, *Hanbatsu shihai no henyō*, p. 175.
21 Itō Miyoji to Itō Hirobumi, 14 June 1897, in *Itō ke monjo*, vol. 28, pp. 337–44.
22 Itō Miyoji to Itō Hirobumi, 8 July 1897, in *Itō ke monjo*, vol. 28, p. 313.
23 See note 17.
24 See note 22.
25 Itagaki Taisuke to Itō Hirobumi, 16 September 1897, in *Itō Hirobumi den*, vol. 3, pp. 317–18.
26 Itō Miyoji to Itō Hirobumi, 31 October 1897, in *Itō ke monjo*, vol. 27, p. 327.
27 Itō Miyoji to Itō Hirobumi, 17 November 1897, in ibid.
28 Itō Miyoji to Itō Hirobumi, 19 November 1897, in ibid.
29 See note 27.
30 See note 28.
31 Itō Miyoji to Itō Hirobumi, 9 January 1898, in *Itō ke monjo*, vol. 30, p. 580.
32 *Segai Inoue kō den*, vol. 4, pp. 594–8.
33 Kabayama Sukenori to Matsukata Masayoshi, 24 June 1898, in *Matsukata Masayoshi monjo*.
34 Hirata Tōsuke kankei monjo, in *Kenseishi hensankai shūshū monjo*. Kokuritsu kokkai toshokan kensei shiryōshitsu.
35 *Segai Inoue kō den*, vol. 4, pp. 567–8.
36 *Dai nihon teikoku gikaishi*, vol. 4, p. 1002.
37 *Kenseitō tōhō*, vol. 1, no. 4, 20 January 1899, p. 177.
38 *Tōkyō nichinichi shinbun*, 8 June 1898.
39 *Dai jūnikai teikoku gikai shūgiin – chiso jōrei chū kaisei hōritsuan hoka ikken shinsa tokubetsu iinkai sokkiroku*, no. 3, p. 23.
40 Pamphlet by Suzuki Gizaemon, 5 August 1898, in *Nemoto Yoshishige ke monjo*.
41 Ibid.
42 Ōura Kanetake to Sasa Tomofusa, 13 June 1898.
43 *Shinpotō tōhō*, no. 27, 5 June 1898, pp. 10–15.
44 Katsura Tarō jiden, in *Katsura Tarō kankei monjo*.
45 *Hirata Tōsuke kankei monjo*.
46 Ibid.
47 According to a letter from Yamagata Aritomo to Matsukata Masayoshi dated 18 June 1898, Hirata Tōsuke's visit to Yamagata was on 12 June, not 13 June, and therefore, Yamagata's visit to Inoue Kaoru was also on 13 June. *Itō Hirobumi den*, vol. 3, p. 371.
48 Ōura Kanetake to Inoue Kaoru, 29 August 1898, in *Inoue Kaoru kankei monjo*.
49 See note 47.
50 Ōura Kanetake ʻto Sasa Tomofusa, 13 June 1898, in *Sasa Tomofusa kankei monjo*.
51 Hirobumi Itō, *Commentaries*, p. 125.
52 There is some ambiguity here concerning which kind of Imperial ordinance Ōura was talking about – that under article 8 of the Constitution or that under article 70. Since, however, article 70 became applicable only

when an extraordinary session could not be convened, it was inapplicable to the tax increase issue.
53 *Itō Hirobumi den*, vol. 3, pp. 374–6.
54 Ōura Kanetake to Sasa Tomofusa, 24 August 1898, in *Sasa Tomofusa kankei monjo*.

6 The collapse of the party Cabinet

1 *Jiji Shinpō*, editorial, 7 July 1898, cited in *Fukuzawa Yukichi zenshū*, vol. 16, p. 425.
2 Hirata Tōsuke to Yamada Nobumichi, 24 June 1898 (enclosed in letter from Yamada to Sasa Tomofusa, 27 June 1898), in *Sasa Tomofusa kankei monjo*.
3 Yamada Nobumichi to Sasa Tomofusa, 27 June 1898, in ibid.
4 Tokutomi Iichirō (ed.), *Kōshaku Katsura Tarō den*, vol. 1, pp. 789–90.
5 Ibid., p. 795.
6 Ibid., p. 810.
7 Draft of letter from Katsura (addressee and date unknown, but from the content appears to have been written in the middle of October 1898), in ibid.
8 *Katsura Tarō jiden*, vol. 3, in ibid.
9 Tsuzuki Keiroku, 'Kizokuin no shokō ni tsugu', drafted July 1898, in *Tsuzuki Keiroku kankei monjo*.
10 Ibid., p. 1.
11 Ibid.
12 Ibid., p. 2.
13 Ibid., pp. 7–9.
14 Ibid., pp. 19–20.
15 Ibid., pp. 21–2.
16 Ōtsu Junichirō, *Dai nihon kenseishi*, vol. 5, p. 55.
17 Tsuzuki, op. cit., p. 16.
18 See note 1.
19 *Hirata Tōsuke kankei monjo*, vol. 1, pp. 98–100, in *Kenseishi hensankai shūshū monjo*.
20 Ibid.
21 Ōura Kanetake, another leader of the Yamagata faction, also expected Inoue Kaoru to take a lead in 'weeding out democrats and restoring the monarchical cabinet'. Ōura to Inoue, 29 August 1898, in *Inoue Kaoru kankei monjo*.
22 Ibid.
23 Inspector-General (Nishiyama Shichō) to Prime Minister (Ōkuma Shigenobu), 13 September 1898, in *Ōkuma monjo*.
24 Kiyoura Keigo to Yamagata Aritomo, 26 October 1898, in *Kōshaku Yamagata Aritomo den*, vol. 3, pp. 329–30.
25 Inspector-General Nishiyama to Prime Minister Ōkuma, 8 October 1898, in *Ōkuma monjo*.
26 Diary entry for 27 June 1898, in *Konoe Atsumaro nikki*, vol. 2, p. 90.
27 Umenokoji Sadayuki, Funabashi Chikuken, Karahashi Arimasa and Kuse Michiakira to Konoe Atsumaro, 1 July 1898, in *Konoe Atsumaro nikki*, vol. 2, p. 95.

28 *Konoe Atsumaro nikki*, vol. 2, pp. 92–3.
29 See note 24.
30 Shumpo kō tsuishōkai (ed.), *Itō Hirobumi den*. Tōseisha, 1940, vol. 3, pp. 386–7.
31 Ibid., p. 387.
32 Ibid., p. 388.
33 *Jiji shinpō*, editorial of 28 June 1898, in *Fukuzawa Yukichi zenshū*, vol. 16, p. 420.
34 *Jiyūtō shi*, Iwanami bunkō, vol. 2, p. 44.
35 Sasahara Masashi, *Teikoku gikai kaisan shi*, Naigaisha, 1932, p. 186.
36 Hara Kei zenshū kankōkai (ed.), *Hara Kei zenshū*, Hara Shobō, 1969, p. 403 (original edition, 1929).
37 Ōtsu, *Dai nihon kenseishi*, vol. 4, p. 816.
38 Tabata Kōzō of Kumamoto Prefecture to Prime Minister Ōkuma Shigenobu, 10 July 1898, in *Ōkuma monjo*.
39 Report from Inspector-General to Prime Minister, 8 September 1898, in *Ōkuma monjo*.
40 *Tōkyō nichinichi shinbun*, 31 August 1898.
41 Ibid., 8 September 1898.
42 Report from Inspector-General to Prime Minister, 8 September 1898, in *Ōkuma monjo*.
43 Ibid., 4 October 1898.
44 Ibid.
45 *Taiyō*, vol. 13, no. 3, p. 119.
46 Ibid., vol. 4, no. 20, 5 October 1898, pp. 49–50.
47 *Kanpō gōgai*, 22 October 1898.
48 *Kanpō*, no. 3103, 31 October 1898.
49 See note 47.
50 *Kenseitō tōhō*, vol. 1, no. 4, 20 January 1899, p. 177.
51 *Meiji zaisei shi*, vol. 3, p. 975.
52 *Sakatani Yoshio kankei monjo*.
53 Ibid.
54 Ibid.
55 See Table 4. Soeda was included among government officials having party origins.
56 See note 52.
57 *Tōyō keizai shinpō*, no. 1, 15 November 1895, pp. 10–11.
58 See note 7.
59 See note 52.
60 Ibid.
61 Ibid.
62 *Tōkyō keizai zasshi*, no. 935, 9 July 1898, cited in *Teiken Taguchi Ukichi zenshū*, vol. 6, p. 451.
63 Matsuyama Moriyoshi to Ōkuma Shigenobu, 15 September 1898, in *Ōkuma monjo*.
64 Opinion paper of Beppu Tamoji to Prime Minister Ōkuma, September 1898, in *Ōkuma monjo*.
65 Report of Inspector-General to Prime Minister, 13 October 1898.
66 Ibid., 13 September 1898.
67 Nakamura Kikuo, *Meijiteki ningenzō – Hoshi Tōru to kindai nihon seiji*,

Keiō tsūshin, 1957, p. 242.
68 Report from Inspector-General to Prime Minister, 19 September 1898, in *Ōkuma monjo*.
69 Ibid., 26 October 1898.
70 Ibid., 18 September 1898.
71 Uzaki Rojō, *Inukai Tsuyoshi den*, Seibundō, 1932, p. 174.
72 *Taiyō*, 5 October 1898, vol. 4, no. 20, pp. 255–6.
73 See note 70.
74 Ōtsu, *Dai nihon kensei shi*, vol. 4, p. 831.
75 Hiraoka Kōtarō to Kojima Kazuo, 28 October 1898, in *Kojima Kazuo kankei monjo*.

7 Concluding the land tax bill

1 *Mainichi Shinbun*, 25 August 1899.
2 *Teiken Taguchi Ukichi zenshū*, vol. 5, p. 398.
3 *Fukuzawa Yukichi zenshū*, vol. 16, p. 152.
4 *Hara Kei zenshū*, vol. 1, p. 359.
5 *Mainichi shinbun*, editorial, 14 February 1899.
6 *Tōkyō keizai zasshi*, 21 May 1898, vol. 39, no. 928, p. 1099.
7 *Tōyō keizai shinpō*, 5 May 1898, no. 88, p. 35.
8 See also chapter 5.
9 Kondō Yoshio, *Inoue Kakugorō sensei den*, Inoue Kakugorō sensei denki hensankai, 1943, p. 249.
10 *Tōyō keizai shinpō*, 15 January 1899, no. 112, p. 5.
11 Kuki Ryūichi to Itō Hirobumi, 28 November 1898, in *Itō ke monjo*, vol. 60, p. 72.
12 Nihon shiseki kyōkai (ed.), *Ōkuma Shigenobu kankei monjo*, Tokyo, 1943, vol. 6, pp. 285–6.
13 Ibid., pp. 289–90.
14 *Kenseitō tōhō*, 20 January 1899, vol. 1, no. 4, p. 177.
15 Fujimura Michio, 'Gunbi kakuchō to kaikyū mujun no tenkai', in Shinobu Seizaburō and Nakayama Jiichi (eds), *Nichiro sensō no kenkyū*. Kawade Shobō shinsha, 1959, p. 79.
16 Morita Shirō, *Jinushi keizai to chihō shihon*. Ochanomizu Shobō, 1963, pp. 165–73.
17 *Kenseihontō tōhō*, no. 3, pp. 50–3.
18 Ibid., no. 2, pp. 96–7.
19 Ibid., p. 97.
20 Ibid., pp. 109–10.
21 *Kenseitō tōhō* no. 3, pp. 135–6.
22 Ibid., p. 136.
23 *Jinmin*, 19 March 1899.
24 Ibid.
25 Hara Keiichirō (ed.), *Hara Kei nikki*. Fukumura shoten, vol. 1, p. 284.
26 Kuki Ryūichi to Itō Hirobumi, 28 November 1898, in *Itō ke monjo*, vol. 28, p. 70.
27 Itō Miyoji to Itō Hirobumi, 31 March 1899, in *Itō ke monjo*, vol. 28, p. 333.
28 Kaneko Kentarō to Itō Hirobumi, 16 November 1898, in *Itō ke monjo*,

vol. 64, p. 185.

29 *Tōkyō shinbun*, 25 May 1898.

30 See Banno Junji, 'Waihan naikaku zengo ni okeru hanbatsu to seitō', in *Shigaku zasshi*, vol. 75, no. 9, 1966, pp. 44–8.

31 Tomita Nobuo, 'Dai jūyonkai teikoku gikai ni okeru senkyohō kaisei', in *Seikei ronsō*, vol. 32, no. 1.

32 *Dai nihon teikoku gikai shi*, vol. 4, pp. 901–2.

33 *Jinmin*, 15 February 1899.

34 *Kenseitō tōhō*, 5 March 1899, vol. 1, no. 7, pp. 401–2.

35 Ibid.

36 *Jinmin*, 19 February 1899.

37 *Kenseihontō tōhō*, 2 February 1899, no. 5, pp. 41–5.

38 *Jinmin*, 3 September 1899.

39 Ibid., 11 April 1899.

40 Ibid.

41 *Mainichi shinbun*, 12 September 1899.

42 *Kenseitō tōhō*, vol. 1, no. 9, 8 April 1899. See also Uno Shunichi, 'Rikken seiyūkai kessei no zentei jōken', in *Nihon rekishi*, no. 209.

43 *Hōchi shinbun*, 23 April 1899, and *Kokumin shinbun*, 13 June 1899.

44 *Kokumin shinbun*, 13 June 1899.

45 *Shinpotō tōhō*, 20 May 1898, no. 26, p. 3.

46 Hiraoka Kōtarō to Kojima Kazuo, 4 December 1898, in *Kojima Kazuo kankei monjo*.

47 Tsunoda Shinpei to Ōkuma Shigenobu and Inukai Tsuyoshi, 3 December 1898, in *Ōkuma Shigenobu kankei monjo*, vol. 6, p. 293.

48 See note 46.

49 See note 46.

50 Tsunoda to Ōkuma, 20 December 1898, in *Ōkuma Shigenobu kankei monjo*, vol. 6, pp. 294–5. The period of increased taxation was to be five years, not seven, which shows how well the secret in the negotiations between Yamagata and Hoshi had been kept, until it was finally made public.

51 *Nippon*, 19 October 1898.

52 Ibid., 5 October 1898.

53 Ibid.

54 Shioda Shōbei, *Zōho, kōtoku Shūsui no nikki to shokan*. Miraisha, 1965, p. 94.

55 Diary entry of 18 November 1899, in ibid., p. 105. See also Mitani Taichirō, 'Taishō shakaishugisha no seiji kan', in *Nenpō seijigaku*, 1968, Iwanami shoten, p. 70.

56 Ibid.

57 Shioda, op. cit., p. 111.

58 See Fujimura, op. cit.

59 *Taiyō*, vol. 6, no. 1, 3 January 1900, p. 39.

60 *Meiji zaiseishi*, vol. 1, pp. 70–1.

61 *Jinmin*, 1 and 4 February 1899.

62 Ibid., 9 February 1899.

63 See note 59.

64 Taketomi Tokitoshi to Ōkuma Shigenobu, 22 April 1899, in *Ōkuma monjo*.

65 Taketomi to Ōkuma, 4 May 1899, in *Ōkuma Shigenobu kankei monjo*, vol. 6, p. 311.
66 See note 64.
67 See note 64.
68 *Jinmin*, 5 September 1899.
69 Ibid.
70 See note 64.
71 *Jinmin*, 3 September 1899.
72 *Meiji zaiseishi*, vol. 3, p. 1034.

Index

Abe Isoo 194, 226n
Abei Iwane 226n
Adachi Kenzō 226n; on unrest in
  Kumamoto Kokkentō 113
administrative reform 158, 160;
  acceptable to *Jijūtō* 64–5
administrative retrenchment 3, 24,
  27, 40–1, 96, 170; and
  expansionism 53, 63–5; and
  Kaishintō 74, 75, 76–7; tax
  reduction and expansionism
  52–3, 54–9; *see also* expenditure
  reduction
Agricultural and Industry Bank 43,
  87
agricultural society law, proposed
  45–6
Aimintō 166
Amemiya Keijirō 173, 226n
anti-foreign feeling 98
anti-foreign movement 72–3
anti-peace campaign 201
Aoki Shūzō 17, 18, 19, 226n
arable land, concentration of 18–19,
  24
Arimatsu Hideyoshi 19
Army and Navy Ministers, *Kenseitō*
  Cabinet 145–6, 147
Asahi Club 153
Asano Nagakoto 27, 28, 29, 226n
Atāmi Conference 16
attack to supersede defence 86

budget: carrying on with previous
  year's 49; and fourth Diet 63–4
Budget Committee, boycotted by
  Kaishintō 74–5

budget investigation, and the Diet
  52–3
budget-law relationship 100–1
budgetary deliberation 33–5, 73–4,
  117
bureaucracy 120, 149, 152; and
  budget cuts 40–1; entry of party
  members 101–2, 150, 152;
  Itō-line 30, 185, 186; and second
  Itō Cabinet 104–7; *see also*
  Yamagata faction bureaucrats
businessmen: and *Jichitō* plan 19;
  and *Kenseitō* 185, 186; protected
  93; *see also* corporation tax
business tax 171–2

cabinets: decision-making before
  Diet inauguration 26–7;
  transcendental 4–5
Chambers of Commerce and
  Industry, Conferences of 92–3,
  94–6
Chambers of Commerce and
  Industry, National League of 187
Chinese indemnity (reparations) 48;
  use of 47, 87–8
Chōshū 156
Chūō Club 103, 108
Chūō Kōshōbu 66; cohesion difficult
  to sustain 68–9
Chūō Shinbun 66, 67
city electorates, separate 187–8,
  191–2
civil servants, and Jichitō plan 19
Civil Service Appointments
  Ordinance 150, 161, 168;
  abolition proposed 159–60; and